THE NEW COMPLETE
Pomeranian

THE NEW COMPLETE
Pomeranian

by VIVA LEONE RICKETTS

ILLUSTRATED

New Expanded Edition

1977 – FIFTH PRINTING

HOWELL BOOK HOUSE

730 FIFTH AVENUE

NEW YORK, N.Y. 10019

English, Canadian, American and Bermudan Champion Pixietown Serenade of Hadleigh, only Pomeranian to be a champion in 4 countries. Bred by Mrs. G. Dyke, England, and owned by Florence, Lady Conyers, Westerleigh Estates, Bermuda, and Ruth Bellick, Baltimore, Md. *Turofsky*

Copyright © 1965, 1962 Howell Book House Inc.
Library of Congress Catalog Card Number 65-28211
ISBN 0-87605-250-2   Printed in U.S.A.

ACKNOWLEDGMENTS

THIS book is respectfully dedicated to the American Pomeranian Club, Inc., and to all the officers and members who have worked so diligently for the improvement of the breed. They are especially to be commended for their foresight in establishing the *Pomeranian Review,* official organ of the parent club, which serves as a medium of communication between members everywhere.

I wish to acknowledge the source of history of the breed. Most of the material was taken from the papers of the late Milo Denlinger, whose love of Pomeranians in general and his own Blue Boy in particular was so well known to Pomeranian lovers everywhere.

Also, I wish to extend my deep appreciation to all those who aided in the compilation of material by giving freely of their knowledge, and by loaning their precious photographs and mementos for use in this book.

VIVA LEONE RICKETTS

Table of Contents

PART I

By Viva Leone Ricketts

PART II

By Elsworth S. Howell

Milo G. Denlinger

A. C. Merrick, D.V.M.

Pomeranian and Girl
Oinochoe (wine-jug).
Late Athenian fabric (4th century B.C.)

HISTORY AND DEVELOPMENT OF THE BREED

IT was but a hundred years ago—in 1859, to be exact—that the first dog show was held in Great Britain. Long before that time there was some effort to sort dogs into breeds and to keep those breeds comparatively pure, but no stud-book was maintained and such pedigree records as were kept were private. The owner of any strain of dogs was at complete liberty to give it a name of his own choice.

It may be conceded that the "small shagged dogs kept by the Suevi, quick to give the alarm at the approach of intruders," spoken of by Tacitus, may have been progenitors of the modern Pomeranian, but they were very remote ones and probably were much unlike the modern Pom in size, coat, and type. Livy also makes mention of a similar German dog, but we are at a loss for any details about it.

There can be no doubt that the Pomeranian is of Central European origin, specifically of German origin, but there is more likelihood that it was developed as a recognizable breed in Würtemberg or some other part of Southern Germany than that it came from the Prussian State or Province of Pomerania. That statement is not intended to imply that no Pomeranian dogs were or are to be found in Pomerania, since it is possible that one or a few of the earliest specimens brought into England

7

came from there and for that reason were called Pomeranians. However, there is no reason to believe that the breed developed in Pomerania, or that it was bred or improved there more than elsewhere.

The Pomeranian was and remains the Spitz dog. This statement may be hard for some breeders and fanciers to accept, since the Spitz tribe is about the most plebian of the races of dogs. But all aristocratic strains of men and dogs have derived from obscure and commonplace beginnings, and the proud Pomeranian is unable to deny his lineage.

The Pomeranian, or Spitz, is believed to be closely related to the Samoyed dog, a large breed developed by the Mongol tribe whose name it bears, which inhabits the vast stretches of icy tundra reaching from the White Sea to the Yenisei River in the eastern part of Siberia. There the Samoyed nomadic tribesmen employ their dogs for various duties, the chief of which are towing their barges when the thaws of their short summers open their rivers to traffic, the drawing of their sledges (at which the dogs are very adept), and the herding of their reindeer, which constitute the chief feature of the economy of the tribe. The Samoyed dogs exhibited in the dog shows are usually cream or white in color, but the dogs in their native habitat are by no means confined to those colors.

The resemblance in type and in coat characteristics and texture between the Pomeranian and the Samoyed dog is so marked that there can be no mistaking it by the person who will face the facts. The difference in size may be discounted when it is realized that the Spitz or Pomeranian has ranged in size from the four- or five-pound Toy dogs we now call Pomeranians to larger dogs up to the size of the true Samoyed. Whether the Spitz or Pomeranian is descended from the Samoyed or the Samoyed descended from the Spitz, we have no sure way of ascertaining. The theory that the two breeds descended from common ancestors at some time before the breeds of dogs were clearly differentiated is as tenable as that one breed descended from the other. That the relationship is close, however it may have been brought about, is not open to doubt. One thing in common that has never changed, is the happy-go-lucky disposition of both Samoyed and Pomeranian.

8

The breed might have had its origin in southern Germany and moved northward and eastward to penetrate and to cross the Siberian wastes and to be adapted to their needs by the Samoyed nomads. This appears likely, since the Samoyed peoples, while essentially Mongols, are also related to the Finns; and the Finns, being more advanced in civilization, are more likely to have contributed their characteristic breed of dogs to their nomadic kinsmen than to have derived it from them.

It is equally clear that the Finkspitz, a Finnish breed, is a close relative to the German Spitz, or Pom. It may be the connective link between the Spitz and the Samoyed. The Norwegian Elkhound is also evidently a kinsman of the Spitz.

The Schipperke is only another version of the Spitz with a different kind of coat. The fundamental structures of the two breeds are much alike. All that is necessary to note the resemblance of the Schip to the Pom is to compare their skeletons. Moreover, the name *Schipperke* in Belgium, the breed's home, was "Spitz" or "Spitske" up until 1888 when the present name was adopted.

In spite of the fact that there were dog shows in England as early as 1859, it was not until 1870 that the Pomeranian was recognized by the English Kennel Club, and the first show to be opened for the breed was the Kennel Club Show in June 1871. There were only three entries in that class—"those entries," according to Miss Lilla Ives, one of the earliest and most important breeders of Pomeranians, "being composed of a trio of large white dogs." The show was judged by Mr. Lort and the class was won by a bitch named Floss, the property of a Mr. Turner. All three dogs were owned by separate exhibitors.

The following year at the same great show there were thirteen entries, all property of different persons, but the following year entries dropped to seven. At the Kennel Club Show of 1890, not a single Pomeranian competed. This failure of the breed to catch on is all the more remarkable because of what was to follow, beginning in 1891.

In February of 1891 at the Agriculture Hall, while the great Crufts Show was in progress, a meeting of Pomeranian exhibitors, breeders, and fanciers was held for the purpose of forming a permanent organization to promote and further the interests

Greek Vase, 400 B.C. Aphrodite and Apollo
Photo, E. Walker.

10

of the Pomeranian. There were only seven persons present at the meeting, but once the Pomeranian Club was organized, many additional recruits joined almost at once. Miss Hamilton of the Roselle prefix was elected the first president of the organization, and Theodore Marples, whose thumb was in every activity that pertained to dogs, was the first secretary.

How much of the success was due to royal patronage of the breed is not known, but it is certainly true that Her Majesty, Queen Victoria, exhibited and won with a Pomeranian known as Windsor Marco in the April show of the Kennel Club two months following the Pomeranian Club's organization. It is very likely that this win by the popular queen gave a fillip to the breed's popularity. From that date onward, the Pomeranian breed made steady progress. Increase in entries was steady until in the October 1905 Kennel Club show there were 125 Poms exhibited by sixty-five exhibitors in the thirty classes provided for the breed. It was the most numerous breed in the entire show.

In 1892 the Pomeranian Club formulated and published its Standard of Perfection in a brochure which had a wide circulation. Prior to that time no Standard of the breed had existed and Poms were adjudged by the ideas, penchants, or whims of whoever happened to act as judge. This resulted in chaos, out of which the publication of the Standard brought a kind of order.

Faulty as the first Standard was, it served as a point of departure. For an instance of its defectiveness, the coat was described in the Standard of 1892 as "silky," which would then and now spoil the show prospects of any Pomeranian that carried such a jacket. The Standard was soon amended to substitute the word "glossy" instead of "silky"; this was but little better. In 1897 another amendment was made in the Standard to describe the coat as "glistening," and the mane and frill were described to be of "long, straight, glossy hair." The top coat was finally and correctly described as "harsh." The "silky" and "glossy" and even "glistening" connoted a soft coat, and a soft coat fails to stand out away from the body as is required in a Pom of any distinction. In the Standard presently in use in England the correct coat is adequately described.

11

In May of 1907 the Pomeranian Club had become strong enough to stage its first specialty show, and was so successful that shows were held annually for many years, to be interrupted, however, by World War I.

For many years the Kennel Club had offered four challenge certificates at each of the major British shows, for dogs and for bitches over eight pounds. In 1908, the number of certificates for the entire breed was reduced to two—one for each sex. Now interest in the breed was confined to the small ones and big Pomeranians disappeared from show rings. "Pomeranian Miniature" became merely "Pomeranian."

The English fanciers had obtained their early exhibits and breeding stock from the Continent—Germany, Belgium, France, and Italy—where pedigree records for Toy dogs were not carefully maintained. Many were shown and won with no known background. It required at least three generations of selective breeding and keeping of accurate records to enable the fanciers to know what was behind specimens and to breed intelligently. The English possess great patience and a way with livestock and they soon were producing true strains of superior dogs. In the process they eliminated the less desirable dogs from their breeding programs and improvement of the breed generally resulted. Judging from old photographs of some of these early English winners, Poms were no paragons of beauty and type as we now know them, but this was the beginning of a trend toward general improvement in the breed.

By the time the breed reached America via England, breeding records were available and American breeders could go forward with certainty. Pomeranians in America were not only established by importations from England, but they were further reinforced and continue to be supplemented by importations, some good and some bad.

In America Poms were first exhibited in the Miscellaneous Classes, so there was no winners class and for that reason the attainment of championships was impossible. The first Pom ever exhibited in the United States is believed to be Sheffield Lad, shown in the Miscellaneous Class at the February show of the Westminster Kennel Club of New York in 1892. There were no further entries until the 1896 show of the same club, when two

Poms were exhibited: Prince Bismarck and Wolfgang, who won second and third, respectively, in the Miscellaneous Class.

In 1899 there were a number of importations from England, largely blues and chocolates, and The American Kennel Club was moved to recognize the breed and admit it to the studbook. The Westminster Kennel Club at its show in February .1900 was the first show-giving organization to provide classes (including winners class) for Pomeranians at an American dog show. Nubian Rebel, a chocolate, property of Mrs. Frank K. Smith, was best of breed and later made his championship. As point ratings at that time were based on dogs in the whole show, some dogs made their championships without ever meeting another dog of their breed, and only ten points were needed, so championships at that time meant less than they do today.

The same year, 1900, the American Pomeranian Society was organized (its history appears elsewhere in this book). White Poms were numerous in those early days and some of them weighed as much as twenty-eight pounds. Blues and chocolates were also numerous and the orange-shaded sable Ch. Dragon Fly established his color in Poms, as distinct from wolf-shaded sables which were common at that time. Much of the brilliant clear orange, so popular today, derives its luminosity from the blood of Dragon Fly. However, the bright clear orange color was slow to find acceptance, although now it is the rage. Mrs. Parker's Ch. Mars, the first sensationally beautiful Pom of that color, set the stage for the continued popularity of clear oranges. Mars, in addition to his beautiful blazing color, was superb in type and showed with the high-headed hackney gait that made him famous and brought about an appreciation of a beautiful flashy orange Pom strutting about the ring as only a Pom can strut when it is superb and knows it. He transmitted his style, type, and color to his progeny.

Where Mars' blazing color came from is problematical, but it undoubtedly was a mixture of ancestry in colors that brought about an accidental clear color that was dominant in Mars and therefore remained. St. Anthony, the sire of Mars, was a warm apricot fawn. He in turn was sired by a blue son of Boy Blue, known as Bit of Blue, and he was out of a daughter of the rusty black Little Nipper. Mars' dam was named Yellow Aster, but was

13

Toy Pomeranian with Child
Greek tombstone from Alexandria, Egypt
(about 3rd century B.C.)

in fact not yellow but of a warm brown shade. She, too, was a daughter of Little Nipper, an unsound black. Out of this hodgepodge of colors came the glowing orange sensation known as Mars.

During World War I no championships were awarded in England and it was then that Gold Blaze of Dara and Greygown of Dara were whelped. Mated, they produced the internationally famous English and American Ch. Flashaway of Dara. After winning the Non-Sporting Group at the great Crufts Show in England, a great triumph for the great Flashaway, he was sold to Charles Gilbert of California at an alleged price of 300 pounds, at that time amounting to approximately $1500 in United States money—an unheard-of price for a dog at that time.

Flashaway's blood still comes down in a straight line in the best Poms of today, here and in Europe. The great producer of champions, Ch. Sealand Moneybox, goes back to Flashaway.

In 1926 Ch. Woodfield Diamond King (by Erimus Re-Echo out of Erimus Merry Dawn) made his appearance on the Pomeranian stage, where he remained to dominate the whole Pomeranian future. Diamond King was bred and owned by Mrs. Jemson's Woodfield Kennels at Birmingham, but his blood was largely Dara strain. His sire, Erimus Re-Echo, was a son of Flashaway Too of Dara, with six generations of Dara blood back of him. His dam, Erimus Golden Dawn, was a daughter of Greygown of Dara, the dam of Flashaway.

Ch. Woodfield Diamond King was the sire of at least nine British champions—Ch. Loveliness of Dara, Ch. Sundawn Invader, Ch. Woodfield Sardonic, Ch. Sealand Career, Ch. Lynley All Gold, Ch. Sealand Gorgeous, Ch. Woodfield Diamond Queen, Ch. Woodfield May King, and Ch. Woodfield Peter Pan.

It was about this time that Mrs. Vincent Matta of Long Island came actively into the Pom picture and remained to dominate it for so many years with her many Garden winners. In the twenties she acquired the great producing bitch Little Houdina Girl, of Goldspeck and Dara bloodlines, all going back to Little Nipper. Acquiring champion after champion, she imported the ever famous Sealand Moneybox, who lived to sire twenty-seven champions, all of which produced noted progeny and many champions. Moneybox' ancestry goes back to Flashaway of Dara.

Ch. Foxfire Joy and Ch. Foxfire Chips

Mary L. Kneisel with U.S. and Can. Ch. Hunt's Gold Boy II

PERSONALITY OF THE POMERANIAN

NO ONE ever possesses a Pomeranian, for once a Pom has stared into your face with elfin look from adoring eyes, and has placed his feathery-light paw-print upon your heart, you are his to have and to hold forever after.

Poms have a way of infiltrating your life and happiness in such a way that they become an integral and important part of the very warp and woof of your existence.

To the aged couple who have passed the milestone of strenuous activity, and who spend a great deal of their time in quietude, the Pomeranian brings life and youth in abundance, and merriment and cunning activity without undue noise, appearing like a dancing sunbeam threading the days.

To the person living alone, the Pomeranian brings love and "togetherness" in that great measure that only an understanding companion can bring. He is a being to which the lonely person can talk, and it is soon evident that the Pomeranian understands, for he responds as though he knows all that is said to him. He may not actually know what all the words mean, but he understands enough to respond as though he DOES know every word. Poms have their own ways of "conversation," understood only by a Pom owner. Their ways of asking and receiving what they want are countless. I have owned many Pomeranians that would

17

not have shocked me for one moment had they suddenly and intelligently answered me in human language when I talked to them.

When I say, "Let's go to the garden," our Poms dance in excitement, for there is nothing they love better than exploring about the garden paths while I cut flowers for the house. When I say: "Let's mail the letters," they dash for the mailbox and watch with bright eyes while I place letters in the box, and their excitement knows no bounds when the mail carrier drives up and places the mail in the roadside box. They whoop joyously to the back door and dance madly until I take the mail from the box and then they settle down around my feet while I read the day's communications. They wait for THEIR mail, as I always give them the advertising letters I never read, and pity the luckless correspondent whose letter somehow gets mixed with the Pom's mail, for it is soon reduced to bits.

Our Poms know our party-line telephone ring is one, and they never come to tell me to answer the phone when it rings more than one time. And when I say I must go to the grocery, they droop—all but my old Nubbin, who is decrepit with age and other troubles, for she is privileged to ride along in the car to the grocery. They all know what "grocery" means, and when I come home again I find them lined up at the door and their joy knows no bounds. When I start placing supplies in their special places, the Poms gather around expectantly, waiting for their "treat," which is raw hamburger. It is hard to know who enjoys this the most, the Poms or me.

To the young couple just establishing a home, the Pom is important. He goes along on every week-end jaunt or hour's stroll and he gains more attention from passers-by than would a mink stole, a diamond necklace, or a natty sports car. Dancing along at the end of a leash, he is the target for all eyes.

The Pomeranian is not an aggressive fighter, unless he is provoked. He is unselfish to a great degree, but he also has a deep sense of possession and will fight to protect what he considers as his very own. He loves toys and a bed of his own, and he loves to cuddle close and be petted and talked to. He returns all affection lavishly, and he is playful even to a very old age. He loves to feel clean and well groomed and will act ashamed and slink out of sight behind the furniture if he has filth upon himself he cannot remove. His sense of cleanliness is remarkable.

The Pom can swell with indignation when an intruder enters the household, and for this reason he makes a good watch dog, his acute sense of hearing and his immediate uproarious outrage providing a very good burglar alarm. He will meet the challenge of the largest dog as though meeting his own wee size and for this reason must be protected from taking on "more than he can successfully chew."

He is quiet and careful around the very young and if he has been raised in a household before a baby arrives, he makes a good companion. But a Pom should never be purchased as a wee puppy for a young child of active age, as he can be ruined for life through a child's grasping his coat and mauling him, no matter how much the child may love him. Very young children do not have the capacity or necessary judgment for handling a young puppy.

The Pom is a very hardy dog once he has become partly grown or has matured, but in the baby stage he is so delicately built that he is no match for the mauling that very young children give a pup if not supervised closely.

Int. Ch. Creider's T-Town's Serenade, bred by Mrs. Norma Creider, and owned by Mrs. M. Allen, Romallen Kennels. *Dan's Photography*

19

Champion Little Timstopper

Originally owned by Mrs. Vincent Matta, then owned by Mrs. James M. Austin, Old Westbury, Long Island.

A Grandson of Ch. Moneybox Gold Coin and a Great-grandson of Ch. Sealand Moneybox and on the mother's side, a Great-grandson of Ch. Moneybox Currency.

Show sensation for two years with two Best in Show all breeds and 28 Best Toy Wins, two at Westminster and one at Morris and Essex Show. Eighteen times Best Toy in 1947 without a defeat. His son, Ch. Little Timstopper's Teeco and a younger brother of Timstopper, Ch. Little Tim's Chipper, both owned by Mrs. Austin, were sensational winners with Chipper twice Best in Show all breeds in 1949.

As you see, all those famous winners trace back to Sealand Moneybox but previous to Moneybox, there were other big winners worth mentioning: Ch. Little Sahib with four Best of all Breeds, Ch. Little Rajah with two Best of all Breeds, Ch. Little Ra with one Best of all Breeds and last but not least, Ch. Little Emir that made history in 1928-29-30 with a total of nine wins as Best of all Breeds.

OFFICIAL STANDARD

STANDARD as adopted by the American Pomeranian Club and published in *Pure-Bred Dogs, American Kennel Gazette,* April 1971.

APPEARANCE—The Pomeranian in build and appearance is a cobby, balanced, short-coupled dog. He exhibits great intelligence in his expression, and is alert in character and deportment.

HEAD—Well-proportioned to the body, wedge-shaped but not domed in outline, with a fox-like expression. There is a pronounced stop with a rather fine but not snipey muzzle, with no lippiness. The pigmentation around the eyes, lips, and on the nose must be black, except self-colored in brown and blue.

TEETH—The teeth meet in a scissors bite, in which part of the inner surface of the upper teeth meets and engages part of the outer surface of the lower teeth. One tooth out of line does not mean an undershot or overshot mouth.

EYES—Bright, dark in color, and medium in size, almond-shaped and not set too wide apart nor too close together.

EARS—Small, carried erect and mounted high on the head, and placed not too far apart.

NECK AND SHOULDERS—The neck is rather short, its base set well back on the shoulders. The Pom is not straight-in-shoulder, but has sufficient lay-back of shoulders to carry the neck proudly and high.

BODY—The back must be short and the top-line level. The body is cobby, being well ribbed and rounded. The brisket is fairly deep and not too wide.

LEGS—The forelegs are straight and parallel, of medium length in proportion to a well balanced frame. The hocks are perpendicular to the ground, parallel to each other from hock to heel, and turning neither in nor out. The Pomeranian stands well-up on toes.

TAIL—The tail is characteristic of the breed. It turns over the back and is carried flat, set high. It is profusely covered with hair.

COAT—Double-coated; a short, soft, thick undercoat, with longer, coarse, glistening outercoat consisting of guard hairs which must be harsh to the touch in order to give the proper texture for the coat to form a frill of profuse, standing-off straight hair. The front legs are well feathered and the hindquarters are clad with long hair or feathering from the top of the rump to the hocks.

COLOR—Acceptable colors to be judged on an equal basis; any solid color, any solid color with lighter or darker shadings of the same color, any solid color with sable or black shadings, parti-color, sable and black and tan. Black and Tan is black with tan or rust, sharply defined, appearing above each eye and on muzzle, throat, and forechest, on all legs and feet and below the tail. Parti-color is white with any other color distributed in even patches on the body and a white blaze on head.

MOVEMENT—The Pomeranian moves with a smooth, free, but not loose action. He does not elbow out in front nor move excessively wide nor cow-hocked behind. He is sound in action.

SIZE—The weight of a Pomeranian for exhibition is 3 to 7 pounds. The ideal size for show specimens is from 4 to 5 pounds.

TRIMMING AND DEWCLAWS—Trimming for neatness is permissible around the feet and up the back of the legs to the first joint; trimming of unruly hairs on the edges of the ears and around the anus is also permitted. Dewclaws, if any, on the hind legs are generally removed. Dewclaws on the forelegs may be removed.

CLASSIFICATIONS—The Open Classes at Specialty shows may be divided by color as follows: Open Red, Orange, Cream and Sable; Open Black, Brown and Blue: Open Any Other Allowed Color.

Ch. Golden Glow Dandy Kitten and Ch. Fraley's Wee Teddy Boy, brother and sister, best-brace winners in all-breed shows. Owner, Mrs. Joe Re.

Ch. Mar-Bi-Lea's Gay Cinderella, bred and owned by Mar-Bi-Lea Kennels. *Alexander Photo*

Ch. Davis Wee Gold Boxie, bred and owned by Stella Davis. *Norton of Kent*

Ch. Kavilla's Captivating Star, bred by Mrs.
E. L. Tankesley and owned by Mrs. V. G. Munz.

Ch. Rider's Wee Chick-A-Dee, bred by Blanche
V. Rider and owned by Armstrong's Kennels.

THE BLUEPRINT OF THE POMERANIAN

THE first thing the breeder or exhibitor must learn in order to find a measure of success is to appraise his own stock intelligently—not as to how well it suits him, but as to how closely a specimen comes to conforming to the official Standard, for that is the criterion by which Pomeranians will be judged.

If the breeding stock conforms closely to the Standard, and only the best is reserved for future breeding, a breeder is bound to produce stock worthy of the show ring.

The dog must be well groomed and properly trimmed if it is to be evaluated honestly. And it must walk proudly on leash and stand for examination. If it has been taught proper stance, this also helps, although most good judges have dropped the practice of judging a Pomeranian while it is posed on the table. But it helps to have the Pom standing up on its feet in tip-toe fashion, head proudly upraised and tail plume flat over its back. When a good Pom stands and walks properly, it fairly shouts "Champion!" no matter how many good Poms are in competition. Professional handlers know this and capitalize on it right down to the last decimal point. That is why they so often win. Give them a good Pomeranian and time to train it and that Pom will be a heavy contender in any ring under any judge.

27

1. Ears set too low down on head.
2. Correct ear set.
3. Excessive trimming in front of ears.

1. Long back.
2. Correct top line.

A good judge will not let a "pose" be the only criterion of his judging, for experience will have taught him that both a professional handler and an experienced breeder-exhibitor know how to handle a Pom in the ring to make its faults less evident. That is the reason the people at ringside may think the judge has erred in passing over a beautifully posed Pomeranian to place one that does not pose so well but that shows in its every movement that it is properly put together, as well as beautiful in outline and general appearance. A wealth of coat can cover a lot of sins that show only in gait and under the examining fingers of the judge. Only close examination detects the light eyes, poor mouth, thin foot pads and splayed toes, or low tail set that has been camouflaged by clever trimming, and many other faults such as open coat, soft coat and overlarge ears hidden in brushed-up neck ruff, wrong base color next to the skin of a sable, or stance aided and supported by a raised leash in the hands of a clever handler.

The "blueprint" for judging is meant as an aid to the newcomer in evaluating his Pomeranian and overcoming that so prevalent disease called "kennel blindness." The owner so afflicted looks at his Pom and thinks of the great purchase price he paid (I once had an irate exhibitor say to me after I had failed to place her dog first: "Madam, I paid $500 for that dog and he has champions all over his pedigree"); and remembering all the champions on his dog's pedigree, the owner sees his specimen through a haze of price-pedigree as a champion when in reality he is but a mediocre specimen at best. Some old-timers never have been cured of this disease, while many newcomers learn fast. It isn't how long you have been breeding and showing that counts, but how much you have learned in the process. There are breeders of only a few years' standing who know far more about evaluating a Pomeranian than some who have been breeding and showing for several decades.

Taking for granted that your Pomeranian has been brought to the peak of quality in coat, grooming, trimming, and training, we are ready to judge him according to the dictates of the official Standard.

Take the Pom outdoors on short grass or into the living room and have someone else parade him as you have seen done in

29

1. Out at elbows.
2. Correct front.

1. Down on pasterns.
2. Correct side front.

the show ring. Note whether or not the dog picks up his feet lightly or merely shambles. Note how he holds his head, whether raised high, or lowered so that he appears to have an elongated body. Note how he holds his tail plume, flat over his back in true fan shape, or half up and half down or over the side. Note if every hair glistens and is stiffly stand-off, not shaggy and unkempt, with knots behind his ears and ruffling his body coat.

When you have done all this you are getting your first overall impression, the same as does the judge in the ring; that is, you are if you observe the Pom as though you had never before laid eyes on him, or if you try believing that he belongs to your worst rival—that usually brings out a lot of faults you haven't seen before.

As the Pom parades before you, circling the room, he should appear as a huge puff-ball of fur with a large mane sweeping from under his jaw to give him a frill to go up over the back of the neck until his ears seem to disappear in fluff. He should be short backed, for this is important to general appearance and gait as well as to adherence to the Standard. A short back and huge coat give the Pom the appearance of a floating ball of fur. A slab-sided Pom, one that has a sparse rib cage (and almost always a long body goes with this type), can be detected the moment he gaits, no matter how cleverly he has been trimmed. He will not have that "prance" that is so desirable and will trot with no semblance of Pom "bounce." And here is another fault hidden by a clever pose, for a long-bodied Pom can be "bunched up" in such a way that when he is posed he appears short bodied.

A slab-sided bitch never makes a good brood, either, and such Poms are prone to heart and respiratory troubles, probably because of improper space to expand both lungs and heart, so slab-sidedness is an important factor and is described in the Standard as a major fault. The slab-sided Pom is also the type that is usually out at the shoulder, which is another major fault. Front legs and shoulders are invariably set too far back on a flat rib cage. Loose shoulders and slab sides and long bodies go together like apple pie and ice cream; where you find one, you usually find the others.

If legs are too long the Pom has a stilted appearance and he

31

1. Low tail set.
2. Correct tail set.
3. Tail over side.

1. Cowhocked.
2. Correct rear.
3. Too wide behind.

32

never gaits with that well-known motion that is to be seen when tiny, cat-like feet are raised quickly and set down again in a twinkling dance step, as though the Pom's feet were barely tapping the floor, almost floating on air. If the legs are too short, again the Pom will appear to be long bodied, due to the fact that his legs are not long enough to square him up, or, as famous, former all-rounder English judge Tom Gascoyne puts it, not long enough to "round him up." The perfect Pom appears to be able to stand in a square or circle.

Next we consider the head. Without a good head you just do not have a good Pomeranian. Head characteristics are strongly hereditary and poor heads will plague a breeding program right down to the sixth generation and beyond. Since general appearance counts for so much in judging the Pom, we cannot have a good Pomeranian with a poor head, no matter if the body is well-nigh perfect.

The official Standard tells us that the head should be somewhat foxy in outline. Note that it says "somewhat foxy." The true fox head has more curve to the jaw than is allowed in the Pomeranian. The good Pom head should be wide at the back of the jaw and come gradually to a delicate muzzle in a medium-short jaw. Too long—and you lose the important wedge and the Pom has a Shepherd-like appearance. Too short—and you have a muzzle more like a Chihuahua's, which does not answer to the Pom Standard's requirements. Too square a jaw and the Pom appears coarse in head. For ultimate beauty, the jaw should be as short as possible, so long as it does not lose the true wedge shape.

The skull should be slightly flattened on top and in no instance should the dog be apple headed; nor should the dog have the round-domed skull that one English judge aptly described as having too much baking powder in it. It should never look like a round-topped biscuit.

The skull should have a little stop but the stop should not be pronounced or the dog will be the apple-headed variety. The coat on face and head should be short and glossy.

Nose leather should be black in all coat colors except blue and chocolate, when the nose should be the same basic color but a little darker in tone. However, if the nose should be black on a chocolate, I don't think any judge would grade the dog down on this account. In no instance should a Pom's nose be pink or spotted. The top line from nose leather to stop must be level and never dished in an upward curve near the end. Nostrils should be well defined but delicate.

Teeth are not so important in the Pom as in some other breeds. Perfect teeth are pearl-like in appearance and clean, and a few out of line do not constitute an undershot or overshot jaw. The Standard asks that they meet in a scissors grip, where the upper teeth close just over the lower ones, and not in a level bite where the edges meet, making a squared jaw. The Standard makes no penalty for a missing tooth.

Eyes should be dark and lustrous and should have that sparkle that proclaims "Mr. Personality" himself; and the eyes should be set wide apart but definitely not so far apart as to give the Pom a vapid expression. The eyes should be at a slight angle and the rims of the eyelids should be black in all but the blues and browns, when again self-color is required.

Ears are most important to the quality and appearance of the Pom. They should be as small as is possible. I have yet to see ears that were too small. They should be set high on the head and close together, facing forward. Ears set too low on the side of the head are even worse than large ears and give the Pom a lamb-like appearance.

Cowhocks are listed in the Standard as a major fault, along with several other flaws, and certainly are not desirable, but they are man-made in most instances and not inheritable in the true sense. Therefore, this condition is not so important in breeding stock as in show stock, although all breeding stock should be of show-stock quality if possible. No Pom is perfect, for all have faults to some degree. And while I prefer and always look for straight legs, I feel that cowhocks are less serious than overlarge ears or a coarse muzzle, when one has to make a choice, for the latter two faults are inheritable. Because cowhocks are not necessarily heritable, they are condoned by many judges who know that low-set ears, large ears, and long bodies are inheritable and therefore more serious faults.

Next comes another highly important point in the evaluation of the Pom: tail set. If the tail is set high on the end of the backbone, it should not have the feel of a hard bone pressing into the palm of the hand when the palm is placed flat against the tail root. Proper high set has no feel of boniness and the tail lies flat on the back and spreads out into a fan that should reach the back of the head. If the tail root has a twist to the set, the tail will not lie flat but will fall over the side, no matter how high the set, with most of the plume falling to one side.

If the tail is set low, the bone will press into the palm of the hand when the test is made, and the root can be seen to protrude outward and upward instead of disappearing into a flat plume over the back. Extremely low tail set will cause the tail to circle upward in a "squirrel" tail, and although often this does not detract alarmingly from the appearance of a heavy-coated Pom, it turns an otherwise good Pom into just a nice pet type that should never be used for breeding purposes. Artful trimming can do much for the appearance of such a Pom and I have seen many judges fooled by a poor tail, but never one who really knows Poms. This type tail is strongly hereditary.

Coat on a Pomeranian is not something you can get by application of a lotion or coat-grower. The proper Pom coat is really two coats: the first, a thick furry under coat; the second, a long outer coat of guard hairs that are stiffly stand-off without application of lotion. The outer coat should glisten with life but be harsh to the touch. The body from the neck to the back of the hind legs should be covered with a thick under coat lighter in tone than body color, supporting the thick outer coat. The coat must never be kinky or curly.

The Standard tells us the weight for show is three to seven pounds, with preference given to the four- to five-pound size, and with this most experienced breeders agree, but, sad to relate, far too many judges still give precious championship points to the undersized Poms. I expect to see the time when underweight and overweight will be listed as disqualifications. It is not fair to disqualify a monorchid male and then to give points to a bitch that is useless as a breeder because of her size. Simply adding fat to bring an underweight Pom up to the three-pound weight is never justified, unless it was skinny in the first place, for a good judge will penalize a Pomeranian for being either too skinny or too fat.

35

The larger size, over seven pounds, run to coarseness. So evaluate your Pom from this standpoint: "Is it good for the breed?"

Last, we come to color. Many fanciers think that if a color is pretty it will get by in the show ring. But that depends upon how you enter the dog. Entering an orange Pomeranian that has sabling over the shoulders but nowhere else, in the orange class that calls for a clear color, is to subject the dog to penalization. Such a Pom will not be a good sable either, and so it is best to enter it in either the American-bred or the bred-by-exhibitor class. Oranges should be clear orange, with lighter under coat. Breechings on an orange should not have a whitish cast, but a lighter shade is permissible. A Pom with color variations as described above is not subject to disqualification, but a judge must take coat coloration into consideration when competition is close.

All colors recognized in the Standard should be good clear colors and not muddy or dull. Colors should not be mixed with a few white or black hairs. So evaluate colors carefully before entering a Pom in competition if you are out for championship points. Of course, if you just love showing your Poms and go in for pure sport, by all means enter any Pom that is not a discredit to the breed.

A Pomeranian should be judged on the basis of his outstanding qualities and not tossed into the discard because he has one or two faults. If dogs were judged for faults instead of for their good qualities, most would lose. It is a bright day when a near-perfect specimen walks into the ring. And it does happen, but not so often as the fond owner-exhibitor would like to believe. If the overall picture is good and your Pomeranian has no disqualifying faults, by all means take him into the show ring. Everyone wins whether or not they achieve the blue ribbon or the coveted purple, for the show ring is the quickest way I know to a thorough education of what constitutes a top quality Pomeranian. The exhibitor always learns if he is open minded and does not listen to the poor losers who immediately state that the judging was fixed. When they tell you, "So-and-so's dog is going to win today," and pretend to have inside information, and the dog does win, it usually has won because the poor-sports-men have lesser quality Poms and they knew it and were preparing an alibi ahead of time.

The show ring is the place not only to educate yourself as to what constitutes a good Pomeranian, but it is also a good advertising medium. Hiding your Pom under a bushel never brings in any customers. So size up your Pom intelligently and honestly and without prejudice, and then show him. If you wear rose-colored glasses when looking at your own stock and then take the glasses off when observing the other fellow's stock, you will **never** advance as a breeder or an exhibitor.

Ch. Pacemaker's Lady Tina

Davis Ricky Money Box Jewel   Ch. Currency's Wee Wonder

Top-flight, seven-week-old show prospects from the kennels of Beatrice Palmer.

CHOOSING A POMERANIAN PUPPY

CHOOSING a puppy is always an exciting experience, even to the old-timer. It is always desirable to buy the very best specimen one can afford, or to choose the best to keep from a litter one has produced, for one good puppy is worth more than several mediocre ones. If you can go to the kennel and choose the puppy yourself, that is always most satisfactory. But if you cannot, you have to rely on the knowledge and honesty of the breeder, so make sure that you choose one that is reliable—not only one that is thoroughly honest but also a breeder who has knowledge to back his judgment. A breeder can be very honest and trustworthy as to intention, but he can be very wrong and unreliable when it comes to assessing the value of a Pom. And, of course, anyone can make mistakes as to what a puppy will be when mature.

If buying for show or breeding purposes, make sure the background of the puppy is good and represents a line known to produce good specimens, with no strongly inheritable faults of a major nature. Any line can produce faults at times, but some lines are known consistently to produce major faults. These are to be avoided. Here is another example of the value of attending shows, whether or not you exhibit, as you can learn the background of each Pomeranian entered in the show merely by

Ch. Bonner's Sunny Showstopper exhibits the short body, good tail placement, heavy coat when shedding, good ear placement, foxy muzzle and good eye size, and, best of all, a bold, unafraid, inquiring expression.

Golden Glow Best Yet, bred and owned by Wilma Smith. This picture illustrates good short body, good front and pert face.

Kloster's Wee Tania, bred and owned by Myrtle Kloster. A good puppy remains good even when in the ragged stage of shedding, as pictured here.

Pup-Pet's Happy Major, bred and owned by Flora Evison.

40

purchasing the show catalogue, which lists the dogs and their sire and dam, also their AKC number, through which you can obtain a complete pedigree from the AKC, if you so desire.

If purchasing by mail, write the selected breeder in detail, telling exactly what type, color, and sex you prefer, and for what purpose the puppy is wanted. This gives the breeder the chance to give you an intelligent reply. Ask for snapshots and pedigree copy but be sure you return them to the breeder.

A puppy should have the same general points of conformation as the Standard requires for the adult dog, but its color may change later, as many reds and orange-sables are covered at the age of eight weeks or more with a wealth of grayish-black hair. A shaded muzzle may clear later or it may not. It all depends upon the background in breeding.

A puppy should carry a heavy coat but it cannot be expected to have a mature type coat. In judging the puppy's potential, some points are a dead giveaway. If the tail, for instance, lies straight down the back so flat it leaves a track in the coat when lifted, the tail set is high and the tail most likely will be good when the dog is mature.

Puppy jaws also give one a pretty good preview of what the mature jaw will look like. A square or stubby jaw with a perfectly even bite may mature into an undershot jaw, or it may stay level. I learned this the hard way and it cost me one hundred and fifty dollars. I sold a pup with a beautiful even bite for three hundred dollars and it matured with a slightly undershot jaw. I took it back and returned the three hundred dollars and later sold the mature dog for one hundred and fifty dollars as a pet. While I was holding the pup for shipment to the original purchaser, I refused to go back on my word to this first buyer and sell the pup to a man who wanted it for a pet at the three hundred, regardless of what it matured into. I have not trusted an even-jawed puppy since.

The puppy that matures to have a nice jaw as an adult usually looks a bit overshot—not with a pronouncedly longer upper jaw, but with the lower jaw slightly shorter than the upper jaw. Teeth should just barely meet, with the upper teeth fitting over the lower ones in a scissors bite.

Look for small and delicate boning throughout, as any sug-

41

This puppy from the kennels of breeder-owner Mrs. Paul Helcamp shows a good front and stance, sweet face, and well-set eyes and ears.

Highland's Merry Legendmaker and Highland's Merry Magic Legend, puppies with good coats, good ears, and sweet faces. Bred and owned by Patricia Hopkins.

Wild Wind's Orange Punch and Wild Wind's Mostly Mischief, bred and owned by Mrs. Ross Hanna. This picture illustrates excellent side views of two good puppies at the age of three months.

gestion of coarseness in a puppy indicates a heavy-boned or coarse adult.

Feet should be small and dainty. Large feet mean that a pup will grow up to match the feet. A puppy that comes forward boldly to be petted at weaning age and up to ten months, will likely mean a friendly and calm mature dog.

Short neck and back are desirable and a short face with wedge-shaped jaw should be looked for. A long-nosed pup never grows up to be anything else. Neither does a big-eared one. Light eyes do not grow dark, and a thin, weedy rib cage never grows into a rounded one. Set the pup on the floor and get down so that you can observe its top line. If its hips stand higher than its shoulders, and this is not because the coat is shedding in patches, pass the pup up for a better specimen. Do not allow a cute face to blind you to the pup's other qualities or faults.

Study the Standard and study the excellent illustrations used to picture what a good Pom puppy looks like. And always remember that the choicest specimens usually come high, but that they are worth the difference in price. It costs no more to raise a good specimen than a poor one, and if you start out with a good one you have the best chance of ending up with a good mature dog.

Four of a kind, all good, at the age of seven and nine weeks, from the kennels of breeder-owner Lois E. Campbell.

Penpom's Nix Von Schneeweiss, heavy coated, beautifully marked white stud. Bred by B. Kenyon and owned by Margaret Penprase.

Ace-Hi Snow Princess and Ace-Hi White Lady, snow white puppies from four generations of white breeding. Bred and owned by Beulah Connors.

Ch. Thunder of Erimus, one of the very few fine blacks in the country today. Owners, Mr. and Mrs. Norman Jerome.

COLOR BREEDING

THE breeding for specific colors is a subject that has always interested fanciers, and in the past, Pomeranians came into show rings in many beautiful colors and each had its devotees. But the craze for oranges overshadowed interest in all other colors, which is a pity, for it has led to almost complete elimination of many beautiful shades. However, in the past few years I have noted several unusual colors and my mail has been heavy with inquiries as to how this and that color can be obtained.

Since the oranges have almost completely eliminated the chocolates, blacks, blues, and whites formerly to be seen, it will take several generations of color breeding to begin to produce consistently true colors in the latter hues. But many of the old-time breeders are currently searching for specimens of the rarer colors to work with. And during the past few years I have examined a fairly excellent chocolate, a beaver, a smoky blue, and a blue with lavender overtones.

There is also a strong revival of interest in blacks, and some very good blacks have been imported from England. Blacks formerly were numerous in England, but the color is now on the wane over there, so top quality blacks are obtainable at a reasonable price. Therefore, now is the time to import blacks, if breeding blacks is your goal. Breeding clear black to black produces blacks and also blues, especially if there is some white or orange sable in the background.

One especially good black has come over from England in recent years—Norman Jerome's Ch. Thunder of Erimus—and Robwood Kennels also have imported some outstanding blacks during the past few years.

While breeding black to black sometimes produces blues, breeding blue to blue is said to almost invariably produce blues. Reports of blues from orange-sable breedings have come in, but these almost always turn orange-sable later. Blue pups are born black, turn to blue later, and while some turn a coppery sheen at about six weeks, the new under coat coming in will show a decided blue color. Only time can tell how a blue will turn out, and repeated breedings of the same cross can be expected to bring the same results.

Browns usually come from breeding black to orange, though one of the old-time strains of browns was established by breeding a black to a white, producing the celebrated Hizza, a great winner of her time and a top producer. She established a brown line, and most of the top brown lines in the United States today can be traced back to Hizza's progeny. At one time browns were more popular than oranges, as were chocolates, which are dilute browns.

Beavers are a deep taupe shade with reddish overcast over the body and are very rare. Reds are technically merely a deeper shade of orange, as red is one of the original colors of the spectrum. Red, to be good, should be clear in color, not merely a dirty dark orange. Oranges are so well known that they need no description, but many ignore the fact that the Standard calls for an orange to be self-colored throughout.

Orange-sables must have a clear orange body color, with lighter orange or creamy under coat, and with black sabling or tipping to the guard hairs on body and tail plume.

True creams of a clear color, not muddy and not merely a poor orange color, are beautiful and much admired by those who see them, but far too many judges pass over the creams for oranges, even though the creams are of a better quality. This should not be, for the Standard makes no distinction in value between any of the recognized solid colors, and more active showing of creams might serve to educate judges to their worth. Creams are secured by judicious choice of breeding stock, breeding together the lighter oranges having good black pigmentation of nose and eye rims. The color is easily maintained in the breeding program by breeding creams to creams or light oranges.

Whites dominated the Pomeranian stage at the turn of the century and one hundred years or more ago all Pomeranians were white, biscuit, or black. The blacks were used by shepherds to guard their flocks because this color was not so quickly detected by predatory wolves, so history tells us.

Parti-colors are rarely seen, but the Standard recognizes white body color with either orange or black patches evenly distributed over the entire body. White on the saddle and a white blaze on the forehead are preferred. The wording of the old Standard caused so much confusion that many judges did not disqualify black and tans, but that situation has now been clarified by the American Pomeranian Club. A black and tan Pom is not recognized as a parti-color. It appeared that the mention of black and tan as a minor fault was meant to recognize black and tans as an allowable color but this was not the case. The Standard should have stated "black and tan Terrier markings." This has recently been cleared up, although there is a sizable following within the parent club that wants all lovely colors recognized by the Standard, as is the case in many other breeds—Pekingese, for instance.

Inclusion of all colors would encourage breeding for the rarer colors and the unusual blendings.

Ch. Nelson's Hot Toddy,
owned by Mae Nelson.

47

TRIMMING CHART

1. Whiskers may be thinned if heavy.
2. If heavy coat protrudes into corners of eyes and causes watery eyes, carefully clip it close and clean from corners of eyes.
3. Proper ear set.
4. Straggling hair evened with ear tip but *not* denuded on inside of ear.
5. Only *straggling hairs* cut away—*not sheared* around tail as on Poodle.
6. Proper back foot clip and stance.
7. Proper front foot clip and stance.

Front feet and legs are trimmed so that front feet resemble cat's paws, nails not showing but all hair clipped around and between toes and up the back to the first joint only. Back feet are trimmed the same and up back of leg to hocks.

At the root of the tail, with tail over the back, straggly hairs above and below anus are snipped away, *but it is not permissible to shear tails from roots all around in Poodle fashion for an inch or two. Neither is it permissible to clip coat on back under the tail to make tail lie flat.*

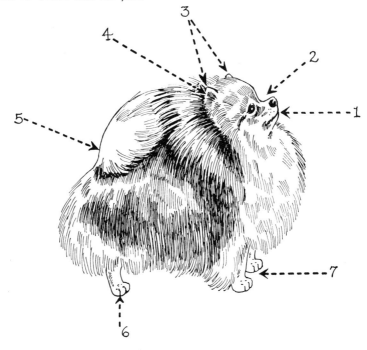

GROOMING THE POMERANIAN

HERE we come to the point that is most worrisome to the novice as well as to many long-time breeders who have never learned to groom and trim a Pomeranian properly. But I think that failure usually comes as a result of too much grooming rather than from too little.

Rules are simple. Grooming is not something to be done the day of a show, or even three days before. Properly, a moderate amount of grooming should be begun before a puppy is weaned. Accustomed to gentle grooming almost from birth, the puppy takes it in stride and without resentment. A Pomeranian loves to be clean, and lavish praise following grooming will transport the Pom into ecstacies of prancing pride. He's a born show-off.

The Pom's first complete grooming should come at weaning age. Trim ear tips as shown in the diagram, placing the nail of the thumb and forefinger over ear leather to prevent cutting the ear, and trim off the fringe of hair that makes ears appear out of proportion when untrimmed. The present Standard states, "trimming unruly hairs on edges of ears permissible." This phrase is so elastic that a judge could not term an exhibit ineligible if its ears were trimmed all the way down to its skull, even though this most certainly would make ears appear enormous and so prominent that overall appearance would be spoiled. So keep ear trimming to a minimum, trimming the tips just enough to show the true outline and size of the ear. Trim the hair on the inside edge of the ear about one-half the length of the hair trim on the outside ear rim. Later on, as the coat becomes long, snipping straggling wisps from behind the ear is permissible and wise. Trimming of the Pom should be considered in the same light as the proper grooming of the owner, and is for the same reason—to present a clean, tidy appearance.

Feet should be cleaned of excessive hair around the toes, but nails must not be exposed. Legs should be trimmed up the back to the first joint. DO NOT shear the leg coat completely around the leg. Straggling hairs anywhere on the body should be snipped off, but be sure you do not shear out large portions of coat. Trim just the few overlong hairs.

Trimming the anal area is necessary for the sake of cleanliness, so snip away all straggling hairs that close over the rectum. Otherwise, you will have a soiled Pom most of the time. Trim away just enough coat that the rectum is clean of hair. Snipping of the unruly hairs beside the tail root is customary and is not penalized, but beware of trimming tails in accordance with old-time practice. Too many Pomeranians come into rings today with tails trimmed at the roots in Poodle fashion, in the mistaken belief that a knowing judge will be fooled into thinking the Pomeranian has a shorter body than it really has. Trimming or shearing the tail root completely around the bone for an inch or two is decidedly objectionable and certainly constitutes excessive trimming, as does trimming too close to show date.

Also, some owners are using thinning shears on the section of back coat that is covered by the tail plume, to make tails lie flatter, and even are shearing plume ends into a fan until they resemble the spread tail of a pigeon. Thinning back coat is objectionable, as is trimming tail plumes into fans. By all means keep all trimming to a minimum, trimming only for neatness.

Teeth should be cleaned from puppyhood, for the dog will not object if it is started early. Dip a dampened soft cloth in powdered pumice stone and rub teeth and gums once or twice a week. When the puppy is shedding his teeth, this procedure once a day is usually soothing. The first attempt at tooth cleaning will be a trial to both puppy and handler but the puppy will soon learn to accept it. Loosened baby teeth can be picked out with the fingers, all but the large canines, which, if they do not come out of their own accord, will probably require use of a veterinarian's forceps.

To bathe or not to bathe bothers most novices. Do not bathe the Pom in a tub of water unless he is actually dirty to the skin or in need of a bath containing an insecticide for lice or fleas. The new lather bombs that contain an insecticide are fine for cleaning purposes and do not soak the coat.

Keep the nails cut back from the start, for when they are allowed to grow long, the heart, or quick, of the nail shoves out and nails cannot then be cut short until the quick has been reduced. Cutting into the quick is very painful and causes profuse bleeding which can become a hemorrhage that ends in death. (For instructions on trimming nails, see page 126, Part II of this book.) Pom nails should be moderately short, as too short nails will stick upward in ugly fashion.

Now comes the all-important brushing. Directions used to be given to brush and re-brush daily, but the most successful breeders and exhibitors in the business of turning out Poms in perfect coat condition, usually brush but once a week, or, in a few instances, twice a week. Use pure bristle brushes with single bristles. The cluster-type tears the coat out too much. And since the advent of nylon I have found that the soft nylon hair brushes made for small children are just right for the brushing back of the hair on the Pom's ears and around the face and the belly area.

Using the bristle type on an adult Pom, the child's type on a puppy, start behind the ears. Take the ear tip between the fingers and brush downward with the soft nylon brush, and on adults, brush with the bristle brush from the back of the neck downward on the body. Part the hair in layers and brush each layer downward toward the tail, avoiding tearing out the under coat, slowly moving back until the whole body has been covered. Lay the tail over the back and brush from the roots with sure, gentle strokes. Too vigorous or too fast brushing will tear out some of the plume and this should never be permitted to happen. Turn the Pom over and lay it with its back downward between your knees, and brush the belly hair with the nylon brush, giving special attention to the leg fringes and pants. Then stand the Pom on a table and brush the pants downward—*not out,* which serves to elongate body appearance. Brush the apron under the chin and brush the neck ruff upward, and beginning again on the back coat, brush from the tail to the neck in a forward motion that raises the coat. After you have groomed every inch of the Pom coat, sprinkle or spray with cold water and rub with a rough towel until the coat is slightly dampened. If hair is curly or straggly behind the ears, as it often has a tendency to be, shake a little amber-colored powder into the coat behind the ears and on neck ruff and front frill or apron, and rub it in thoroughly. Then brush it completely out again and the coat will be beautiful, with every hair standing off in shining beauty. Powder must always be brushed out thoroughly until no cloud arises when the dog is patted smartly in the show ring, as this will get your entry disqualified. So do a good job of brushing out the talcum (not face powder) if you use it. Face powder has a cream base that sticks to the coat hair and should never be used. The talcum put out for men to use after shaving is usually just right.

Keep your Pom well groomed and trimmed at all times and never trim ears and legs just prior to a show. Trim at least ten days before a show so the "new haircut" look will have vanished.

Whiskers can be thinned or untrimmed (although the APC frowns on trimming), but they usually are trimmed when the Pomeranian has such a profusion of whiskers that he appears frowsy and coarse of muzzle. Muzzles must never be clipped down to make them appear more delicate. If you try it and get caught and penalized, don't blame the judge.

Chalking or coloring the coat to cover unwanted light spots is "faking" and a judge MUST mark you ineligible to compete if you are guilty of this offense, and you will be subject to a fine or suspension or both by the AKC.

Keep ears clean, for dirty ears cause dogs to dig at them with their hind feet and ugly knots will form in the coat behind the ears. An adult dog should be watched closely and the moment it starts casting its coat in hot weather the loose patches should be gently plucked, not yanked out, with a comb. Daily brushing at this time is advisable to remove loose hair and under coat, but brush gently. Do not dig out the coat, or permanent damage may be done to the under coat. If the skin is dry and flaky at shedding time, rubbing a little fresh olive oil or lanolin into the skin is beneficial. The feeding of wheat germ oil will prevent this condition from arising.

EAR TRIMMING

Cut #1 is made straight across ear tip with thumb nail and forefinger protecting ear leather.

Cut #2 is made about 1/8 inch down inside edge of ear. Cutting too far down on this one appears to widen ear set.

Cut #3 is made about 1/2 inch down outside edge of ear, depending upon head size of Pom. Small, 3 lb. Pom cut would be smaller, 5 lb. Pom perhaps longer. This is medium size, about 4 lb. Pom.

.1

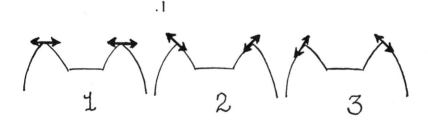

Ch. Sealand Good Brandy of Gold Blackacre, owned by Miss Helen Nowicki.

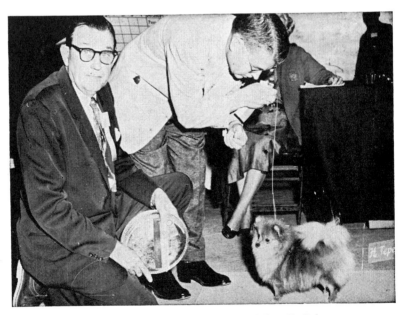

Aristic Dainty Delight, bred by Mrs. I. Schoenberg and owned by C. V. (Shorty) Harwood.

AMERICAN POMERANIAN BREEDERS

IN WRITING of American breeders, it is difficult to know where to begin or where to leave off, but there is an end to space available when writing a book. Furthermore, so much has been accomplished by so many that a writer can only scratch the surface.

Mrs. Roy Webber of Newton Center, Massachusetts, is one of the earlier breeders in Pomeranian history in the United States about whom a book could be written. She has owned and bred outstanding Westminster winners and again has scored in being active in breeding and exhibiting. Among her many champions are Premier Crown Prince, Cairndhu Realization, and Premier Crown Jewel. These outstanding champions appear in the background of many of today's top winners. Ch. Little Prize Package, BOB at the Garden in 1952 and 1953, and Ch. Premier Crown Pippins Joan are among her recent champions. Mrs. Webber is an astute breeder and exhibitor, never bringing a Pomeranian into the ring until it is in full glory of coat and excels in ring training. Her Ch. Cairndhu Realization was BOW in 1936 at the Garden over ninety-six Pomeranians. Mrs. Webber has been a pillar of support in the American Pomeranian Club, Inc., and still works hard to support the breed.

Grace Rishell of Bridgeville, Pennsylvania, is another old-time breeder and professional handler of whom much could be written. Her first Pom, presented her by her father, was imported, and like so many of that era, little was known about the dog's background. But her image remained in Mrs. Rishell's memory and became her goal in breeding, so in 1934 she began buying Poms from Dara, Perivale Memento, and Bonny Ideal lines that resembled her first Pom. She owned Ch. Day Dawn of Beaumanor, Ashburn, and Whyteheather Betsierone, purchased from the late Reuben Clark. Ch. Best Yet of Ashburn, whose gleaming red color runs in the lines of most of the good reds today, was one of her outstanding Poms and she also had Chs. Reighlayn's Merriment and Reighlayn Little Dano, among many others.

Violet Boucher, professional handler-breeder and owner of Firland Kennels, purchased her first Pom in 1931 and has finished more than one hundred Toy dog champions. She bred many of the old-time champions and finished many for other owners, among them Chs. Shining Gold Dragon, Shining Gold Tad, and Polly Prim of Skyline. Her Ch. Moneybox Monkeyshine was the first Pom to win a West Coast BIS. Monkeyshine is still alive and full of vim and vigor.

Glad Days Kennels of Gladys M. Wright of Bloomington, Indiana, began when Mrs. Wright's physician recommended a hobby because her health broke down under the stress of public life (Mr. Wright is a minister). Mrs. Wright purchased a son of Ch. Sealand Moneybox from Mrs. Matta and the success she has since attained is proof of the good sense of buying top foundation stock. Ch. Jem's Double Ace and Ch. Glad Day's Red Robin both finished their championships quickly and I had the pleasure of awarding majors to both. Mrs. Wright's Ch. Moneybox Show Boy finished in four shows, winning twelve points in one week. Her first champion was Glad's Victoria, a granddaughter of Rob Moneybox.

Great Elms Kennels, owned and operated by Ruth Beam of Pineville, North Carolina, is one of the outstanding kennels in America. Ruth consistently produces top stock and when I visited her some time ago after awarding winners bitch to one of her fine broods and watching it attain the same award at another show the following day under an all-breed judge, I was

Tiny Tot's Dandy Mite
Owners, Messer & Hoffman
Breeder, Mrs. R. J. Wilson

Messer's Frisky Mite
Owner, Dr. Pearl E. LeMay
Breeder, Irene H. Messer

Reighlynn's Reynita
Owners, Mr. and Mrs. Cox
Breeder, Mrs. Grace Rishell

Dee's Own Ducal Desire
Owners, Mr. and Mrs. James Sutton

U.S. & Can. Ch. Jo Jac Dandy Duke
Owner, Mrs. W. R. Pitts
Breeder, Mrs. Hughes

Ch. Thelcolynn's Showstopper
Breeder-Owner, Mrs. Thelma Gunter

much impressed with the overall quality of her breeding stock. Ch. Great Elms Little Timstopper, then nine years old, was still beautiful and still producing. He carried a huge stand-off coat of brilliant color and by December 1960 his sixteenth champion progeny had been certified by the AKC. I chose Ch. Great Elms Little Buddy, a son of "Timmy," from a group of more than a dozen puppies at the time of my kennel visit, as even then, though shedding his puppy coat and being in that raggedy state that only a shedding Pom puppy takes on at three or four months of age, he looked like a coming champion and time proved his worth.

Ruth Beam's Great Elms Kennels was established back in 1937 with a black bitch, and the kennel name was taken from the great old elms surrounding the house and kennels. While she was searching for a Toy breed to produce, Ruth's brother called her attention to the picture of a beautiful little dog that was winner of the Toy Group at the Madison Square Garden Show—Mrs. Matta's great little Pom, Ch. Little Sahib. He was the inspiration that began Great Elms and gave the kennels such a high mark to shoot at, and I think that even Little Sahib would be proud of the Poms that come out of Great Elms. Schoenberg and Dixieland stock formed the foundation of the kennel. Many home-bred champions have been finished by Ruth Beam, with many more on their way. She shows only at shows within easy driving distance of her kennels, or many more of her Poms would have been finished. She does not employ handlers, preferring to take her Poms personally into show rings, but many sold to others have become champions. She has been awarded the Gaines award for good sportsmanship, voted her by her home club, Piedmont Kennel Club, and she was voted the Dog World award for accomplishment in breeding and the production of champions.

Pauline Hughes of San Diego, California, so well known as a breeder, columnist, and judge, began in Poms back in 1939 with an Aristic brood that was bred to Gladys Youngdahl's Hemmer's Treasure of Skipit. The first litter of one, a lovely cream show type, Wee Gold Teddy, was bred back to his dam and produced two pups, Chs. Tiny Teena and Sir Robinhood. Teena was too tiny to breed and Sir Robinhood contracted distemper and became sterile, but the full sister from a following litter gave Mrs. Hughes Ch. Sable Symphony, who appears in many pedigrees of champions. In 1951 Mrs. Hughes purchased Golden Glow Molly, a daughter of Ch. Golden Glow Dandy, and in 1953 imported Ch. Preservenes Gold Marvel, a son of English Ch. Preservenes Dainty Boy, who became the sire of her Ch. Sir Percy of Point Loma, outstanding stud and sire of several show dogs of championship quality. Some of his present champions are Little Sahuaro of Arizone, Adora of Point Loma, and Celia of Point Loma. Due to city ordinances, Mrs. Hughes is unable to keep a large kennel, but this is good, for when a kennel is kept small by such an enthusiastic Pom fancier as Mrs. Hughes, the resultant quality is always high.

Mrs. Gladys Schoenberg of San Antonio, Texas, wife of the eminent show judge, Isidore Schoenberg, has been a Pomeranian fancier and breeder since 1926. Her Aristic Kennels have become world famous and the kennels that owe their success of today to foundation stock from her kennels are legion. Mrs. Schoenberg has a record of being the breeder and owner of more than sixty champions. A great asset to the breed, she has bred intelligently throughout the years and with such purpose and ideals in mind, that today an Aristic-bred Pomeranian can easily be recognized for its compact body, huge coat, wedge-shaped muzzle, and the overall qualities so desired in a Pomeranian. Her kennels, located on a beautiful tract of land near the edge of San Antonio, are the finest in the world and completely air conditioned, with display rooms that are a revelation and pleasure to the many visitors who see them each year. Over one hundred fine Pomeranians can be seen at any time. Twenty years ago, Ch. Aristic Gold Trinket, at one year of age, was Mrs. Schoenberg's first BIS, all breeds, winner. Since that time she has personally won the coveted honor more than fifteen times and has had dozens of best Toy wins. Poms sold by Mrs. Schoenberg have also gone BIS many times.

Mrs. Schoenberg believes in strengthening breeding programs by adding outstanding specimens to her kennels, as was shown when she purchased Ch. Wilmscote Wee Conquest right after he won as best Toy dog at the Chicago International. The following week Mrs. Schoenberg personally handled him to BIS

59

at Beaumont, Texas, and many such wins followed. He was carefully used in breeding patterns, producing, among others, such winning dogs as Ch. Aristic Conquests Flambeau, Ch. Mayking Blazing Conquest, Ch. Blackacre Wee Dandy II, and Ch. Halthoms Wee Thanksgiving. After having produced a large stock of beautiful sons and daughters which are used as foundation stock, he was sold to Mrs. C. A. Ellis of Grand Prairie, Texas.

When Mrs. Schoenberg started her Pomeranian kennels more than thirty years ago, she used outstanding show winners of the day with dogs of the celebrated English Ch. Woodfield Diamond King, Sun Cherub of England, Ch. Sealand Career, and Ch. Sealand Moneybox lines. This stock transmitted huge show coats and corrected large eyes and ears so prevalent at the time. By careful breeding and hewing to the line of strict requirements, the Aristic line of Pomeranians has become a distinct and recognizable bloodline. Some of the later famous Pomeranians bred or owned by Mrs. Schoenberg were Ch. Aristic Wee Sensation (called Little Thing), who was best American-bred Toy at Westminster in 1955 and top winning Pom for 1954, with five BIS wins and twenty-eight Group wins; Ch. Aristic Wee Pepper Pod, who had two BIS wins and four Toy Group firsts out of four times shown in 1956; Ch. Aristic Moneybox Gold Button, BIS winner and sire of many champions; also, Ch. Aristic Timothy, Ch. Aristic Wee Gold Chip, and many others of like quality. Too much credit cannot be given Gladys Schoenberg of Aristic fame, for out of her careful breeding practices have come the foundation stock of many fine kennels.

Dorothy Lee McDonald, of Sunset Beach, California, is a Pom hobbyist turned breeder. She runs a very successful motel but still has time to care for Poms. Her Ch. Fonda of Foxlawn, a gorgeous, heavy-coated orange, has Gladys Youngdahl's Poms in the background. Ch. Glad's Miss Stinkey is a short-coupled, heavy-coated, superb little Pom.

Gladys Youngdahl is one of the early California breeders still very active in both breeding and showing good ones. Her kennel houses more than one hundred Poms most of the time. One of her earliest outstanding broods was Glad's Goldie O'Flame, going back to Ch. Little Minegold, Ch. Gold Dragon of Gaybee, Int. Ch. Flashaway of Dara, and Offley Honeydew. Ch. Shining Gold Tad also figures heavily in the background of Youngdahl Poms. Ch. Glad's Mister Glad was perhaps the kennel's most potent stud for good, and many West Coast champions bear his name in their ancestry. He died recently at the age of seventeen years.

Dixieland Kennels of Mrs. Margaret Tankesley of Chattanooga, Tennessee, is known throughout the land. Mrs. Tankesley bred the great Ch. Dixieland's Shining Gold, who, after being purchased by Mrs. Vincent Matta shortly after he won his title, was taken out of show rings and used extensively at stud. Hence, it was left to his progeny to make his name great, for what a champion produces is more important to the breed than are his show wins. He was the sire of three-times BIS winners Ch. Little Timstopper and Ch. Little Timsun, and two-times BIS winner Ch. Little Tim's Chipper. Ch. Little Tim's Sunburst and his litter brother, Ch. Little Tim's Chipper, were the same breeding as Timstopper. In fact, the prefix *Tim* was taken from the kennel name of Shining Gold, who was affectionately called "Timmy." Another of Mrs. Tankesley's outstanding studs is Ch. Dixieland's Xmas Box, still lovely though past thirteen years of age. His sire was the ever famous Ch. Best Yet of Ashburn, whose glorious orange-red color runs through the strains of so many flashily colored Poms of today. Ch. Dixieland's Shining Gold was sired by Dixieland's Dandy Gold out of Dixieland's Golden Fantasy, who in turn goes back to Ch. Eastney Sable Dandy and Ch. Pomwin's Little Onederful. To name here all the prepotent-for-good type Poms that have come out of Margaret Tankesley's Dixieland Kennels would be impossible, but she has done as much for the Pomeranian breed in the United States as any other one person in Pom history. Breeders of the present should ever be grateful to those breeders of the past who so steadfastly held to their high ideals of the perfect Pom and never stopped trying to breed the perfect specimen.

Mrs. Edwin Sivori and Miss Virginia Sivori are two who have done much for the breed. Both are Pomeranian judges as well as judges of other Toy breeds. Mrs. Sivori gave me a great deal of help in assembling data about the parent club.

Miss Elsie Blum, another of the earlier fanciers who is still active in the parent club, although no longer breeding Poms, will live on in Pom history. She is known for her unfailing kindness and help to new breeders and exhibitors and for her great Poms of the past. I have her to thank for the records of specialty shows back to the beginning, which entailed a great deal of research and record-keeping on her part. Following is a quotation from a letter the American Pomeranian Club sent to Gaines' Award Committee for Good Sportsmanship (an award she speedily received): "Active member of the APC since 1913, Miss Blum's purpose was to promote the owning, breeding and exhibiting of Poms of the true type and to urge the adoption of this type upon judges. Some of her well-known Poms were Duke of Kent; Mephista, a litter brother to Poquito; Master Reynard; Fox Trot; and Ch. Sable Sun. A Pom of her breeding won first honors in this country and then went on to capture first honors in France. This great little dog, Ch. Pall Mall His Majesty, was the fourth generation of Miss Blum's breeding by the noted Mona Vanna.

"He was sold to Mrs. Andrew Rose and became the only American-bred Pomeranian to ever win top honors in a foreign country, Paris, France, where before only English-bred Poms had won. He was from several generations of American-bred Poms, proving that our own can more than hold their ground against foreign-bred specimen of the breed." (Author's note: quarantine regulations in effect in Europe keep our good Poms from competing over there as no one wants to subject a good Pom to six-months' quarantine in strange hands.) "Miss Blum had several Pomeranians win top awards and winning BIS was her experience on more than one occasion. The great Ch. Emir, owned by Mrs. Vincent Matta, was out of Little Houdina Girl, whose sire was Miss Blum's Lovely Fox Trot. Houdina Girl was the dam of five champions."

Mrs. Vincent Matta is known to everyone in the Pomeranian fancy as a moving light and force in the APC in years past and in breeding, in exhibiting, and in importing and exporting. She bred the famous Chs. Little Emir and Little Rajah and has many more to her credit. There is not the space to list all her achievements, but if she had accomplished but one thing, the importation of all-time famous Ch. Sealand Moneybox, sire of twenty-seven champions (all of which have sired many champions and left their stamp for good on the breed for all time), she would still take her place as one of the peeresses of the Pom fancy. I have been unable to find one American-bred champion of outstanding achievement that does not go back in several crosses to the famous Sealand Moneybox line. Sometimes the line is obscured by the names of various lines whose breeders used their own prefix in registrations, but careful research takes one slowly but surely back to the ever-famous Ch. Sealand Moneybox or his immediate ancestry.

Shared's Kennels, owned by Mr. and Mrs. C. E. Harris of Memphis, Tennessee, have made a flying start with a brood bitch, Little Buster's Judy, sired by Ruth Beam's Ch. Great Elms Buster. This fine little bitch has produced two outstanding champion bitches, Ch. Shared's Cinderella and Ch. Shared's Mighty Miss. "Cinder" is by Ch. Gold Toy's Gay Flame and "Missy" is by Ch. Gold Toy's Elfin Idol. Such an auspicious beginning for any kennel points toward a most successful future.

The kennels of Mr. and Mrs. D. C. Cloninger of Fort Worth, Texas, house some outstanding Pomeranians. Ch. Aristic Little Pepper Pod, a son of Ch. Aristic Wee Pepper Pod, is their pride and joy. Little Pepper Pod made his championship quickly and his story is of a steady climb to that coveted best in show award. He at present has won the Toy Group top award twelve times and best American-bred Toy four times. The Cloninger's kennel houses thirty to forty Poms at all times and they finished four champions up to 1961. They have Aristic background breeding and many fine Poms come out of their kennels.

Ch. Aristic Little Pepper Pod has two champions to his credit, one a Canadian and American champion who has a BIS, also.

Mohawk Valley Kennels, owned by Mildred A. Strait of Ilion, New York, has an interesting beginning that shows the pull of the personality of Pomeranians.

Mildred Strait's sister presented her with a Pomeranian as a gift when she graduated from Oneonta Teachers College. She so loved the little dog that she purchased the kennel of Arthur Taylor when he retired in his 80's, as he was still judging and had little time for kennel work. He had Nibroc, Julo, and

Aristic stock and this gave Mohawk Valley Kennels a flying start. Ch. Strait's Perry Winkle came out of this breeding background. He is a three and one-half pound brilliant orange with a most cobby style and sweet face. Perry Winkle was followed by Ch. Strait's Wee Pollyanna, who finished at the age of ten months. Ch. Little Red Tango is another fine Strait Pomeranian. The kennels have recently imported Madeline of Hadleigh from England.

Hu-Lo Kennels of Parsons, Tennessee, had an interesting beginning. Early in 1954 Hugh and Lorraine Parsons happened to see a Pomeranian in a Jerry Lewis comedy and then and there decided that they were going to breed Pomeranians. Hugh Parsons had majored in genetics in college and wished to apply his knowledge of breeding principles. Their first breeding stock was a son of imported Ch. Dandy of Erimus and a daughter of Ch. Gold Toy's Elfin Idol, a granddaughter of Ch. Sealand Moneybox. Choice of basic breeding stock shows how Hugh Parson's knowledge of genetics paid off with a flying start. Breeding charts are kept and there are no hit-and-miss breedings. The Parsons have a typey bitch in Sungold's Miss Prim, who is sent out to outstanding studs for breeding. Miss Prim is line-bred from Ch. Julo Wee Wonder.

Sun Wink Kennels of San Francisco, California, is one of the older kennels still active. The owner, Loretta Elkins, a licensed AKC judge, and her Sun Wink Poms have been a familiar sight at shows for many years. Among her many fine champions are Sun Wink's Tiny Spark, Sun Wink's Dancing Sun, Sun Wink's Tiny, Sun Wink's Dancing Twinkle, Dancing Star, Star Dust IV, Red Shadow's Radiant Girl, and Little Chickie Dee.

Kavilla Kennels of Mrs. V. G. Munz of Sacramento, California, began in Poms in 1949 and has risen to be one of the leading show contenders on the West Coast. Ch. Kavilla's Captivating Star was purchased as a puppy from Margaret Tankesley's Kennels in Tennessee and was the first Pom in Mrs. Munz's kennels. Canadian and American Ch. Cavilla's Diamond Chip has brought further fame, and Ch. Kavilla's Elegent Pandora, sold as a puppy to Mrs. Margaret Carlos, made her Mexican championship at the age of ten months. Kavilla Poms also excel in obedience rings.

Ruth and Robert Bellick of Ricochet Kennels of Hanson, Massachusetts, were Poodle breeders who could not resist buying a cute Pom puppy. In three short years after this first purchase, Pomeranians were their major breed and they have more than forty Poms at all times. They began exhibiting Poms in 1955 and in 1957 finished five Pomeranian champions. Today this kennel could boast of the many champions to their credit, but they modestly call themselves novices. I know of a lot of old-time breeders who would like to equal the Bellick's record of achievement. A few of their outstanding champions are: Ricochet's Margaret Ruby, Little Kandy Kiss of Ricochet, Radiant Star, Little Flashaway, and Ricochet Li'l Abner, a son of their first Pom, Ch. Little Miss Twinkletoes, who at retirement from exhibition had six best Toy awards and many other honors.

In late fall of 1960, the Bellicks imported Ch. Pixietown Serenade of Hadleigh from England and he went BIS in two of the Bermuda shows en route to the United States under the expert handling of the noted handler Ben Burwell. And on arrival in the United States he was shown at the Easton and Talmage shows in Maryland and went BIS at both.

Irene Messer of Byron, California, is another old-time breeder still active, having bred Poms for over twenty years. As a school teacher she has had little time for training and showing and her puppies have usually been sold as pets and breeding stock. One of the most outstanding champions she has produced is Ch. Messer's Frisky Mite. All of her Poms are line-bred from old Goldwin and Shining Gold Tad lines, her first Pom being white. She also is the proud owner of Ch. Lu-Oaks Jingle Bells. She exported to Japan, to Dr. Li, a fine puppy bitch, registered as Messer's Dungaree Doll, who finished her Japanese title.

Viola Children of Kent, Washington, is another breeder producing good ones but doing little personal exhibiting. Her stock is of the best, being line-bred to Ch. Sealand Moneybox.

Mary Katherine Griffin of Nashville, Tennessee, has been breeding Poms since 1930. She bred Ch. Muffin's Little Shining Gold, and in 1943 she purchased Ch. Dixieland's Crown Prince as a puppy and later traded him back to Mrs. Tankesley, who bred him. She also purchased Ch. O-Hi-Land's Little Sir Echo. Her Ch. Sungold's Sensational Kid is a fine little Pom with a blazing orange-red coat. Ch. Sungold's Gay Cavalier is another good one.

Dresden Pomeranians began back in 1926 with Ella V. Applegate, the mother of Veola Herzog of Los Angeles, California. Mrs. Applegate passed away in 1938 and since that time her daughter Veola has carried on the kennel. The first stud dog was Veola's Don Q, from the famous Ch. Flashaway of Dara. Many winning Poms of today can trace their ancestry back to Don Q and Ch. Flashaway. Dresden Pomeranians include three champions, among them the winsome Ch. Dresden Cheridoll.

Wild Wind Pomeranians, the kennel of Mrs. Ross Hanna of Lubbock, Texas, began with a Pom from Diamond Dromore King and Best Yet of Ashburn. In 1946 Mrs. Hanna purchased a grandson of Ch. Sealand Moneybox, and in 1953 she purchased from Mrs. Matta of New York a grandson of Ch. Little Timstopper's Teeco, a son of the famous Ch. Little Timstopper, who in turn is a son of Ch. Dixieland's Shining Gold, bred by Margaret Tankesley of Tennessee.

Gray-Lyn Kennels in Ohio purchased the entire stock of Jo Beth Kennels, also of Ohio. They now own Ch. Jo-Beth Rebel Rickey, of Nibrock and Dee background. Their Ch. Su Su Thumper of Jo-Beth is by Int. Ch. Golden Glow Dandy out of Trade Wind's Princess Su Su, a fine-boned orange bitch of my own breeding, with Aristic and Dara background. Their English import, Ch. Wilmscote Whirlaway, was repeatedly bred to bitches with Ch. Su Su Thumper and Ch. Rebel Rickey background with outstanding success.

Dee's Kennels of Dolores Hughes of Troy, Ohio, is one of the largest Pomeranian kennels in the Midwest. More than a hundred Poms are kept at all times. Dee purchased her first Pom in 1930 and since that time has produced and sold hundreds of puppies.

Some of Mrs. Hughes' champions are Lochryan Little Caesar, Jo Jac Dandy Duke, Dee's Prince Royal, Trade Wind's Rock-A-By Rebecca, Nibrock Little Sunglow, the imported English bitch Wilmscote Wayward Miss, and Wilmscote Wee Classic.

Ken-Gay Kennels of Kenneth and Gayle Burton of Orleans, Indiana, has been in existence but a few years but already has built up a small but select stock of fine Poms. Ch. Ken-Gay

Ch. Lady B-Dee, bred by Beulah Connors and owned by Blanche Rider.

Ch. Moneybox Tiddlywink, owned by Violet Isabelle Boucher.

Bonnie Buttons is a fine specimen and a good stud, producing show winner Gold Toy Nickey Buttons.

Shady Grove Kennels, owned by Mrs. C. A. Ellis of Grand Prairie, Texas, began breeding Poms about 1940 and has accomplished much in that time. Forty to fifty Poms are kept at all times. Mrs. Ellis purchased the famous English import, Ch. Wilmscote Wee Conquest, who won two BIS awards while gaining his title. He won several BIS awards for Aristic Kennels in Texas before being sold to Mrs. Ellis. Mrs. Ellis bred Ch. Fluffy of Shady Grove and among other outstanding champions owned and bred by this kennel is Ch. Julo Gold Boy of Shady Grove.

Neal Kennels, owned by Mr. and Mrs. Gene Neal of New Martinsville, West Virginia, have many fine Poms. Their first, purchased as a pet, was shown (just for fun) and came out a winner. Gene Neal writes me: "That was the day the show bug bit us," and he might have added that was the day a pair of fine breeders and exhibitors were born. The Neal Kennels send good ones into the ring and they have quality imports as well as outstanding home-breds. They have Erimus, Passfield, and Wilmscote imported bloodlines. BIS winner Ch. Tim of Erimus is their greatest winner and a fine little showman he is (I judged him at the Marion, Ohio, show a few years ago). His type and coat are exquisite and his disposition of the best.

Davis Kennels, owned by Stella Davis of Urbana, Ohio, has been in existence only a few years, but already this kennel is sending into show rings some excellent specimens: they have Moneybox, imported Wilmscote, and Ch. Sir Thomas of Pom Chee Bue background. Ch. Davis' Wee Gold Teena is their pride and joy.

Atwater Kennels, of Jacksonville, Florida, began, as did so many fine kennels, with a pet. She was a granddaughter of the famous Ch. Great Elms Little Timsun, owned by Ruth Beam and the sire of many champions. The Atwaters just could not resist raising one litter and have become outstanding by keeping the kennel small and keeping the best they produce as foundation stock. They have Canadian and American Ch. Dromore Bombardier, and Ch. Princess Candy Jade, and Ch. Great Elms Little Timstopper background.

68

Grose Kennels, owned by Hazel Grose of Longview, Washington, have many good ones. One of their home-breds was recently purchased by Elva McGilbry (nee Cohen), judge and long-time breeder of note. Ch. Grose's Robin Hood is heavy in imported Hadley blood and Ch. Golden Glow lines. All of the ancestry of the Grose Kennels' Poms goes back to Ch. Best Yet of Ashburn.

Eloise Chandler of Berkley, Michigan, is one of the newer breeder-exhibitors. Her Ch. Adora Sir Bullet is a typey orange. Adora El-O-Dee is also an outstanding Pom.

Highland Pomeranians, the kennel of Patricia Hopkins of Altoona, Pennsylvania, was begun in 1954. Bloodlines are mostly Little Timstopper and Julo, with one outstanding stud sired by the great Ch. Great Elms Little Timstopper. The kennel owns the English import, Ch. Bourneville Golden Legend.

Connors Kennels of Beulah Connors of Cameron, Missouri, began in 1936 with sons and daughters of Ch. Sealand Moneybox and Dara lines and of late have been specializing in color breeding. Good blacks, excellent whites, and some good blues have been produced.

Pristine Kennels, hobby kennels of Attorney and Mrs. Edward F. Sweeney, began when they attended a New York show and fell in love with the famous Little Timstopper. Their first specimen came from the Aristic Kennels of Gladys Schoenberg in Texas. This was Aristic Little Spitfire, sire of many show Poms, including Ch. Pristine Ginger Fizz, who remains Pristine's most outstanding stud. He is the sire of Mrs. Webber's Ch. Pristine Tiffany. The Sweeneys also have bloodlines of Ch. Little Timstopper and Ch. Mi-Lo Sable Dandy.

The name *Pristine* has an interesting background. The Sweeneys' first Pom was lifted from the crate at the airport just as the sun was rising, and as the sunlight gleamed on the beautiful orange coat of their first Pom, Mr. Sweeney quoted: "in all its pristine glory," and the kennel name was born.

Mrs. I. D. Van Metre of Martinsburg, West Virginia, has been breeding Poms for many years, having Money Box and Dromore Diamond King lines, which speak for themselves as to quality of background.

Flaming Fluff Kennels of Jo Ann Schroeder of El Sobrante, California, began in 1951 with Bonner stock and she has been very successful. The first champion, Bonner's Blissful, a gorgeous red bitch of typical heavy Bonner coat, was followed quickly by Ch. Bonner's Little Luscious, an adorable cream bitch. And Ch. Bonner's Moneybox also streaked to the title. Ch. Sealand Moneybox and Ch. Latham's Gay Sahib figure heavily in background, and Bonner stock goes back to Aristic stock.

Alnor Kennels of Norma Fraley of Edison, Ohio, specializes in good creams of wonderful coat. She also produces oranges and sables. One of my own bitches was her first brood, and one of my studs, Aristic Little Gold Whizzer, sired her first puppy. Progeny of this mating was crossed to good cream stock from Mrs. Fraley's son's kennels and the basis for good clear creams was forged.

Davon-Shire Kennels of Mr. and Mrs. Norman Jerome of Hallandale, Florida, began in 1938. They soon became avid exhibitors and importers. A few of the champions finished by this kennel are Passfield Patrice, Passfield Petite, Wilmscote Whimsical, Wilmscote Wee Crispin, Davonshire Precious Gem, and the great black, Thunder of Erimus. Thunder was bred in England by Harold Young and is a double cross back to noted English Ch. The Nonpareil. Thunder is a cobby, jet black with none of the rustiness of coat so common at maturity in blacks. He has small ears and the high tail set necessary to a really good Pom in any color. He has a winsome, sweet face that also is not so common in blacks.

La Peer Kennels owned by Mrs. W. H. Fleming of Papeer, Michigan, has been breeding Poms for a number of years. Bitches from this kennel are dams of Ch. Foxfire Emmy and Ch. Foxfire Scot. Mrs. Fleming breeds good clear creams as well as the more commonly seen colors.

Jo-Jac Kennels of Hollywood, Florida, owned by Mr. and Mrs. W. R. Pitts, began when they purchased a Pom as a pet. He was entered in a puppy match and won BIM, and the Pitts were in as far as breeding and exhibiting are concerned. Among outstanding specimens owned by this kennel is Ch. Jo-Jac Dandy Duke.

Pacemaker Kennels of Mr. and Mrs. Charles Edwards, Jr., of Tipton, Indiana, were little known until they purchased the entire kennel of Mrs. Alma Staley of Summitville, Indiana. Ch.

70

Ch. Highland Strutaway, bred by Patricia M. Hopkins, and
owned by Sandra Thallon.   *Erwin H. Frank*

Ch. Richochet Triumphal March and Ch. Surprise Box Black
Eyed Susan. owned by Mrs. Floy Sledge.   *Harold Lowe, Jr.*

Gold Toy's Top Tune is their most outstanding stud, being the sire of their Ch. Pacemaker's Lady Tina, who is now owned by Mrs. Hazel Rasche of Orleans, Indiana. Charles Edwards has a college degree in animal husbandry, which helps account for the deep interest in quality stock. The Edwards have Dixieland and Ru-La-Vir as well as Gold Toy lines.

Joan Innis of Hagerstown, Indiana, finished her first Pom champion, Gold Toy's Gay Toy, in 1957. This is a very typey little bitch, as I can attest, for I once judged her—when she was just starting her show career. Joan is now affiliated with Mrs. Edith Hutchison and they own Hi-Lite Kennels, located at Hagerstown. Ch. Gold Toy's Petite Melody and Ch. Pacemaker's Molly B add to their prestige as breeder-exhibitors to be reckoned with.

Mrs. Sam Thole of Marion, Kansas, began as a producer of pet stock but exhibiting in shows brought about a great interest in improving her stock. Her top champion is Van Hoosers Lucky Wee Max, who has six champion half-brothers. Mrs. Thole also has imported stock from Preservenes lines. She has Julo Wee Wonder and Mrs. McKamey's Ch. Aristic Sunbeau lines as well.

Bell Star Kennels of Mr. and Mrs. Samuel Miller of Lima, Ohio, is another hobby kennel turned professional. The Millers have a tiny, typey Pom matron who has produced more than thirty puppies.

Mrs. Ollie Hauger of Cameron, Missouri, also has a Pom matron who has produced well over thirty puppies. And Mrs. Hauger has found time to exhibit a home-bred champion.

Maple Woods Kennels, owned by Mrs. Joe Kauffman of Urbana, Ohio, produce quality stock. Mrs. Kauffman has Gold Toy, Trade Winds, and Nibroc stock, all with the Sealand Moneybox background.

Mrs. Eleanor Miller of Mt. Vernon, Ohio, is a school teacher with a hobby of raising exhibition Pomeranians. She is the owner of Ch. Gold Toy's Red Flame, a huge-coated orange with beautiful face and conformation. Flame has sired many typey puppies. He was bred by Joyce Brown of Gold Toy Kennels.

Rock A Bye Kennels of Mr. and Mrs. James Sutton of Columbus, Ohio, achieved their first champion during their first year of breeding and exhibiting. Rock A Bye was the prefix I chose years ago for my most outstanding stock in Pomeranians and as the Suttons took over most of my stock when I retired from breeding and judging to guide the destinies of two small, motherless grandchildren, I also gave the Suttons the Rock A Bye prefix. Ch. Trade Wind's Rock A Bye Rebecca was their first champion. Their next champion, Rock A Bye's Bonnie Belle, a gorgeous orange who made her championship in three straight shows (one a specialty), is out of a fine brood bitch I practically forced upon them, as I knew she was prepotent for outstanding progeny. Her background is good and she is a consistent producer of good ones. They have many other Poms of exhibition quality in their kennels at all times.

Edd E. Bivin, owner of Edward's Kennels of Fort Worth, Texas, is another breeder it is a pleasure to write about. Edd is of the younger generation of breeder-exhibitors, beginning in registered dogs at the age of twelve back in 1953. His first and last love in dogs is Pomeranians of exhibition quality. He bred and still owns Ch. Edward's Reddy Teddy, a handsome four-pound orange son of Ch. Topper's Little Corkie, who finished by going BOW at the Chicago International, where there is always tough competition. A son of Reddy Teddy won the Puppy Sweepstakes and went on to best puppy in show at the Pomeranian specialty at Westminster in 1961. This puppy was bred by Edward's Kennels and sold to Mary Brewster of Robwood fame. Many more good ones can be expected to come out of Edward's Kennels. Edd Bivin reluctantly cut down his breeding and exhibition stock to attend college but no doubt will be a force to be again reckoned with when he is back full time with his Pomeranians. He served for three years as president of the Fort Worth Pomeranian Club.

Happy Hill Kennels of Mr. and Mrs. Tom Evison of El Cajon, California, began in 1954 in Colorado. Their very first show wins of note were under Pauline Hughes, Pomeranian specialist, when she judged the Pomeranian specialty of the Silver Bay Show, where Pup-Pet Penny Candee, bred by the Evisons, and Pup-Pet Billy Little Wonder, bred by the Evisons and sold as a puppy, went winners dog and winners bitch for five points each. Both of the Evisons are very active in Pom

73

circles and are supporting members of the San Diego Pomeranian Club. The Evison's kennels were almost wiped out by distemper but they managed to save Penny Candee from the debacle.

Mrs. Jeanette Fickeissen of Gardena, California, is an avid Pom breeder and fancier, owner of the superb showman and stud, Canadian and American Ch. Teeco's Little Topper, sire and grandsire of many champions, and the grandsire of the famous Ch. Rider's Sparklin' Gold Nugget. Topper is the sire of Chs. Topper's Wee Doll, Topper's Little Corkie, Topper's Little Moppet, Sungold's Little Teeco, Sungold's Wee Desire, Sungold's Prissy Lou, Edward's Reddy Teddy and others.

Beverley and James Griffiths of San Diego, California, have been breeding Poms about a dozen years and have several fine show specimens as the result of their efforts. Foundation stock was purchased from the Latham Kennels, their first stud being Ch. Latham's Wee Wonder, whose grandson, Ch. Sahib's Gay Gadabout, made his championship in four majors. Jolly Acres Breezin' By went winners for five points at his first show.

Marianne Melville of Spokane, Washington, purchased her first Pom as a pet in 1951 and by 1954 she had two outstanding specimens in show rings: Hinshaw's Mighty Midget, a son of Int. Ch. Golden Glow Dandy, and Aristic Sir Buttons, purchased from Gladys Schoenberg. Both Poms streaked to their titles and in 1957 Buttons became a Canadian champion also. This kennel has Golden Glow and Aristic bloodlines and has crossed these two outstanding lines with high success.

Lillian Kjeldgaard of Spokane, Washington, has been in Poms since 1952 and is active in Pom promotion, breeding, and exhibiting. She keeps upward of a hundred Pomeranians of Julo, Latham, and Moneybox lines. She is the owner of one of the most sensational braces ever to be shown on the West Coast—a brace which won in competition against as many as eighteen braces under nationally known judges. One of the brace, a fine Setter-red bitch, had thirteen points toward her title when a hip injury ended her show career.

Mrs. Elizabeth Davis, also of Spokane, Washington, began showing Poms about 1957 but already has earned an enviable reputation for quality. Her Int. Ch. Latham's Banginway, a son of Ch. Latham's Tryanpass, handled by Canadian handler Gene Hahnlen, quickly finished his titles in Canada and the United States.

Mrs. William Bigelow of Philadelphia, Pennsylvania, owner of the long-famous Twin Oaks Kennels, is known far and wide for her superb blacks. She began exhibiting at the Garden in 1919.

The Latham Kennels first began breeding Pomeranians in 1938 with Moneybox and Julo lines, going back to the famous old Ch. Sahib, owned by Mrs. Vincent Matta. Marvin Latham was a keen student of line breeding and the success he found attested to the soundness of his policies. The most famous of the Lathams' Poms was Ch. Latham's Gay Sahib, a pure golden orange of three and a half pounds. Gay Sahib was the sire of six champions: Haltom's Gay Sahib, Aristic Gay Little Sue, Sahib's Gay Gadabout, Sahib's Mitzie, Miteycute It's a Darling, and Miteycute It's a Honey. Darling and Honey were litter mates. Ch. Latham's Gay Sahib's background was heavy in heritage from Ch. Little Emir, Ch. Little Rajah's Pearl, Ch. Woodfield May King, and Ch. Sealand Moneybox. It is easy to see what made him great.

Glennie Hart began showing Poms at the age of twelve and after several years showing he had started the famous Ch. Aristic Big Pay Check to his title. But his country called him into service and Pay Check was finished by Anna La Fortune. When Glennie left the service, he and Mrs. La Fortune joined forces in exhibiting and both are familiar figures at West Coast shows.

Sungold Kennels, owned by Anna La Fortune, are well known. Some of the champions under the Sungold banner are: Sungold's Wee Desire, Sungold's Little Teeco, Sungold's Lady Melba, Sungold's Supreme, Sungold's Prissy Lou, Sungold's Lu Lu, and Sungold's Phoebe, all home-breds. Ch. Gold Mist of Waverly, also owned by this kennel, is a BIS winner. Chs. Echo of Waverly, Aristic Major Mite, and Timsun's Gold of Waverly help make up the impressive list of Sungold champions.

Mrs. Norris McKamey of Davenport, Iowa, began in Pomeranians in 1946 and has outstanding bloodlines, her stock being strong in Ch. Dixieland Shining Gold and English Ch. Preservenes Live Wire lines. Live Wire is considered by many to be

Ch. Sungold's Sensational Kid, bred by Mrs. Anna
La Fortune and owned by Mrs. G. A. Griffin.

Int. Ch. Moneybox Token's Trustee, bred by
Mrs. John Smith and owned by Duane H. Knapp

the most outstanding Pomeranian in English history. Ch. Dixie-land Shining Gold goes back to the old Eastney Red Boy line of his sire's side and to Ch. Moneybox on his dam's side. Ch. Aristic Sunbeau, one of Mrs. McKamey's studs, was a son of imported Sunglory and a grandson of Suncherub, who was BIS many times during the war in England when no champions were made or allowed, and this line goes directly back to Bonny Ideal. On the dam's side, Sunbeau goes back to Chs. Little Sahib and Sealand Career. Among champions of Mrs. McKamey's breedings are: McKamey's Sunbeau's Just Me, McKamey's Sundawn Enchanting, McKamey's Commander, McKamey's Sundawn Serenade, McKamey's Margaret Rose, and McKamey's Sunbeau's Beauty.

Rider's Sungold's Timstopper, another of Mrs. McKamey's studs, is a son of Int. Ch. Sungold's Wee Desire, a BIS winner.

Adora Kennels of Mrs. Margaret Leader of Detroit, Michigan, began in 1934, but it was not until 1943 that Mrs. Leader really began serious breeding for show stock with a granddaughter of Ch. Sealand Moneybox. Leader's Surprise Money, when bred back to her grandsire, produced Ch. Leader's Money Box Sunny, who became the twenty-seventh and last champion sired by the great Ch. Sealand Moneybox. Sunny was much like his famous sire and has left his mark for good on much of his progeny through several generations. He won his title in two and a half weeks. Among his champion descendants are: Adora Sir Gay, and Little Gem, who in turn produced Chs. Adora El-O-Dee and Adora Honey Doll. Puppies sold that gained their championships are: Gorgeous Little Joy, Gold Toy's Gold Puff, Adora Sun Toy, and Gold Toy's Gay Flame. All go back to the famous old Canadian and American Ch. Kitch Tumble Lad, whose strain runs strongly in many of the show Poms in Canada and central United States.

The kennels of Mrs. Joe Re of The Dalles, Oregon, although in operation less than a dozen years, show the wisdom of beginning with the very best stock procurable, for Mrs. Re's background stock is from Elva Cohen McGilbry's stock, Canadian and American Ch. Dromore Bombardier, Ch. Little Timsun, and the old Ch. Best Yet of Ashburn. Mrs. Re produced seven champions in her first seven years of breeding and exhibiting.

77

There also are Ch. Re's Wee Delight and Ch. Re's Ima Cute Trinket (by Corkey), of recent titles. Mrs. Re's first bitch of note was heavy in Ch. Little Sahib and Ch. Best Yet of Ashburn bloodlines. By judicious inbreeding and line breeding, Mrs. Re has produced consistently fine stock.

Reese Kennels began in 1909 but it was not until 1929 that Pomeranians became their main breed. Most of the old names of the past appear in pedigrees of this kennel. They have bred almost all of the now almost extinct colors—whites, blues, chocolates, and blacks. They still have blues and some good blacks, granddaughters of one of my own Trade Wind bitches that were shown at the Garden in 1958.

Mrs. Reese and Jeanne Ver Hage, well-known breeder-handler, are co-owners of several fine Pomeranians and all show stock is personally handled by Mrs. Ver Hage.

Bonner Pomeranians of San Antonio, Texas, began in 1928 with a pet. Since that time, many, many champions have gone out from this kennel. Among Bonner studs of prominence is Ch. Bonner's Tiny Showstopper, owned by Helen Pushing of Orlando, Florida. Ch. Bonner's Sunny Showstopper, owned by Bernice Francisco, also came from the Bonner Kennels. Dam of these two outstanding champions is Ch. Bonner's Sunny Cherub, sired by an Aristic stud. Streaking his way through numerous wins in California from 1956 on, is Ch. Bonner's Moneybox Sunny, owned by Jo Ann Schroeder. Other Bonner home-breds quickly gaining their championships include Chs. Bonner's Wee Gold Bug, Bonner's Bo-Peep Darling, Bonner's Gold Doll Flame, and Bonner's Wee Lollypop. Jo Ann Schroeder also recently finished Chs. Bonner's Little Luscious and Bonner's Blissful. Among others are Ch. Bonner's Valsette, Ch. Bonner's Coqueta Cara, and Ch. Bonner's Gay Golden.

Surprisebox Pomeranians of James and Midora Arima, formerly of Glenn Hills, Rockville, Maryland, but now of Northbrook, Illinois, began appearing in shows in 1953. This kennel is known for its Poms of sound structure and true Pomeranian character. The Arimas demand verve and style in their Pomeranians and have produced some very outstanding Poms, one of their most valued home-breds being Ch. Crown Princess Candy Jade, who garnered five points at her first show. Their

78

Poms go back to the famous strain of Elva Cohen McGilbry's Int. Ch. Golden Glow Dandy and Int. Ch. Bombardier. In 1957 the Arimas' imported stud, Ch. Wilmscote Wee Caress, went BOW at the Garden and they followed up their successes by importing English Ch. Golden Penny of Morrell, who, when bred back to her sire, Ch. Zambo of Zanow, produced English Ch. Glamour Girl of Morrell, now in South Africa. Other of their bitches of this same Zambo line include Margo of Hadleigh, Jasmine of Hadleigh, and Surprisebox Sweet Sassafras.

James Arima is a guiding light in the American Pomeranian Club and editor of *Pomeranian Review,* official magazine of the club. It is outstanding among magazines of national breed clubs and has been a force in the fast expansion of the national Pom club.

Golden Glow Pomeranians of the former Elva Cohen (now Mrs. "Sallie" McGilbry, as she has remarried) are known far and wide. Mrs. McGilbry's kennels, long located at Vancouver, Washington, are known for the many outstanding champions that they have produced. Elva began showing Poms in 1935. Her first blue ribbon winner was a female called the "Dutchess," a wolf-sable, a rich color rarely seen nowadays. The Pom that did the most for Golden Glow Pomeranians is Canadian and American Ch. Dromore Bombardier. Elva purchased him as a ten-month-old reserve winner at the Westminster Show, from Earnest Sharland, after Bombardier ("Timmy") had gone from puppy classes to reserve dog in competition with twenty-two other males.

Earnest Sharland became a real friend, giving advice and sharing knowledge gained during fifty years' experience breeding Poms in this country and in England. Bombardier's sire was Ch. Best Yet of Ashburn, who was given to Earnest Sharland by Reuben Clark, another famous Pom fancier. Mrs. McGilbry's first champion sired by Bombardier was a deep orange bitch, Canadian and American Ch. Golden Glow Velvet, who won her title at ten months of age with many Toy Group wins to her credit. When bred back to her sire, she produced Canadian and American Ch. Golden Glow Luckey, now owned by Mae Bresser of Chicago.

Later on came the exciting show winner Canadian and American Ch. Golden Glow Dandy, who won several BIS in both the United States and Canada before he was a year old. Dandy was a flashy showman who held the eyes of judge and ringside. He was shown twenty-nine times and was best of breed twenty-eight times, won first in the Toy Group nineteen times, and was best in show six times, all by the age of nine months, with the exception of some BIS. He was retired on his fourth birthday with a BIS win, to stand at stud for the good of all Pomdom. Mrs. McGilbry should have an accolade for placing him at stud for the good of Pomeranians everywhere, for all too many BIS winners are kept on the road picking up show laurels to the glory of their home kennels, and many fine progeny are thus lost to the breed, for a stud cannot be used extensively and kept in full glory of show coat at one and the same time.

Dandy, as a six-weeks-old puppy, came to Elva in a crate with a bitch sent for breeding, the owner wanting Elva to see just what her stock was producing for the owner. Dandy was unconscious when lifted from the crate and a veterinarian gave no hope for his survival, but Mrs. McGilbry lived with the sick puppy for the next two weeks, feeding him goat's milk, drop by drop, until he was strong enough to feed by himself. It was months before he was in normal health again and Mrs. McGilbry writes that her only mistake was in naming him, as he should have been called "My Reward." Mrs. McGilbry purchased Dandy from his breeder shortly after he regained his health as a puppy, for she had grown so attached to him by that time that she could not bear to be parted from him. His worth is evidenced by the fact that he has sired many champions.

One of Mrs. McGilbry's later outstanding studs and show winners is Ch. Rougeland's Silver Bomber, who finished his championship and went BIS on the same day.

Sally, as Mrs. McGilbry is affectionately called by friends, has a strict code of ethics, both as a breeder and as a judge. She never has kept a mónorchid or an undershot Pom in her kennels, and she never fails to give advice or aid in grooming to a novice exhibitor, and, for that matter, to give aid in any way possible to all breeders and exhibitors. "International Champion" should prefix the name of Elva Cohen McGilbry, as she appears to be a champion in every sense of the word.

C. V. Harwood, better known as "Shorty" Harwood, began showing and breeding Poms in 1946. His first Pom, purchased from Gladys Schoenberg at the age of two months, was BOB for four points at Fort Worth, Texas, in her first show, two days before she was eight months old.

Lois Z. Campbell's Timber Acres Kennels began about 1948 and has been finishing champions pretty steadily ever since. The kennels' first Pom to gain its title was Ch. Merrily, and within a few years the breeding stock included six champions, five of them home-bred. Among champions of this kennel are Ch. Timber Acres Mr. Wonderful, Ch. Timber Acres Jimi Jon, and Ch. Timber Acres Sugar Plum Faery.

Wilma Smith, of Rougeland Kennels, Applegate, Washington, is a breeder who does not show her Poms, preferring to sell them to good homes as breeding and show stock. The many of her breeding that have gone to their titles under the prefixes of other kennels attest to her status as a breeder of top quality stock.

Gold Toy Kennels of Mrs. Donald Brown, formerly of Indianapolis but now of Cumberland, Indiana, was established in 1948. Many fine show specimens have come out of her Gold Toy Kennels. Mrs. Brown's first show prospect was Gold Toy's Crown Prince, who quickly became a champion. Her Dixieland's Southern Star not only sired Ch. Crown Prince but also sired Ch. Wee Bit O Stardust. Miggenburg's Hubba Hubba was a son of imported Ch. Eastney Red Boy and Hubba Hubba's daughters produced Chs. Gold Toy's Miss Peppermint and Lady Cindy IV. In 1949 Gold Toy Kennels purchased Pope's Little Stormy Knight, who sired Chs. Gold Toy's Elfin Idol, Shining Star, Scarlett, Mary's Kentucky Babe, and Little Honey Girl. Ch. Gold Toy's Gay Flame has sired many champions, among them being Chs. Reynita's Sparkling Flame, Gold Toy's Red Flame, Gold Toy's Gay Toy, and Gold Toy's Gay Starette, all of which finished for the title in 1958. Mrs. Brown's Poms are almost all bred down from Sealand Moneybox lines.

Among enthusiastic Pom fanciers is Mrs. Barbara Buckley. Her Himself of Toyhaven is a beautiful orange-red grandson of Ch. Little Sahib and out of a daughter of my own Trade Wind line, going back to Ch. Sealand Moneybox and Ch. Dixieland Shining Gold breeding.

Foxfire Kennels of Mrs. Ralph Myers of Lincoln, Nebraska, is a kennel purposely kept small, with quality of prime importance. Out of this kennel featuring line breeding have come Chs. Foxfire Chips, Foxfire Emmy, and Foxfire Scot. Scot was purchased by Mrs. Roy Webber and finished for the title at Westminster. Scot has been followed by Ch. Foxfire Joy and Foxfire Red.

Margaret Penprase' Poms, under the prefix of Penpoms, have been around for about a dozen years and whites are a specialty. Penpoms' whites are of good type and are small size, which in itself is quite an achievement, as most typey whites of the past have been large and tinged with cream.

Mrs. John Voltz of St. Louis, Missouri, began in Poms in 1933. She made her first sensational win with a tiny red male named Pine Perch Pepper Pod, who usually was referred to as "Strut" because of his beautiful prancing strut in the show ring. He had won several Toy Group awards when his career was cut short by pneumonia. The next big winner was Ch. Aristic Surprise Box, purchased from Gladys Schoenberg. After winning several Toy Groups, Surprise Box went BIS at Land O' Lakes Toy Dog Show in Minnesota. He was a son of Ch. Sealand Moneybox, and his dam was a daughter of Ch. Sealand Career. Mrs. Voltz has line-bred from the Sealand line, doubling and tripling the line in most breedings. She has owned many champions over the years, including Ch. Aristic Moneybox Daintiness, the eighteenth champion produced by Ch. Sealand Moneybox. She has imported English Ch. Wilmscote Wee Conquest lines. Her Aristic Petite Chonquette is sired by Ch. Aristic Wee Pepper Pod.

Norman and Marjorie Kneisel of Portland, Oregon, are breeders who began with the best to be obtained and who have line-bred with marked success. They are known best for their home-bred United States and Canadian Ch. Hunt's Gold Boy II, better known as "Little Frisky." Frisky is now at home in the kennels of Elva Cohen McGilbry and he has won nine Toy Groups, two specialties, and one BIS.

A listing of outstanding breeders would not be complete without the name of Mrs. Jeanette E. Fickeissen of Gardena, California, who is the owner-breeder of the famous Int. Ch. Teeco's Little Topper, who in turn is the sire of the following champions: Topper's Wee Doll, Topper's Little Corky, Topper's Little Moppet, Sungold's Wee Desire, Sungold's Little Teevo, and Sungold's Prissy Lou. Also, last but not least, he is the grandsire of the sensational Ch. Rider's Sparklin' Gold Nugget, winner of more than forty-five best in show awards.

The name of Blanche Rider will always be remembered in Pom history because of her having raised Ch. Rider's Sparklin' Gold Nugget and trained him for his fabulous show career. Nugget was bred by Lee Johnson of Coronado, California, out of a bitch bred by Blanche Rider. Some time ago, Mrs. Rider bought back the dam of "Sparky," as Gold Nugget is called. Mrs. Rider had purchased the litter of three, recognizing the promise of "Sparky" when he was still a nursing puppy. She began showing him in puppy matches, where he immediately began to win. She took him on shopping trips to accustom him to all kinds of conditions and he soon became very much the "man about town." As a judge in a major show, Sally Cohen, of Golden Glow fame, gave "Sparky" his first big push toward stardom and he was sold to Porter Washington at that show. Washington, who is one of today's outstanding professional handlers, purchased "Sparky" for a birthday present for his bride, owner of the Flakee Kennels, and "Sparky" never stopped in his sensational rise to what is perhaps an all-time BIS record in Pomeranians.

A study of "Sparky's" background shows why he was not an accident, but a quality-bred Pomeranian who should leave his stamp for all time on his progeny. His show career has kept him from being used much at stud but it is hoped that he will be retired from the show ring and placed at stud for the sake of all Pomdom.

"Sparky's" champion sires' background includes: Ch. Topper's Little Corkie, Ch. Timstopper's Teeco, Ch. Little Timstopper, and Ch. Dixieland's Shining Gold. He has a heavy cross to Ch. Julo Wee Wonder on the dam's sire's side and all of his ancestry goes back to Ch. Sealand Moneybox in several crosses, with Ch. Seacroft Sealass tossed in. Such a background cannot help but produce champions of note. "Sparky" is a brilliant orange of unexcelled stand-off coat and his showmanship is superb. His forty-odd BIS wins cannot help but go up as time passes, for he is still going strong. He long ago surpassed the record of his famous ancestor, Ch. Sealand Moneybox, in show wins of note, but he has yet to surpass Sealand Moneybox' record of twenty-seven champion progeny, perhaps because he has not yet been offered at public stud.

Duane Knapp of West Sacramento, California, is one of the West Coast's enthusiastic Pom boosters. He works diligently for the breed, and not for personal show glory. He helped to organize one of the top Pom Specialty Clubs in the Northwest, and while he modestly states he is just a novice, he is the owner of Int. Ch. Moneybox Token's Trustee, Ch. Golden Glow Masquerade, Ch. Sassy Sol-Oro (a home-bred), and Ch. Hinshaws Mighty Midget. Amber Glow Bit-O-Fluff is perhaps the best he has ever owned but, unfortunately, had bad teeth when she was purchased and as a result she has never been exhibited.

The Skylark Kennel name is an old one, made famous by Frenchwoman Marie Lyon, but owned for some time now by Shirley Ann Hoffman of Richmond, California. Of fifteen champions owned by Mrs. Lyon, all were home-breds but one. Mrs. Lyon's first Pomeranian was the old and famous Princess Hula, a daughter of Blue Boy. Uninformed about good points of a Pomeranian when she first became interested in the breed, Marie Lyon was told that ALL good Poms had curled tails, and Hula had a markedly curled tail. When Shirley Hoffman asked her if she was ever so green about Pom points as Mrs. Hoffman was at the time, Mrs. Lyon replied: "Green? I was so green I thought they were called Poms because they were supposed to carry their tails in a little doughnut pom pom curled over their backs! I spent HOURS twisting Hula's tail into a tight curl over her back and I sure succeeded. Hula had the tightest curl you ever saw in a Pom's tail."

Hula, however, produced some of the leaders in old Pomeranian history, evidently not being potent for the passing on of that curled doughnut tail. Mrs. Hoffman is experimenting in color-breeding good blues.

Kenneth Mayes of San Antonio is one of the early breeders

of many champions who is still active in producing good ones. He specializes in brilliant oranges and reds, Chs. Mayken's Zante, Mayken's Little Moneta, and Mayken's Little Enchantress being good examples.

Mr. and Mrs. Gray Swaim of Winston-Salem, North Carolina, have good basic stock from Ruth Beam's Great Elms Kennels. I have had the pleasure of examining their stock, all of which have the run of one of the show places of the Old South, for Gray and Billie Swaim are specialists in the restoration of antique Southern treasures. Their home is a treasure-house of almost priceless furnishings and each Pom sleeps in a child's antique miniature playroom bed, and has bedroom furniture to match the bed. Their most oustanding Pom is Swaim's Tar Heel Teddy, called "Troubles." I awarded him BOB at the Winston-Salem show in 1958, for he was superb, with tiny ears and stiff, stand-off coat. He showed gallantly and with spirit despite eleven two-day-old stitches in his abdomen—the result of being attacked and almost killed by an obedience Poodle. "Troubles" has been retired from the ring because the experience caused him to develop a fear of large dogs and ruined him for further showing. This points up one of the drawbacks to Toy breeders at unbenched shows. Too many owners of unruly large dogs exhibit them with complete disregard for the rights of people with smaller dogs. This was not the first time this large dog had attacked another and smaller dog at a public gathering.

Mr. and Mrs. James Horton, also of Winston-Salem, are Pom breeders aiming at the best. In addition to breeding Poms, they have one of the outstanding Maltese Kennels in the United States.

Mrs. Florence Rhoads of Marion, Ohio, has been breeding Poms since the thirties and has good bloodlines. One of her champions, Echo's Prince Charming, of imported Erimus breeding, left several fine sons and daughters to carry on before his untimely death from a heart attack. Mrs. Rhoads and her daughter Eula are co-owners of a kennel and the daughter breeds champion Shelties.

Mrs. Grace Zoll of South Vienna, Ohio, is owner of Sunnyside Kennels. Many champions have been a part of her kennels, which are co-operated by her daughter, breeder-handler Thelma

Ch. Adora Sir Bullet, bred by Margaret
Leader and owned by Eloise Chandler.

Ch. Pristine Ginger Fizz, bred and owned by Victoria B. Sweeney.

Minnick. One of Mrs. Zoll's most noted champions was Ch. Moneybox Two Bits of Nibrock, bred by Mrs. Corbin of the East. Ch. Zoll's Red Bud has a handsome stand-off red coat and shows superbly. Ch. Zoll's Cricket is one of Mrs. Zoll's latest Poms.

Mrs. Dorothy Husted, secretary-treasurer of the American Pomeranian Club for many years and club president for 1961, does not have a large kennel, due to her inability to keep many dogs in her New York apartment. But she is a Pomeranian lover and breeder who has worked hard to forward the progress of the breed through her work for the parent club. One of her finest and perhaps her most valuable broods was Princess Shining Gold, a half-sister of Ch. Little Timstopper and a daughter of Ch. Dixieland Shining Gold. Mrs. Husted is the proud owner of Ch. Currency Wee Wonder.

Georgian Farm Kennels of Mrs. Georgia M. Shepperd has been breeding and exhibiting top quality Pomeranians since 1910. This perhaps is the record for any breeder still active in breeding and showing champions. Mrs. Shepperd has served the APC in many capacities and has always been a booster for the fancy, and at present she serves on the executive committee of the APC. She was club president in 1957-1958.

Among the champions to come from Georgian Farm Kennels are: Ch. Georgian Copper King, Ch. Georgian Gadfly, Ch. Georgian Gadaway, Ch. Georgian Sir Penny Bit, Ch. Georgian Bronze Penny Sonny, Ch. Fairfax Wee Bronze Penny, and many, many others of note.

Miss Burneice Lovelace is another solid booster of Pomeranians and the American Pomeranian Club. She has been circulation manager of the *Pomeranian Review* since its very first year. Her kennel prefix of Stoneleigh is well known and Miss Lovelace has long been a familiar figure at Westminster Shows. Ch. Zein of Zanow, lovingly called "Timmy," is the first American champion of English Ch. Zein of Zanow. "Timmy" is a grandson of English Ch. Hadleigh Brilliant Flame. Ch. Sweet Lady of Arlyd is a tiny true sable of beautiful conformation and winner of two CC's in England and BIS at the South Eastern Counties Toy Dog Society open show in England. Both "Timmy" and Sweet Lady are imported dogs.

Mr. and Mrs. W. C. Horner of Massilon, Ohio, have both conformation and obedience Pomeranians. They believe in the slogan "Beauty plus brains!" Their Ch. Horner's Sir Joe of Genoa, a tiny red sable male, made his title in late 1958. Sir Joe is a son of the Horner's obedience title holder Eveningstar's Jeanie Girl, C.D. Sir Joe was followed to the title by Horner's Empress Carol and Horner's Princess Ellielou, who also is out of Eveningstar's Jeanie Girl. C.D. Carol is out of Ch. Ellielou, and made her championship the same year as her dam did.

Helen Nowicki of Blackacre Kennels, Chicago, Illinois, has long been a familiar figure in Mid-Western shows, having finished many champions in her long career in exhibiting. Most of her Poms are imported from Blackacre bloodlines in England, as she often imports in litter lots from English kennels. She also has bred many champions.

Jack and Shirley Woodall of Memphis, Tennessee, are the proud owners of Ch. Topper's Little Corkie, who is the sire of the exquisite little Ch. Exquisite Corkie's Sunrise. Corkie also is the sire of the famous BIS winner Ch. Rider's Sparkling Gold Nugget, Edd Bivin's sensational Ch. Edward's Reddy Teddy, and Mrs. Joe Re's Ch. Re's Ima Cute Trinket.

Mr. and Mrs. Willard K. Denton of Mt. Kisco, New York, are owners of Ardencaple Kennels. Their Ch. Ardencaple's Mighty Might is a tiny, typey Group winner and his litter brother is another quality Pom. Ch. Georgian Pocket Piece was winners dog at the Florida Pomeranian Specialty Club's Miami show in January 1960. The Denton's dogs have been handled exclusively by Mr. Frank Ashbey.

In writing the history of America's outstanding kennels and breeders, it has been impossible to name all of them. It would take several volumes to tell the complete story of Pomeranians and their breeders. And the listing of all champions and outstanding Poms would in itself be a monumental task. A few breeders who are doing much in importing and breeding good Poms did not come forth with necessary information, and there are others I was unable to contact for lack of proper addresses. Mexico, Canada, Bermuda, and Latin-American countries have many fanciers very active in Pomeranian exhibition and breeding, but no attempt is made to include such data in depth here. For information on the latest breeders and dogs see the chapter entitled "Poms and Breeders of the 1960's" later in this book.

Dorothy Bonner with Honey Chile.

Ch. Preservenes Live Wire, bred and owned by Mrs. E. Shrewsbury.

Ch. Ricochet Marguerite's Ruby, Bred by Mrs.
Marguerite Dolan and owned by Ruth H. Bellick.

THE POMS BEHIND OUR BRITISH IMPORTS

TO WRITE about Pomeranians in England, one must first know something about how the English judge them. Tom Gascoyne was a long-time breeder of outstanding winning Poms in England and his passing in 1960 was a loss to Pom fanciers everywhere. He was an eminent judge of all breeds and kindly consented to write the following short statement on judging Poms in England, although he was quick to point out that this is only how HE judged them, and that he spoke only for himself regarding the judging of Pomeranians.

"I am asked for an article on how the English judge a good Pomeranian. Many people, many minds—I would not dare! How I personally judge a Pom, yes. This is what I look for: first and absolutely essential that majestic mien, which proclaims a monarch in any realm! That poise, flair, verve, style, which is condensed in the term 'Pom character,' and which earned him the title 'King of Toys.' Second in importance—movement, another characteristic peculiar to the breed. High stepping, straight, true, bouncing off his hocks. Then coat, double texture with straight top coat; a substitute which often gets past is the dense, single texture, fuzzy coat, found in some oranges, which stands without the brush but is inclined to frizz.

91

"Style in trimming at present—i.e., shaping a dog out of its coat to look like a miniature Chow—handicaps a sable because it means cutting off all black tips, which mutilates color—and sables usually have the best coats! Conformation: in most breeds this should come first, but a Pom that is made right but lacks character is just a Pom! Hence my priorities. Short, well-ribbed body (a good coat is rarely grown on a flat body), and unless there is something between the shoulder blades there is a tendency to weave in front movement. Short neck on a nicely laid shoulder means a head set on to look up without over-showing. High-set, straight strunt (a high-set tail as 'strunt' is a term used in England and Scotland for root of tail). I like a round, tight Pom. A low-set or loosely carried plume spoils the circle. Good bend of stifle and hock are a must if he is to bounce off his hocks as if on springs. Fine, straight bone, cat feet, head with a medium face, slightly flat skull. I detest any semblance of apple. Small ears, kindly expression and orthodox color. The craze for orange breeding and breeding orange to orange has impaired pigmentation and texture of coat. I have painted my ideal Pomeranian. Points in order of merit. When I find one which measures up I will give a king's ransom.

"Tom Gascoyne"

I feel that the whole Pomeranian fancy on both sides of the Atlantic is fortunate in having the ideals of such an outstanding breeder and judge painted so graphically for them.

Mrs. Gascoyne has written about their own kennel operations, saying Mr. Gascoyne was breeding Poms before World War I. After the war he went in for a number of breeds but always had a good Pom for variety classes. When she came upon the scene (Mrs. Gascoyne is a daughter of Mrs. Butler of Zanow affix), Poms again took priority. Blacks were concentrated upon and the best black in England was owned for four generations. He was The Nonpariel, the ancestor of all good blacks of today, and wartime winner of 369 firsts and forty-two best in show awards. Debonair of Morrell Opal was exported to India for a record price, as were Domino of Morrell and Black Opal of Morrell.

Colors were introduced after World War II. Ch. Humphrey of the Vines of Morrell was winner of eight championships and was best in Toy Group twice. Gentleman of Morrell, winner of one championship and ten reserves, and sire of two champions, was accidentally poisoned at three years of age. His son Zambo of Zanow is the sire of champions. Lucky Star of Morrell, winner of one championship and best of breed, died at the age of eighteen months. Ch. Solitaire of Morrell was winner of seven championships, was four times best of breed, and was a champion at nine and a half months. He was exported to Mrs. Brewster of Robwood Kennels in the United States.

Mrs. G. Dyke of Hadleigh Pomeranians has bred many champions and of her first eighteen champions, five became international champions. Hadleigh Poms have won more than a hundred challenge certificates, which is a record in the breed in England. During 1957 Mrs. Dyke took three Poms to the title: Ch. Wee Model of Hadleigh, Ch. Lady's Jewel of Hadleigh, and Ch. Lovely Lady of Hadleigh. At Crufts in 1958 she showed a ten-month-old puppy, Lady Fair of Hadleigh, who won the CC for best puppy bitch, edging out two former unbeaten bitches, Sylvia of Hadleigh and Angela of Hadleigh, both of which won their classes at Crufts and each of which holds one challenge certificate.

It takes three challenge certificates, or CC's, as they are usually listed in England, for an English championship. The point system we have in the United States is not used and listing of wins sometimes is confusing to American readers.

Ch. Sweet Lady of Hadleigh is the dam of Ch. Lady's Jewel of Hadleigh, Ch. Lovely Lady of Hadleigh, and Ch. Lady Fair of Hadleigh. Sweet Lady's sire is Ch. Hadleigh Brilliant Flame. Ch. Hadleigh Brilliant Flame has sired many champions, including English and American Ch. Rose Marie of Hadleigh, AKC Ch. Sweet William of Hadleigh, Ch. Tiny Tot of Hadleigh, and Ch. Sweet Lady of Hadleigh. Bonny Boy of Hadleigh is the sire of Ch. Dimples of Hadleigh, Ch. Billy Button of Hadleigh, and Int. Ch. Annabell of Hadleigh. Hadleigh's Pride is the sire of English and AKC Ch. Cuddles of Hadleigh, Ch. Hadleigh's Golden Wonder, Ch. Foritta of Hadleigh, and AKC Ch. Hadleigh Prince Charming.

Mrs. Dyke states that much of her success is due to careful breeding to the best bloodlines, care being taken to have really top-class, well-bred brood bitches. Grooming and trimming always play a part in the presentation of the Pom and Mrs. Dyke always dampens her Poms' coats with cold water and brushes well, powdering a little behind the ears and on breechings and plume, then brushing the powder out. Showmanship is also essential, she states, and she feels that too much grooming or brushing is inclined to tear out the coat of a Pom. She brushes with a good bristle brush about twice a week, unless the dogs are casting their coats, in which case all dead hair must be taken out.

Mrs. Dyke also states that she always endeavors to send abroad something that is a credit to her kennel and always gives honest and true description of what she offers for sale. Many buyers from overseas have purchased as many as twelve Pomeranians from Mrs. Dyke, and she states that they have been highly satisfied.

Preservenes Kennels of Mrs. E. E. J. Shrewsbury goes back three generations, as both the mother and grandmother of Mrs. Shrewsbury have bred Pomeranians. Mrs. Morton (her grandmother) began the kennel and handed it down to Mrs. Gilbert (her mother), who in turn handed it down to Mrs. Shrewsbury. All have been very successful and are noted breeders of quality Pomeranians. Preservenes' Poms have reached near-perfection in many instances and are heavy contenders at the larger English shows where three to six thousand entries, all-breeds, are not unusual. We in the United States must remember that in England each dog is usually entered in several classes, whereas over here each dog is usually entered but once. In England three thousand entries does not mean three thousand dogs. For instance, if each dog entered at Madison Square Garden or Chicago International were to be entered in five or six classes, there would be eight or ten thousand entries.

Mrs. Shrewsbury's biggest winner is the famous Ch. Preservenes Live Wire, a small-eared, sweet-faced, huge-coated Pom of medium size. He was twenty-four times winner of the challenge certificate at Crufts, and he won forty best in show awards and over 600 prizes before being retired. His breeding goes back to Riverleigh, Bobby Ideal, old Tollgate and Eastney lines.

Many Preservenes Pomeranians have won championships and

Ch. Humphrey of the Vines of Morrell
Owner, Mrs. A. M. Gascoyne

Agasicles of Coronne
Breeder-owner, Mrs. Scandrett

Ch. Dimple of Hadleigh, bred and owned by Mrs. G. Dyke.

many good ones have been exported to all parts of the world.

Wilmscote is the prefix of Robert Flavell. Dogs from his kennel figuring heavily in the background of Poms being exported to the United States are Wilmscote Wild Wind (dam of AKC Ch. Wilmscote Wee Conquest), Chs. W. Wee Contender, W. Wee Companion, W. Wee Cyrano, and Wilmscote Wee Cyclone. Wilmscote Wee Companion is the sire of AKC Ch. Wilmscote Wee Craftsman, Wilmscote Wayward Miss, Wilmscote Worthwhile, Wilmscote Weaver, and Wilmscote Wink.

Coronne Pomeranians is the kennel of Mrs. F. K. Scandrett, a leading producer of black Poms and a well-known exhibitor. Because she is unable to attend shows outside her local area, she does not make as many of the big shows as do some breeders. However, she shows at Crufts in London. Her Ch. Jewel of Jet is the sire of Agasicles of Coronne, who went best in show at the South of England Pomeranian Specialty. She is a short-bodied, heavy-coated Pom of jet black coat. Diogenes of Coronne was sired by Rudi of Coronne and is out of Demelza of Coronne, who also has several nice show wins. Mrs. Scandrett has been a Pom breeder since 1934 and a great lover of blacks, a color in which she specializes.

POMS IN CANADA

There are many good Pomeranian breeders in Canada, but the vast area of Canada and the deep snows of the winters keep many would-be exhibitors at home, so while their kennels house many Poms of championship quality, they lack opportunity to show. Among breeders who do exhibit are W. W. and R. B. Laskey of Fredericton, N. B. They also exhibit at a few United States shows and their winsome little Crown Princess Julie of Jargon made the title in 1960. Crown Princess is a daughter of Ch. Hunt's Golden Boy II, out of Little Lulie IV, a Canadian champion and winner of five Toy Groups as well as BOB and winner of Group placings in the United States.

Pat and Evelyn Kenny of Calgary, Alberta, Canada, are owners of the Kenlynn Kennels. They own Chs. Corkie's Golden Glow Topper, Renfrew Jewel (C. D.), Kenlynn's Golden Dawn, and Pacemaker's Little Caesar.

POMS IN BERMUDA

Here in the United States we have begun to hear much of Bermuda's Pomeranians. Florence, Lady Conyers, of Westerleigh, Pembroke, Bermuda, has become a heavy contender for United States honors and in February 1960 her Bermuda Ch. Shadow of Hadleigh won her third five-point major at the Westminster Show, to finish her AKC championship. She was winner for five points the previous day at the New York Specialty Show of the American Pomeranian Club, Inc.

The Bermuda shows at which numerous United States breeders now contend for Pomeranian honors are run under the rules and regulations of the governing body in Canada.

Am. and Can. Ch. Tiralin Dark of the Moon,
owned and handled by Mrs. Joy LeCompte.

Ch. Nino of Thelcolynn, U.D., and Sourdough Timothy, U.D., owned by Mrs. E. P. Lambert, Arlington, Virginia. Ch. Nino has been confirmed by the AKC to be the first Pomeranian to earn both the breed-ring championship and U.D. title. She has two Canine Awards for high scores while earning her C.D. and C.D.X.

THE POMERANIAN AND OBEDIENCE

POMERANIANS more than hold their own in advanced obedience training. Several of them have finished to their title and won top scores. Experienced trainers have learned not to smile in a patronizing manner when someone asks to enter a Pomeranian in obedience school.

Several Pomeranian kennels have obedience Poms holding the highest obedience degree, and some have titles in two or three countries. There is not enough space to do justice to their honors and I mention a few of them in later paragraphs to stand as examples as to what can be done with Poms in obedience training and exhibition.

When the puppy reaches the age for obedience training (six months of age or over), he should, if possible, be taken to obedience school. If this is out of the question, a good book on home obedience should be purchased and studied and directions followed.* You will find it fascinating as you watch your puppy's eagerness to learn and his pride when he has finished a perform-

* See *The Complete Novice Obedience Course,* by Blanche Saunders, published by Howell Book House Inc.

The Complete Open Obedience Course, by Blanche Saunders, published by Howell Book House Inc.

The Complete Utility Obedience Course, by Blanche Saunders, published by Howell Book House Inc.

ance and has won your praise. There is a lot of "ham" in all Pomeranians and they love to capture attention.

Sophia Mayes of Wellesley Hills, Massachusetts, was a well-known obedience trainer who had worked several large breeds to titles. Her son begged for a little dog as a pet, for he had been bitten by a large dog and was afraid of large breeds for that reason. So "Spark," a Pomeranian, was purchased and she proved so smart that Mrs. Mayes decided to take her to obedience school, and, in her own words, Mrs. Mayes says, "What a furor it created when I appeared in class with a Toy dog." But owners of the larger dogs soon stopped smiling in amusement. Spark, registered as Susie O' The Avenue, quickly earned her title of C.D., went on to C.D.X., to T.D., and had completed her U.D. when she developed a congenital eye cataract and was unable to judge distances for jumps, so had to be retired.

Starlite's Betty Lue, known as "Dixie," was purchased and trained by Mrs. Mayes and earned her C.D. in June of 1955. She completed her C.D.X. in March 1957 and her T.D. in October 1957. Meanwhile, she produced a litter of puppies, so her maternal duties interrupted her obedience work for the time being. Mrs. Mayes did not rest on her laurels with Betty Lue but went on training Poms in obedience, loving to see the tiny bits of fluff outdoing their larger brethren. In March 1960, with Dixie and Robin, she won the brace class at the Dog Owner's Training Club of Baltimore trials, the brace finishing with a score of $196\frac{1}{2}$, with seven braces competing. The judge, commenting on Dixie and Robin's exhibition, remarked that in all his years of judging such competitions, this was the best brace he had ever seen.

The following April, Sophie Mayes' May Morning Waltzing Matilda, affectionately known as "Terry," passed the tracking test of the New England Dog Training Club to earn her T.D. degree, becoming the fifth Pomeranian ever to receive this title. Three of the five Poms that won the T.D. degrees were owned and trained by Sophie Mayes, the first being Susie O' The Avenue, C.D.X., T.D., and the second Starlite's Betty Lue, U.D.T., who finished her numerous titles after she had raised a litter of puppies. In 1960 Mrs. Mayes began the training of Robin (May Morning Robin Redbreast) for tracking.

Mrs. Joy Lecompte, owner of Goldpaz Kennels, Salem, Oregon, is the owner of AKC and CKC Ch. Beach's Brightest Angel, who is the holder of Canadian and United States C.D. titles, proving that Pomeranians can win in conformation rings and go on to pick up laurels in obedience rings. Angel is also the holder of the Dog World Award of Canine Distinction for obedience and 1959 winner of the American Pomeranian Club Annual Specials in Novice A obedience, with a perfect score.

Buttons Rubel, U.D., is a six-pound orange Pom with loads of personality, who is owned and handled by Mrs. Gladys Dykstra of Springfield, Massachusetts. In August 1954, she received the Utility Degree. Buttons is one of the highest scoring dogs of any breed in the East. Her scores have always been in the high 190's, with many perfect scores of 200. She was the highest scoring dog in the show of the Otter Valley Obedience Club at Rutland, Vermont, where there is much competition from Canadian obedience dogs as well as the best in the United States. Buttons also won at the shows of the Obedience Training Club at Cranston, Rhode Island, and at the Springfield Kennel Club trials at Springfield, Massachusetts.

There is always a large audience at ringside when Buttons performs, which shows that most people like to see a small dog in action. And she is a willing and flashy worker. She has been trained by her owner at "Bea's" K.9 Obedience Training School in Springfield under the direction of Mrs. Beatrice Connelly.

Many people think of obedience training as only for the larger dogs, the unmanageable dogs, and the dogs that are a problem to their owners and handlers. But that is not true. Any dog is a better dog at home or on the street when it has had some obedience training, Mrs. Dykstra writes, and in this all can agree. Poms are quick to learn and seem to retain training longer than many other breeds. Their desire to learn makes them a joy to work with, and, while the number of Poms in obedience is not great, the percentage of excellent workers with top scores is very high. Mrs. Dykstra continues: "The size of the Pom is of little concern. Three to four pounders do just as good work as the larger ones. If one feels that his Pom is too large for breed competition in conformation, he should consider training him for obedience."

101

Buttons is known to thousands of children in the Springfield area, having been shown in the thirty-three public schools of the city in connection with the Humane Society's program to show children how dogs can be trained in simple obedience for the protection of themselves and their owners. Over 14,000 children had seen Buttons in this program up to 1958. Teachers have used Buttons as a subject for story telling, story writing, drawing, and even modeling. Buttons demonstrated at each semester of Mr. Corbin's "Problems of Democracy Classes" at the Classical High School in Springfield, and at the Shriners' Hospital for Crippled Children and Westover Hospital for War Veterans.

Buttons has participated in library story-telling hours at most of Springfield's branch libraries, as well as at the children's center of the main library. It is at these gatherings that she usually dons an outfit to suit the occasion—Easter outfit, St. Patrick's day outfit, or Santa Claus costume.

In their work for their pet badges, Girl Scouts and Brownies have benefited by the demonstrations. Buttons also has visited a dozen different churches, either in obedience class demonstrations or alone with her mistress. Fair grounds in Massachusetts and Northern Connecticut also are her haunts, as well as Christmas parties for the Girls Clubs, and many other children's parties. She has been on television several times as guest of the SPCA and The Western Massachusetts Electric Company.

Buttons was whelped at the Rossmoyne Kennels, formerly of Mt. Vernon, New York, and currently at Medford Station, L. I., New York. Her sire was Bialek's Tiny Tim and her dam was Rossmoyne Marie. Buttons was ten years old in 1961. All her demonstrations are free and the whole Pom fancy owes a debt of gratitude to Mrs. Dykstra for her wonderful work.

Another outstanding obedience Pom of the Dorchester, Massachusetts, area was Paula Goulston's Dantar Pizzucato, C.D., who illustrates to perfection a Pomeranian's adaptability to advanced training. He was trained for further titles when he contracted a virus and was lost.

Mr. and Mrs. W. C. Horner of Massilon, Ohio, are the owners of another fine obedience Pom, Evening Star's Jeanie Girl, C.D. (called Mimi), as she has repeatedly been high-scoring dog at show after show, often attaining that perfect score of 200. She delights crowds by outscoring many larger breeds, doing her work with such enthusiasm that the ringside never fails to give their approval in thunderous applause.

Mr. and Mrs. Frank Blankenship of Muskogee, Oklahoma, and their animal nurse and housekeeper, Jan Leslie, have done much with Poms in obedience. They first worked with Junior E. Nunn, who has more than thirty years' experience in the Army Training Corps for dogs. Junior put Bo-Jingles in training after Jan Leslie had put his C.D. on him in Oklahoma City. Junior put a C.D.X. on Bo-Jingles at three straight shows, with a score of 199½ at each of the three. Of all the dogs Junior Nunn has trained (which include many breeds), the Blankenships state that he considers Poms in general, and Bo-Jingles in particular, the most intelligent and valuable. Anywhere they go, the general comment is, "There is our competition."

Jan Leslie started Bo-Jingles, when he was eight months old, in obedience classes in Oklahoma City. He had eight weeks of training, then graduation. There were seventeen dogs in the graduating class, judged by an out-of-town judge, and Bo-Jingles placed first with a score of 196. In his next three shows he finished his first degree, then Nunn took over. Later the Blankenships started obedience classes of their own in Muskogee, Oklahoma, with Frank Blankenship as the director and Mrs. Blankenship as the instructor. Jan worked with Ch. Fancy Mittens and Ch. Darling Debbie, and in three straight shows after they completed obedience school, both Poms earned their C.D.'s. Mr. and Mrs. Blankenship state that after working with many breeds in classes, they are convinced Poms outrank all other breeds when it comes to learning rapidly, and they feel Poms are more precise in every exercise they are called upon to do. They are happy workers and therefore do not hesitate to obey commands.

Jan Leslie is a great asset to the Blankenships. She was orphaned at the age of two years and placed in an orphanage in Boston. There she stayed until she was nineteen. Then she left to train as an animal nurse at the famous Angell Memorial Animal Hospital and she worked there for eight years with top doctors and interns. Mrs. Blankenship writes: "It happened one Sunday morning as we were coming out of Our Lady's

103

Cathedral that this little person tapped me on the shoulder. I just know for many reasons now, that God put here there. She wanted directions to a home where she was to work for a time." This was the home of a heart specialist with a wife and three children, who had met Miss Leslie and had asked her if she would like to come to Oklahoma City to work. But she had found that she did not care for just housework and was homesick for dogs. The Blankenships then and there made arrangements with her to come and work for them in their home and kennel. Poms were chosen for their future major breed because the Blankenships admired their beauty and Jan loved Poms above all other breeds. Together they gradually built the Pom kennel, starting with Tasty Cupcake, who presented them with Bo-Jingles. Then Sparkie-Boi was added. Soon they had over forty Poms, but later, after they had purchased a smaller place, they had to reduce the size of the kennel. Mr. Blankenship travels a great deal and two trained Poms go with him on trips, since he says that he would feel undressed without them.

Mrs. Gail B. Niper of Clifton, New Jersey, is an avid booster for obedience in Pomeranians and has done much to publicize the breed's ability in this field. Foxie XI, a five-pound male, excels in training. The holder of the C.D.X. award in obedience, he is the sire of conformation point-winner Elfin Autumn Glory.

Another enthusiastic obedience fan is Pat McManus of Columbus, Ohio. Her most outstanding obedience Pom is Dandy Bug of Glo Toy. He has acquired all the obedience degrees and has been awarded the Canine Award of Distinction for his outstanding work in obedience. He did all this after only thirteen weeks' training.

Captain and Mrs. E. P. Lambert of Arlington, Virginia, are the proud owners of the winsome Sourdough Timmie. Captain Lambert was stationed in Anchorage, Alaska, at the time they acquired Timmie, hence his Alaskan name of Sourdough Timmie. Mrs. Lambert had trained and handled dogs as a professional handler for more than twenty years and was long associated with the Elsie Muir Chihuahua and Pekingese kennels in New Mexico.

When Timmie's dam lost her milk when Timmie was but a scant five weeks old, he was turned over to Mrs. Lambert as

Eveningstar's Jeanie Girl, C.D., bred and owned by Mr. and Mrs. W. C. Horner. Jeanie Girl scored 200 consistently in winning her title in obedience. The Horners also own fine conformation champions.

Bo-Jingles, C.D., C.D.X., owned by Mr. and Mrs. Frank N. Blankenship and shown here with his trainer-handler, Jan Leslie.

she was known to have "a way with dogs" and was thought to have the best chance of saving the tiny tyke. The breeder had had to make an emergency trip to Seattle, also, and could not take Timmie and his litter mate along. Mrs. Lambert had not had the two puppies more than a week when she noticed Timmie's unusual intelligence, and she decided to purchase him. She states that Timmie has been the most compensating purchase she has ever made. Timmie was eager to learn and Mrs. Lambert found it hard to keep up with him. At the age of five months he was in an obedience demonstration. Since only puppies six months old could be entered in obedience school, Mrs. Lambert began Timmie's training with Blanche Saunder's book, *Training You to Train Your Dog.* Her success attests to what can be done at home with a good Pom and a good book, and, I should add, a good trainer.

At the obedience exhibition when Timmie was but five months old, he did C.D.X. and U.D. work with specially built jumps of 12 x 18 inches. Unfortunately, the Alaskan Club held only one trial a year and the Lamberts had to take Timmie to Tacoma, Washington, for a trial just so Timmie could get his C.D. before he was two years old. Timmie got one of his legs for his C.D. under the noted trainer and judge Blanche Saunders, with a perfect score of 200. Timmie now has streaked through his final titles, since the Lamberts have returned to the United States, where obedience trials are plentiful.

Timmie also has been trained as an entertainer at hospitals and schools, having appeared before thousands of school children and veterans in hospitals from Alaska down to the States. In fact, he has so much "ham" in him that Mrs. Lambert states this is his only fault, as he loves so dearly to "perform" that he sometimes is too much of an "eager beaver" ham.

Pomeranians and owner-handler-trainers such as Mrs. Lambert do much for the Pomeranian breed, for they prove beyond the shadow of a doubt that Poms are powerhouses of brains and love and ability. Atoms of dogs they may be, but like atoms, they are second to none in achievement.

106

Dancing Sammy, C.D., C.D.X., U.D., and winner of Canine Award of Distinction, is shown with a few of his many trophies. Dancing Sammy is owned and trained by Pat McManus.

Ch. Gold Toy's Top Tune, bred by Mary Bond
and owned by Mrs. Charles Edwards, Jr.

Ch. Gay Sahib's Pride, bred and owned by Mrs. Kathryn W.
Haltom.

SPECIALTY CLUBS

IN COMPILING authentic data of the American Pomeranian Club, Inc., the parent club, the task has been difficult. There undoubtedly has been a loss of a great many important details, for complete records have not been kept for some years in the past when the club was mostly inactive except for holding a show and a meeting each year in New York. Such data as is given here can be traced to an authentic source of information, and if important details are missing, it is unavoidable, as some principals have passed away and others have forgotten. If after publication of this book, important missing details are reported to me or to the APC secretary, they will be included in the next edition of this book.

Miss Elsie Blum, one of the long-time boosters of the parent club, and Dorothy Husted, secretary for many years and 1961 president of APC, have worked long and diligently in tracing facts, and to them I owe a debt of gratitude. Mrs. Elsie Sivori also sent important information, including the extract from an article by Vincent Matta which appeared in the Golden Jubilee issue of *The American Kennel Gazette* of September 1934. In the article Mr. Matta states that the American Pomeranian Club was founded in 1900, just about the time the breed was formally recognized by The American Kennel Club. Poms for some years

109

had been shown in the Miscellaneous Class and before that had been confused with the Spitz dog.

The New York show in 1900 was the first to give winners classes for Poms and L. P .C. Astley, an English judge and Pom breeder, came over from England to judge the breed. No record was given by Matta as to the number of entries, but it probably was small. Mrs. Frank Smythe's Nubian Rebel, a brown Pomeranian, was adjudged best of breed. Rebel again went BOB at the club specialty in 1902, and later became a champion.

Vincent Matta also reported that club after club followed suit in giving classes for Poms, so that the formation of the parent club was the lever which gave impetus to the upward climb of Pomeranians. The large entries in the days following the formation of the parent club are no longer a reality, as everything that could be called a Pomeranian was then shown, while today's Pomeranian entries, though smaller in number, are far superior.

Dorothy Husted writes that records state that the parent club held its first specialty show in 1910, so that specialty spoken of by Mr. Matta must have been of an informal type. Mrs. Hartley Williamson and Mrs. Frank Smythe are given credit for the formation of the American Pomeranian Club (the club did not become incorporated until July of 1921). At the first specialty, held in 1910, Mrs. L. C. Dyer came over from England to judge the breed and 138 Poms were entered. Ch. Canner Prince Charming, a black, was awarded best of breed.

Miss Elsie Blum sent information taken from old show catalogues, indicating that in January 1914 there were 174 entries, but that 1915 entries dropped to seventy-two, while in 1916 entries were back over the one hundred mark to 107. In 1917 there were 110. In 1918 entries rose to 128, and in 1919 went back to 105. Up until 1928 entries averaged over one hundred annually and then gradually dropped as competition became keener and quality higher.

The parent club soon became active in promoting specialty clubs in various parts of the country and in 1912 the Western Pomeranian Club was formed in Chicago by Mrs. Hebden, formerly Mrs. Arbuckle. This club is still active, holding a specialty each year.

In June of 1958, the American Pomeranian Club issued its

first edition of *Pomeranian Review,* a quarterly magazine of excellent quality and content, produced under the editorship of Mr. James Arima, who still is at the helm. Many members had dropped out of the club because meetings were not accessible to them. Since no regular communication medium was available, they lost interest. The appearance of the *Pomeranian Review* almost immediately changed all this and membership and show entries began to climb everywhere, until present membership as of 1962 stands at an all-time high of over 260 members and membership still is climbing. Entry at the Westminster Specialty in February 1961 was seventy-eight and this is amazing when it is considered that the entry five or six years earlier was almost at the disappearing point, in one instance being only eight entries.

Mrs. Husted, who was elected 1961 president with Mrs. Josephine Leonardis as secretary-treasurer, writes that not only are entries climbing but that quality of Pomeranians entered is 500 percent better than in former years when entries were so low. Of course, a very few good Poms always have been entered, but Mrs. Husted speaks of overall quality of entry in general.

The San Diego Pomeranian Club was organized in April of 1949, with seventeen charter members. Gerald K. House was charter president. Pauline Hughes and Mildred Collins originated the club. Peter J. and Gladys Youngdahl of Temple City, California, acted as advisers in the organization and were the first honorary members. A puppy match has been held each year, and the first specialty show was held in conjunction with the Silver Bay Kennel Club Show (all-breed) in 1952 with an entry of fifty-seven Poms. A specialty is now held annually and entries are high, never fewer than twenty-seven Pomeranians. In San Diego, as elsewhere, overall quality rises higher each year and competition is keen. In 1957 associate memberships were inaugurated and the club's list includes members from all over the United States and Canada, and from French Morocco. In May 1957 the club published its first *Newsletter,* which is now issued monthly. The club has furthered the interest in Pomeranians not only locally, but also nationally. Those members who have worked diligently through the years include Tom and

Flora Evison, Beverly and James Griffiths, Jean Higgins, Pauline Hughes, Lee Johnson, and Anna and Ray La Fortune.

The New England Pomeranian Club, which was recently formed, had as its very first president Mrs. Roy Webber, who is known to all Pom lovers. Charter members include Mrs. Sophia Mayes, of obedience fame, Mrs. Esther Martin, who also served as president, and Mrs. Ruth Bellick, who finished five Pom champions in 1957. This club has raised Pom entries in New England shows from nothing at many shows to majors at most of them now. They began with thirty members and the number is growing.

The Columbian Pomeranian Club was organized in 1953 and since that time has held several puppy matches and specialty shows, all of them outstanding successes. With Elva Cohen McGilbry as supporter, they could hardly fail to be anything but successes, for she is known as one of the best boosters of the breed. Judge as well as breeder-exhibitor, she encourages beginners and this spells success for any club. The club has associate memberships as well as voting memberships and issues a club newsletter. My thanks go to Bertha Garrison and Marjorie Kneisel, who have sent me interesting information regarding the club.

The Pacific Northwest Pomeranian Club does not hold a specialty show but instead supports the Island Empire Association all-breed shows each year with entries and trophies. This club has a program of help that is second to none and one that is rarely equaled in any breed. Marianne Melville, Elnora Johnson, Mildred Robinson, and Lillian Kjeldgaard are the four charter members still with the club, and their work for the breed is commendable. Their enthusiasm has spread to the complete membership and this enterprising group works closely with each other in any problems an individual may have, supports surrounding shows with entries and trophies, and holds out a helping hand to all newcomers in the district. As a group they have made an intensive study of nutrition and they are fortunate in having Dr. Robert Carlson, a young local veterinarian, as an enthusiastic member whose help and advice have been of great value. Classes are conducted by Marianne Melville in grooming and training, and in preparation for puppy matches and all-breed shows. The group, as a gesture of hospitality, always serves lunch to all Pomeranian breeders and exhibitors at their shows. This is a wonderful program and I think might well be copied by all specialty or breed clubs.

Miami, Florida, also has a specialty club but I have been unable to secure any data regarding the formation or program of the club. They have good entries each year at their shows, which are held in conjunction with those of the combined specialty clubs of Florida the day preceding the Miami all-breed show.

The Fort Worth Pomeranian Club is a very active specialty club, having held its second specialty show in 1961. Their membership at that time was sixty and still growing fast. They get together for their meetings with a dinner served afterward. Beautiful trophies for most blue-ribbon as well as purple-and-gold winners and majors in both sexes can be expected at their shows.

Ch. Rougeland's Red Rascal, owned by Mrs. Veola Herzog.   Ch. Strait's Perry Winkle, owned by Mildred A. Strait.

Ch. Sir Percy of Point Loma, bred by Alvie C. Grimmer, and Ch. Motet of Point Loma, bred by Pauline B. Hughes, who owns both dogs.

WORTHWHILE READING MATERIAL

THE New Art of Breeding Better Dogs, by Kyle and Philip Onstott, first issued in 1946 (revised in the new edition published by Howell Book House Inc.) was one of my very first dog library books. It remains the leading book on the breeding of dogs. The Mendelian theory of heredity is explained so simply that even the amateur can easily grasp its fundamentals. Inbreeding, line breeding and out breeding are fully explained, as are the effects of heredity and environment. This is a book no serious breeder can afford to be without.

The International Encyclopedia of Dogs, edited by Stanley Dangerfield and Elsworth Howell with special contributions by Maxwell Riddle, is undoubtedly one of the finest reference works available on dogs anywhere. Within its 480 pages are alphabetical entries on everything pertaining to dogs as well as a profusion of color and black and white photographs to delight any dog enthusiast.

Gaines Dog Research Center, 250 North Street, White Plains, N.Y. puts out several fine aids to the breeder, among them *Gaines Dog Research Progress,* a free bulletin with important veterinarian articles and laboratory reports.

The Complete Dog Book, published by The American Kennel Club, is a must, as it gives all official breed Standard information and other worthwhile data on dogs in general. The Pomer-

Ch. Mayken's Zante
Breeder, Kenneth Mayes
Owner, Mrs. F. B. Ross

Sungold's Miss Prim
Breeder, Anna La Fortune
Owner, Hugh Huston

Ch. Gold Toy's Gay Toy
Breeder, Joyce Brown
Owners, Hutchison & Innis

Ch. Majack Sugar Plum
Owner, Mrs. Wadsworth

Ch. Su Su Thumper of Jo Beth
Breeder, Elizabeth Smith
Owner, Grace Shackelford

Ch. Latham's Banginway
Breeder, Marvin Latham
Owner, Elizabeth Davis

116

anian Standard as published in this book is the only official Standard and the yardstick a judge is obligated to follow in adjudicating dogs in the ring. This Standard is written by the parent club, approved or amended by the AKC, and published by them. Amendments may be added later and published in the official magazine of The American Kennel Club, which may be secured by yearly subscription. This magazine is *Pure-Bred Dogs, American Kennel Gazette,* published at 51 Madison Ave., New York, New York 10010.

The magazine is published monthly and along with interesting articles, includes records of all AKC show wins throughout the United States, the minutes of all AKC Board meetings, announcements of official changes in any breed Standard or rules pertaining to showing, etc. Armed with this official magazine of the AKC, anyone can be informed instead of misinformed, as is so often the case where hearsay is the rule. If a ruling is published as official in this magazine, it *is* official until such time as it is amended or revoked and so published.

Pomeranian Review, official publication of the American Pomeranian Club, Inc., is also a must for Pomeranian owners. As described under the chapter on specialty clubs and their official publications, *Pomeranian Review* tells all about Pomeranians and their owners. It is edited at 1052 Meadow Road, Northbrook, Illinois, and the circulation manager is Miss Burneice F. Lovelace, 7113 Oxford Road, Baltimore 12, Maryland.

Ch. Schirman Oaks Golden Timsun, bred and owned by Mr. and Mrs. Harry Schirman.

Bertha Disher and Kathryn Birk with lapfuls of Disher puppies.

Rob Moneybox, Glad Days Taffy, Dee's Lassie, Glad Days Gipsy Rose, Toody Gold Dust, and Ch. Glad's Victoria with their owner, Mrs. Gladys M. Wright.

Int. Ch. Aristic Suntoy, Int. Ch. Dromore Bombardier, and Int. Ch. Golden Glow Dandy being held by Mrs. Elva McGilbry of Golden Glow Pomeranian Kennels.

SOME FACETS OF SPECIAL CARE AND
HANDLING OF POMERANIANS

POMERANIANS are exceptionally hardy dogs, since they are descended from the Huskies of the Far North. They comprise a breed that can "take it," as veterinarians can attest.

However, all breeds have their peculiarities and the Pomeranian is no exception. For example, breeds having a very short nose are prone to respiratory trouble; those having large protruding eyes are subject to eye injury and infection; and Toy breeds, whose newborn puppies often (as in the case of the Pomeranian) weigh less than three ounces, sometimes need special attention.

Many Toy breeds have been bred down in a short span of time from about thirty-five pounds to less than three, as is the case with the Pomeranian of today. Because of this, they sometimes suffer whelping troubles. Many owners believe that they can keep the Pomeranian diminutive by feeding sparingly, and this is especially regrettable because underfeeding only results in poor bone structure and weakened bodies.

Proper knowledge of feeding and care of newborn litters, and attention to whelping peculiarities when they arise are of paramount importance to the owner of Pomeranians, whether he has one or a dozen.

The feeding of plentiful amounts of meat (beef and poultry),

119

commercial dry dog food, dried skim milk, and a good concentrated all-purpose vitamin product will keep a Pomeranian in the pink of health. The simpler the diet the better, so long as a vitamin concentrate is fed regularly. I say this, having taken into consideration human weakness and inability to resist the Pom's cunning way of begging table scraps and meat. Including a good vitamin product is the surest way of insuring proper nutrition under average conditions.

I mention the more important problems that Pom owners sometimes have to face, and the methods used to counteract them that have proved successful for many, including myself. I sincerely hope that the following summation of information gathered throughout thirty years of dog breeding will be of value to Pomeranian breeders, new *and* old, for we are never too old to learn the new, nor do we ever gain so much experience that we cannot be helped along the way by someone else.

During the first six weeks of a Pom puppy's life, never forget that in his requirements he is just a wee replica of any larger breed. Proper food, proper rest, exercise, and clean comfortable living quarters, with plenty of personal attention are necessary if you want him to develop at his best. Human companionship and attention bring out the best in a Pomeranian puppy and condition him to take his proper place in later life. His whole outlook on life in general is in the formative period during his first six months and especially in his first eight weeks, so during that period you are molding puppy character as well as building a strong healthy body.

No one would continue to ply a twelve- to eighteen-month-old child with baby cereal and strained baby food, yet that is what too many owners do with a Pom puppy several months old. Comparatively speaking, a Pom at six weeks is as old in growth of body and mind as the human child of one year. At six to eight months a Pomeranian compares with a child in its early teens, and at nine to ten months the Pomeranian is mature in mind and body. Feed him accordingly, and at nine to ten months start giving him plenty of outdoor exercise, summer *and* winter. Poms love the snow and it does them no harm to play in it if upon being brought into the house they are toweled of

120

excess wetness and the tiny balls of snow their coat gathers on every wisp of hair.

Pom puppies, if fed solid food as soon as they will eat it, thrive like little weeds. Pomeranians mature in from nine to ten months and this fact must always be taken into consideration as against advice on the larger breeds that require two or three years to mature. At weaning age a Pom's tiny body needs more solid food than milk, baby cereal, and strained baby foods; otherwise, Mother Nature would have made sure that Pom mothers produced good rich milk for a year or more, instead of from four to six weeks.

Puppies and pregnant and lactating bitches have additional nutritional needs which are discussed in Part II of this book.

It is true that a Pom could get sufficient protein and vitamins and minerals by eating additional foods, but this method often upsets digestion and leads to more trouble, so a vitamin product is a necessity. A Pomeranian is such an active animal it burns up more energy than a quiet type dog and therefore cannot be expected to eat sufficient food to take care of its needs when stress factors are present, such as during growth, teething, pregnancies, etc. (A stress factor is anything outside the regular routine that brings on the need for extra food, special diet, or veterinarian treatment.)

The manner in which a puppy survives his first six weeks will determine much of his health and vigor for months to come. The first three days after whelping usually determines whether or not the puppy is going to thrive without special attention from the breeder. Watch a litter as they nurse and if one nurses angrily, constantly yanking at a nipple and making little scolding sounds, examine it after several minutes. If the stomach has remained flat even though the pup nursed steadily, you can be sure it is not getting sufficient milk. The puppy may be too weak or too tiny to wrap its tongue around the nipple in the manner necessary to properly draw the milk. It may be trying to nurse a teat too large for its tiny mouth. In this case, whatever the reason, proper measures must immediately be taken if the puppy is not steadily to grow weaker from its efforts and from lack of nourishment. At this point it must be kept warmer than usual, for weakened puppies lack body warmth. If

White Star's Bo Peep & White Star's Miss Muffet, famous brace bred by Jean Blackler and owned by Lillian Kjeldgaard.

Ch. Shared's Mighty Miss Owners, Mr. & Mrs. Harris

Ch. Jolly Acres Breezin' By Breeder-Owners, B. & J. Griffiths

From kennels of Viola Children, puppies from triple Sealand Moneybox breeding.

Lou-Lan's Petite Pixie, dam of 2 chs., owned by Louise Lanouette.

Scotia Cavalier's Biddie Boo, owned by Frank Welsh and Roy Marin, Jr.

122

chilled at this point, they simply give up and the battle is lost. These factors just mentioned are a result of the fast reduction in Pom body size and the consequent variation in size of puppies within a litter—some large, some tiny. The tiny ones are not runts, as would be the case in litters produced by the large sized breeds, but are puppies that will vary just as greatly at maturity. This is a point that is often overlooked by those more familiar with the large breeds, when writing about puppy care. Neither are the teats of many Pom bitches uniform in size. This is a bad combination when a newborn Pom puppy is very tiny and often spells the difference between a profit or a loss to the breeder. (It is the very tiny ones that usually bring in the three and four figure prices.)

If the puppy is trying to nurse a too-large nipple, change it to a smaller one from which the milk flows readily when it is stripped between thumb and forefinger. If the puppy is too weak to provide proper suction on the teat, it must be fed artificially for a few days or until it gains strength.

When a puppy nurses properly, drawing milk in a satisfactory amount, it nurses quietly and its stomach takes on the rounded appearance of a miniature football. With the weak ones it is wise to give one drop of vitamins daily, and the vitamin preparation should be given at blood-warm temperature. If the puppy is very tiny, under two ounces, a half-drop is sufficient. Place a drop of the vitamin preparation on the end of a finger and wipe part of it off in the puppy's mouth. A weak puppy so managed may gain sufficient strength in a day to get along all right. It is amazing how soon a small puppy learns to outmaneuver his larger litter mates by diving under the squirming mass to seize and hold a nipple. But the first day is important; often it is the dividing line between a pup that lives and one that fades and dies.

For the first three weeks after whelping most Pom bitches take good care of their offspring and the owner's time is best spent in seeing that the mother is well fed and cared for, with most puppy care left to the dam's capabilities.

Begin the introduction of solid food at three weeks by scraping a piece of red meat—beefsteak—against the dull side of a knife or a spoon. This way you get tender meat and juices with-

Ch. Premier Little Prize Package
Breeder-owner, Mrs, Roy Webber

Ch. Glad's Miss Stinkey
Breeder, Gladys Youngdahl
Owner, Dorothy Lee McDonald

Ch. Tim of Erimus Gold Blackacre, English import owned by Gene
Neal, imported and shown to championship by Gold Blackacre Kennels.

out any of the tough fiber that is hard for a young puppy to digest. About one-fourth teaspoon of scraped beef and juice is sufficient for a first feeding. Take a wisp of scraped meat on the tip of a finger and hold it against the puppy's nose. Usually the puppy will eagerly lick the meat from your finger. If it does not, open its mouth and deposit the meat inside the puppy's mouth. This usually will start it off. From this time on, introduce solid food as fast as the puppy will take it. Let the puppy eat from the dam's saucer, if she will permit, for this is a good way to introduce commercial dog food. And from now on, give vitamins daily according to directions on the bottle.

Meat given to Pom puppies should always be minced or ground to prevent choking if puppies are crowding for food, because Pom throats are very tiny and a too-large chunk of meat can cause the Pom to choke to death. Don't learn the hard way through loss of a valuable puppy.

Whelping is sometimes a troublesome point in Poms. Puppies vary in size at birth and a large puppy and a tiny dam make a bad combination. However, nature usually takes care of the situation if the bitch is left to herself; but all too often the new breeder becomes frightened and rushes the dam to a veterinarian who all too often gives pituitrin to induce heavier labor, with the result that the pup is rushed too fast and dies. For some reason, Pomeranians in labor seem to dilate very slowly. With large breeds, puppies will usually emerge a few minutes apart. Not so the Pomeranian. Two to three hours is not unusual, and especially if a puppy is large or coming backwards. I believe that more pups are lost through being rushed than from any other one factor. I have had dams who took all day to deliver four pups. As long as the dam does not appear exceptionally weakened or exhausted, it is best to have patience.

When the bitch has whelped all her litter, she will curl contentedly around them and take care of their needs. Watch the flow from the bitch's vulva for from eighteen to twenty-four hours. If the flow is red blood mixed with mucus, she is in good condition. If it is greenish black and the bitch acts nauseated and refuses to eat, there is in all probability a retained placenta or a dead pup and she must be taken to the veterinarian at once or poisoning will result in death.

125

Very often a puppy will appear dead when whelped, due to a difficult or prolonged passage. The question of whether or not the pup is alive is one that even long-experienced breeders and veterinarians ask themselves. The answer should always be assumed to be "yes" and the breeder should take immediate steps to revive the puppy. Vigorously towel the pup in front of direct heat, clear its mouth and nasal passages and apply artificial respiration with thumb and forefinger on its tiny rib cage. Hang it head downward and swing it back and forth, as this gives the same motion as do the tumbling beds used for polio patients whose lungs are paralyzed.

Several drops of liquid may drip from the pup's mouth and nostrils and then it will gasp as air enters its lungs, which were collapsed at birth. The puppy will be limp and flaccid until its lungs inflate. Then its muscles will draw up and the pup will appear to shrink but it will now feel firm and plump. When the pup cries out and squirms actively, give it to its mother. She will do the rest.

If a bitch is whelping her first litter and is overtired or suffering from shock, as sometimes happens, she will make little or no effort to clean her puppies as they arrive. In this case the attendant will have to do the whole job, including starting kidneys and bowel to working for the first time. Take a piece of warm, sterilized cotton, dip it in olive oil and gently stroke the penis or vulva of the newborn puppy and immediately its kidneys will respond. Apply the same treatment to the rectum and the puppy will strain and its bowels will move. A newborn puppy's bowel is filled with a substance appearing like a shining dark brown string of beads. Once this has started it can be pulled from the puppy. And this is important, for once the substance remains overlong, it dries to a waxy hardness and seals the bowel. The puppy will die within a week's time, often within days.

A dam in shock may remain in that condition for several hours, or as long as three days. (Many bitches have been unfairly branded as poor mothers when they really were suffering from shock and were incapable of performing or realizing their duties.) After shock has worn off, the dam will be an excellent mother. Shock is due to difficult or prolonged labor and happens

126

Ch. Simmerman's Joy, shown here by Clara Alford.
Breeder-owner, Mrs. Norris McKamey.

more often with a very tiny or new mother. Most bitches never suffer shock, but the breeder should be prepared to combat the condition should it occur.

When a puppy reaches its sixth week, begin accustoming it to a leash by tying a soft silken cloth lightly around its neck and letting other puppies tug at the cloth as you oversee their play. If this is done for a short period each day the puppy will become accustomed to having something around its neck and will not become frightened or stubborn when the real leash is used. A leash for a Pom must always be a silken one, very light, because a leather, chain, or other type of heavy leash is unpleasant and will cause the Pom to hate the leash. More Pomeranians than I like to state have lost in the show ring simply because they hated the leash and failed to travel with that proud uplift of head which is an intrinsic feature of a good Pom. So supply yourself with a proper leash, a light nylon leash, and your Pom will show proudly, with head held high, as a Pomeranian should.

At left, Ch. Great Elm's Rumple's Tom Thumb, owned by Kathryn Griffiths of Jilltara Poms.

Fa Rob's Red Buttons, bred and owned by Phyllis A. Picksley.

POMS AND BREEDERS OF THE 1960's

THE PAST few years since the first edition of *The New Complete Pomeranian* was written have brought about many changes in the Pomeranian picture. New faces, new Poms, and new kennels have come to national prominence, some to international fame. *Pomeranian Review,* official organ of The American Pomeranian Club, Inc., has mainly been responsible in bringing these kennels and new faces to the attention of the Pomeranian fancy. In its pages miles do not exist and breeders and fanciers have been brought close together in one huge family.

In obedience, Poms are still walking away with top honors in competition with all comers. It is always a delight to audiences to see a diminutive fluff of fur and vivacity go through obedience trial exercises with aplomb and precision, besting dogs weighing twenty times as much. There was a time when trainers scorned the arrival of a Pom in obedience training, but no longer.

During 1964, according to Sophie Mayes writing in *Pomeranian Review,* statistics show that Poms earned 30 C.D. and 7 C.D.X. degrees.

New specialty clubs have also come to the fore in the past few years. Much of the upsurge in Pomeranian exhibition can be traced directly to interest aroused by the many fine and hard working specialty clubs in various localities. Almost any section of the United States now has its regional specialty club, operating under the watchful eye of the American Pomeranian Club.

One of the newer ones to be organized is the Northern California Pomeranian Club, Inc. Qualifying matches were held in 1963 and their first specialty show was held as a part of the Golden Gate KC Show in San Francisco in January of 1964.

Memphis Tennessee Pomeranian Club held its first Specialty in 1963 which was an outstanding success both in entries and enthusiasm engendered. This club is going places fast.

The Bay Colony Club of New England is quite active, holding successful specialties each year with outstanding judges. They had an entry of 33 at their last show, judged by Mary Brewster.

The Pomeranian Club of Florida in Miami holds one of the show pieces of the year with heavy entries and glittering trophies at Hialeah each year. I had the pleasure of judging there in 1963. This is an upcoming club with genuine Pomeranian lovers as their "local classes" prove.

The Pomeranian Club of Milwaukee offers another of the fine Specialties of the year. Other and older clubs are listed under "Specialty Clubs" in an earlier chapter.

Minor changes were made in the official Standard as approved by A.K.C. on April 12, 1960. Changes are mainly in colors and in faults. Beaver is described as a "dark beige" which fits my original description.

Major faults are listed as: "Round, domey skull. Too large ears. Undershot. Pink eye rims. Light or Dudley nose. Out at elbows or shoulders. Flat sided dogs. Down in pasterns. Whole-colored dogs with white chest or white foot or leg. Black mask on an orange."

Listed as objectional: "Overshot. Large, round or light eyes. High or low on legs. Long toes. Too wide in hind legs. Trimming too close to show date. Tail set too low on rump. Black, brown, blue, and sable should be free from lemon or any other color. Black and tan. Underweight or overweight."

Minor faults: "Must be free from lippiness, wide chest. Tail should not curl back. Black mast on sable. White shadings on orange."

130

Colors allowed in the official Pomeranian Standard, continue to be hotly controversial. Many breeders continue to demand that all colors be allowed and the ban on black and tans removed. But certain fanciers continue to keep a firm "thumbs down" attitude. In days gone by, all colors were recognized, just as in Pekingese, and many beautiful colors were common. But the craze for orange and red Pomeranians has almost banished blacks, chocolates, whites, beavers, and the beautiful blues. Many breeders of today have never seen many of these rare colors and if the present position is continued by some members of the official board some colors will pass into oblivion. The darker colors have always carried genes for harsh stand-off guard hairs in coats and the loss of the darker colors may result in a softening of coats that will have to be treated to be stand-off. Several generations of orange to orange may produce just such a result. In the author's opinion, the time to guard the beautiful stand-off coats that need no help in standing erect without entanglement is *now*.

Leading background bloodlines have changed for the better. Pomeranians are consistently and more uniformly of better quality. Size has become more stable. No longer do we see the huge Poms formerly brought into the ring and the useless tiny-ettes have almost disappeared. The three and a half to five pounders now dominate the scene.

Aristic, Great Elms, Golden Glow, Sunglow, La Rita, Creider and McCamey lines lead the field in United States background and abroad, Hadleigh and Passfield. The Schoenberg Aristic line continues to be prominent in pedigrees of BIS winners. Dorothy Bonner based her line on Aristic stock and many of her champions have taken BIS in the past years. Outstanding among them is Dorothy Guild's Amer., Can., and Bermuda champion Bonner's Prettytune Petit, an illustrious grandson of Schoenberg's famous Ch. Aristic Wee Pepper Pod who has many BIS wins and a myriad of champion children and grand children. This great little stud, who graces the cover of this book, has stamped his type on Poms for all time.

Anna La Fortune continues to own and produce great show winners who are themselves producing champions. Among her greats is Ch. Sungold's Gay Cavalier who has accounted for two dozen champions under the Scotia banner as he was sold to Scotia Kennel as a small puppy. Anna's Ch. Sungold Jessie and Ch. Sungold's Darling Spectacular, co-owned by Anna and Marion Darling, are big winners.

Ruth Beam's Great Elms line goes back to Ch. Little Timstopper who also had Aristic background. Ch. Great Elm's Little Timstopper sired 22 champions and his get are carrying on their illustrious sire's successes. Ch. Great Elm's Timstopper Again while under five years of age sired seven champions and shows promise of outproducing his famous sire's record. This line might lead the field in champions produced if Great Elms showed more but this is a one-woman kennel whose owner likes to do her own showing which makes it limited in scope.

Edna Girardot of Scotia Kennels, Scotia, New York, accounts for many a champion as a result of having a large kennel of fine Pomeranians and exhibiting consistently, often having several Poms showing at the same time.

Golden Glow and McCamey Poms appear in many pedigrees of note, as these two of the older lines going back to Julo and other imported lines are still actively showing and producing many fine champions.

Creider's T-Town Kennel continues to produce some sensational champions. A small kennel, it nevertheless produces some of the outstanding champions that take BIS wins.

In Bermuda the Westerleigh Kennels of Florence, Lady Conyers, dominate the field and in recent years have successfully invaded the American continent. In the first edition of *The New Complete Pomeranian* the great International Champion Pixietown Serenade of Hadleigh, credited to Ruth Bellick as sole owner, is co-owned by these two ladies.

It was Lady Conyers who first obtained Serenade from Gladys Dyke with whom Lady Conyers is acquainted. Serenade is at this writing the only living Pomeranian to be a champion in four countries: England, Bermuda, Canada, and the United States, with BIS wins in all of them. Serenade was a runner-up at the great Crufts show in 1960, where five thousand dogs is an average entry, and he has 3 English BIS wins. He came to Bermuda and won 2 BIS's and made his title there in three shows. He went to the United States with the Bellicks and in one year

132

swept 5 Specialties, 42 Groups and 15 BIS's. In Canada he won 2 BIS awards. He then was retired after winning the Toy Group at Westminster in 1962. He is producing consistently high quality progeny and his sons and daughters are accounting for many BIS wins and are themselves producing outstanding progeny. We in the United States owe an eternal debt of gratitude to Lady Conyers for bringing him to the United States and placing him at limited stud to outstanding bitches.

At present date Serenade has 12 champion sons and daughters in four countries. Westerleigh Kennels usually house a dozen or more champions of various countries.

Lady Conyer's late husband, Sir Reginald, was Speaker of the House of Assembly and Lady Conyers has headed most of the important governing boards in Bermuda. She has orchids, among other hobbies, being a lover of natural beauty and her 18 or more Poms all live in her beautiful home on Westerleigh Estates and sleep on a specially constructed sun porch just off Lady Conyer's own bedroom where she can hear the slightest unrest among her beloved Poms. They have a landscaped tropical Paradise to play and exercise in. Lucky Poms.

In England, Hadleigh and Passfield continue to lead the field. Back in the United States so many new faces have become known for fine Pomeranians at shows that it is impossible for lack of space, to name but a few.

Romallen Kennels, owned by Maybelle C. Allen, has a "doggy" history from way back, according to Mrs. Allen. The kennel was established in the United States when the Allens returned from Japan where General Allen had served as Chief of Staff for Korean Operations on General McArthur's staff and afterward as Commanding General of the XVI Corps. Before that General Allen had served as Commanding General of the 12th Armored Division in combat during World War II, and later as G.3 of the European Command. Two handsome German Shepherds accompanied the Allens from Germany to add to their Samoyedes and Shetland Sheepdog family of canines.

After their stay of duty in Japan and Korea, Mrs. Allen became interested in Pomeranians. She states she "simply could not resist these small charmers" and after having purchased several as gifts to friends and relatives, she found she had "quite lost her heart to the breed." Blair's Anthel Showstopper, bred by Mrs. Blair, was Mrs. Allen's first champion which she purchased as a tiny puppy. After that there was no stopping her. Thelcolyn's Scarlet Flame of Romallyn, purchased from Thelma Gunter and bred to the famous Eng., Bermuda, Canadian and United States Ch. Pixietown Serenade of Hadleigh, produced three handsome male puppies. Joudy, the most promising, was practically perfect but he and his brother Robin died of an obscure infection a year ago. The remaining male, Romallen Rollicking Rufus, a rich red of huge coat, is now being shown and on his way to a speedy title.

Creider's T-Town Serenade, another son of the famous Int. Ch. Pixietown Serenade, of Hadleigh, was purchased from his breeder Norma Creider, and soon became an international champion with BIS wins here and in Bermuda. Romallen's latest purchase is English and American Ch. Cherrie of Hadleigh. Since Cherrie is a granddaughter of Int. Ch. Pixietown Serenade of Hadleigh, and was heralded in England as "the outstanding toy of the year," some marvelous puppies should come out of this kennel.

Cherrie is the only toy to have won the supreme awards during 1963, with three BIS's to her credit in England. Romallen has corraled some of the best bloodlines in England, the United States, and Bermuda.

A $40.00 bird and a guilty conscience were the beginning of Bertha Disher's Pom-Pals Kennels in Indianapolis, Indiana. Her husband had for some time longed for a Pomeranian puppy and to soften him up for the news of her forty dollar bird, Bertha stopped on her way home and purchased her husband a Pom puppy. However, the puppy "took" to Bertha, so on Mother's Day Ralph Disher bought himself another Pom puppy; with the ice thus broken he went out two weeks later and purchased still another, according to "Birk," writing in *Pomeranian Review*.

Now, a few years later, the Disher's Kennel houses several topnotch champions, among them Ch. Disher's Top Brass of Pom-Pals and Ch. Pom-Pals Sir Gala Laddie; of Aristic, Gold Toy, and Amber Lo bloodlines.

Kathryn Birk, the "Birk" of above, is known to *Review* readers for her fine doggy articles about shows and showing as she and her husband are avid owner-fanciers and are to be seen surrounded by Pomeranians at most Midwest shows.

Elizabeth Troxler of Pineburr Kennels, Greensboro, North Carolina, has been breeding Poms for thirty years and has a select line of imported background, mostly Hadleigh. Her latest champion is Ch. Starmist of Hadleigh and Pineburr; of Morrel, Shamrock, and Zanow background.

Millamor Kennels, owned by Eleanor and Ken Miller of Mt. Vernon, is an outstanding Ohio kennel with five champions at stud. Their home and kennel on Route 2 is a mecca for Pom people on vacation from all over the United States. Hospitality is the keynote here and this small but select line of Pomeranians is a delight to see. Here, love of fine Poms and pride of achievement abound, and well it might for within a few years this kennel has gone to the top with fine Poms. Their Ch. Millamor's Music Man, a homebred, went from the classes to Best of Winners at the New York Specialty of the A.P.C. in 1965, with an entry of more than 100 fine Poms under Isadore Schoenberg, one of the best Pomeranian judges today. With Ken Miller handling Music Man repeated his win the following day at Westminster under Mrs. Yan Paul, a well-known Canadian judge of toys.

The story of Ch. Millamor's Music Man began in 1959 with the purchase of Thelcolyn's Tiny Ring Master from Thelma Gunter who in turn had secured him from breeder Louise Lanouette. Ring Master soon became a champion for the Millers and they went back to this same breeder for Ch. Thelcolyn's Tiny Sun Dance. Upon acquiring Sun Dance the Millers bred him to Millamor's Red Mist, a daughter of Ch. Ringmaster. From this breeding came four puppies, but only two of them survived, and they became Ch. Millamor's Music Man and Ch. Millamor's Jitterbug, finishing within a few weeks of each other. Not wanting to be left out of top billing, their grand-dam, Millamor's Gold Flame, took time off from maternal duties to become a champion.

At present the Millers have four females of the same breeding as Music Man and Jitterbug, and much is expected from inbreeding when these females mature. Music Man at the age of 18 months had won 4 Group firsts, four seconds, 3 thirds, and one fourth. I gave Ch. Music Man a Best of Breed. A most handsome lad, he is brilliant orange, so bright it almost verges on red; three pounds in weight and of marvelous coat even during the heat of summer. Music Man never fails to thrill and delight audiences as he proudly struts around the ring. Ring-presence and showiness appears to be bred into Millamor Poms, a kennel housing about 24 Pomeranians of all ages at most times. Remember Millamor. It may well be future stiff competition for anyone . . . anywhere.

Louise Lanouette of Lou-Lan's Pomeranians, Newport, Virginia, was "taken over by Poms" in 1957 when she purchased a good one as a pet and later could not resist producing "just one litter." Her kennels have now produced many fine specimens from Thelcolyn Showstopper and Millamor stock. She is building on the premise of keeping the very best female and breeding to the best stud she can afford. This may lead this kennel to become one of the successful kennels of the future. Her Lou-Lans Petite Pixie is the dam of Ch. Thelcolyn's Tiny Ringmaster. She has consistently bred to the best of Thelma Gunter's stock and now is line breeding to Millamor stock which in turn goes back to her own and Gunter or Thelcolyn stock and this is producing some fine Pomeranians.

Roadoke Pomeranian Kennels of Salem, Virginia, is co-owned by Frank Welsh and Roy Morton, Jr. They operate a select boarding kennel in summer and fall and have Cavalier, Showstopper, and Billie Button bloodlines. Much will be heard from this partnership in the future as both are genuine lovers of good Poms and are enthusiastic exhibitors.

Minnick's Pomeranian Kennel is a continuation of Grace Zoll's Sunnyside Kennels, an old and well-known name. Carried on by Grace's daughter Thelma, of South Vienna, Ohio, the kennel is now headed by Ch. Tumble Toy's Wee Whisper who sired Ch. Zoll's Golden Charm and Zoll's Tumble Toy's Freddie, nearing his own title. A small but select kennel of excellent Pomeranians, Minnick's has housed many champions and many of the champions of today have Grace Zoll's Sunnyside stock in their background. Daughter Thelma has exhibited her mother's Pomeranians and now her own. She holds a professional handler's license, being expert at handling toy dogs in the ring.

136

Joanne Hanika is one of the newer breeders now coming to national notice through *Pomeranian Review,* especially in the mid-west. She has Gold Toy, Pom-Pals females, with a son of Ch. Edward's Reddy Teddy and Ch. Thelcolyn's Sun Dance as show and stud stock.

Mrs. Neil Baldwin of Stow, Ohio, is a newcomer who received her baptism of fire at Madison Square Garden last February when she came out with Winners' Bitch, a record to be proud of especially as she did her own handling. She has Rossmoyne, Passfield, Gold Toy, Aristic and Davis bloodlines.

Kathryn Griffiths of Jilltara Pomeranians, Kannapolis, North Carolina, has been breeding Poms eight years and her bloodlines are exclusively Ruth Beam's Great Elms. Her bitches are Great Elms and she breeds to Ruth's top studs. Her kennel is small and exclusive as she has more than two thousands orchids to care for. She is active in national orchid societies in official capacity, and she holds offices in the local kennel club.

W. W. Steinhauer, Audubon, New Jersey, better known to the Pom fancy as "Winkie" of Boxwink Kennels, is carrying on the famous bloodlines of Marguerite Dolan whose champions of the past bring up nostalgic memories to oldtimers who saw them so superbly handled by Joe Rabba whom oldtimers called "Mr. Pomeranian."

Champions Little Dutch Master, Little Enchore, Little Sir Winston, Little Red Shadow, Little Bambi, Little Lord Willing and Little Topper Bit are a few stars out of the past whose offspring loom large in the background of Boxwink Kennels. Mrs. Dolan, the master mind behind these breedings, still is quite active and coming up with winners as well as passing along her fine bloodlines to Boxwink.

Ch. Boxwink's Little Wee One, which I had the pleasure of judging on two occasions carrying her to BIS at the Hialeah, Florida Specialty in 1963, is an outstanding example of sound breeding for coat, style, and personality.

Winkie is A.K.C. representative of the American Pomeranian Club. His efforts in behalf of A.P.C. Specialty shows in the past few years have been largely responsible for their marvelous climb in entries with 109 in February of 1965.

Macherie Pomeranians owned by Dorothy Guild, a health department school nurse of Spokane, Washington, is a small but high-quality kennel; small of necessity due to Dorothy's nursing duties. She keeps an average of a dozen fine broods with International Champion Bonner's Prettytune Petit as lord and master. "Robbie" streaked to his championship with two five point majors to his credit and with Porter Washington handling him. He then invaded Canada with handler Pat Tripp and finished his Canadian Championship at the Working Dog Association of British Columbia, show and went BIS which must have been a shock to working dog owners. He added another Canadian BIS and came back to the United States to add still 2 more BIS's. He then went to Bermuda and won his title there with a Group first, 2 Group seconds and four Best of Breeds. He was third high point winning toy dog in Phillips' ratings and was nominated by the West Coast Professional Handlers Association as one of the 5 top toy dogs being shown on the West Coast. He was whelped November 11, 1961 at the Bonner Kennels and was sold to Macherie Kennels as a puppy. He rolled up his fabulous record in 47 showings during eleven months of 1964 while still but two years of age.

Thanks to training as a registered nurse, Dorothy has worked out a system for preventing premature loss of litters and attacks of eclampsia. The appetite of a pregnant bitch is watched closely and if it wanes, or shows signs of upset connected with pregnancy, she is immediately placed on a schedule of daily doses of $\frac{1}{2}$ teaspoonful Formula 222, a vitamin-mineral formula of high potency. If the pregnant bitch suffers loss of appetite after whelping, she is given daily, one capsule of Vitemia, Formula 178, an "all-in-one" vitamin-mineral capsule having a high content of iron.

If the bitch is eating well after whelping, she is given 1 calcium tablet of $7\frac{1}{2}$ grains to supplement the 222 formula. If not eating well, she is given a calcium tablet plus 1 Vitemia. Usually appetite is restored in two to three days' time under this treatment. Dorothy feels that acidosis develops within 24 to 48 hours after loss of appetite.

I have long been convinced that so-called false pregnancy in bitches is actually absorption of fetuses in the womb due to lack of sufficient nutritional elements to support both dam and

138

litter. Medical science has proven that a body will absorb what it cannot sustain, or abort it.

I once had a bitch caesarianed when she did not labor properly and she was found to have five whelps in her womb, with only one living and that one died soon after birth. The other four were in various stages of absorption, the smallest a tiny ball the size of a marble, and mummified, showing a perfect minute skeleton with ribs of threadlike proportions. The above treatment as outlined by Dorothy might have prevented this loss.

When a bitch's appetite is "picky," Dorothy gives 2½ tp 5 grains daily of Soda Bicarbonate. This comes in 5 and 10 grain tablets and induces intake of water to flush the system. I consider this new finding of Dorothy's so important that I include it here.

Pashdohl Pomeranians of Phyllis W. Seeley of Norwalk, Connecticut, while comparatively new to breeding on her own, really go back to her childhood when in 1912 her mother, Ada Maxwell Wagner, remembered by old-timers, began winning with blacks, winning a New England show with a 7 pound black. Mrs. Seeley still treasures this ribbon and pedigree. Specializing in blacks today, she also has most other colors including some good chocolates which today are rare, oranges, sables and whites. About 40 Poms are usually housed at Pashdohl.

Highland Kennels of Patricia Hopkins of Ashville, Pennsylvania, lie in a beautiful wooded section that provides a veritable paradise for Pomeranians. This kennel, built on Aristic bloodlines, is line-bred back to Ch. Aristic Wee Pepper Pod. Aristic Terriana is the backbone of the Highland line, producing Ch. Aristic Sunboy of Highland and point winner Aristic Suntoy of Highland who subsequently produced Ch. Highland Strutaway and Ch. Highland Ristic Delectable. In 1962 Bonner's Pepperkorn, also a grandson of Pepper Pod, was purchased and quickly finished to the title. Another from this kennel, Ch. Highland Brilliance, has finished his championship in Canada.

El-O-C Kennels owned by Oren and Eloise Chandler of Grand Rapids, Michigan, have come a long way since the first edition was written. They are a small but excellent kennel, building their stock on quality, rather than on quantity. Several home-bred champions live at El-O-C Kennels, among them Ch. Adora

Sir Bullet and Ch. El-O-Dee. Sir Bullet has points in Canada but never was finished due to the serious illness of Mr. Chandler that lingered on. They recently finished a pair of puppies from a litter out of a black and tan bitch, El-O-C's Sir Harry, an orange sable, and El-O-C's Sir Richard, a cream. A winsome puppy, soon to be shown is El-O-C's Sir Johnny pictured with Mrs. Chandler.

Eve-Ron Kennels, owned by Evelyn and Ronald Schaeffer of Cortland, Ohio, began in 1942 but only started breeding and showing Pomeranians since 1955. Evelyn is a professional handler, well-known in the Midwest and South. At present she has about 45 excellent Pomeranians and a few Maltese and Pekingese. Her Pomeranian line was founded on Adora and Aristic lines and are known for their sweet baby faces and their daintiness. The kennel is connected to their home but has its own furnace, and an air conditioning system for summer. Runs, 50 feet long and 8 feet wide, are constructed to give proper exercise to inmates for proper development of legs. Evelyn has finished many a champion of various toy breeds for others, but her own pride and joy is their Ch. Eve-Ron's Toy Ba Bee, a deep red with a baby face. Some of their other Pom champions are: Chs. Eve-Ron's Wee Little Mystery, Eve-Ron's Tiny Timothy, Eveningstar's Gae Fantasy, Eve-Ron's Miss Judy, Eve-Ron's Tiny Bubbles and Adora Eve-Ron's Little Sonny.

Rocky Homer, owner of Star Don Kennels, Route 1, Transfer, Pennsylvania, with about 20 Pomeranians, has been breeding Poms for five years and has acted as assistant to Mrs. Schaefer for the past three years. He has several show specimens with points and he is the owner of Ch. Highland Delectable.

Mary and Bill Auer own a very successful kennel with much accomplishment in less than five years, all because they sought experienced advice from the old *Complete Pomeranian,* written by Milo Denlinger, and followed through.

They purchased a good bitch from the Thelcolyn line and bred her to one of Bob Goodrich's studs. From a three-pup litter they kept the two females. They showed the most promising one and in an elapsed time of 61 days "Bunny" became Ch. Auer's Houri Dancer. The other female from this litter, "Buttons," was bred to Ch. Thelcolyn's Tiny Sundance with Ch. Auer's Calypso

140

Kid, now owned by Anna La Fortune, as the result. "Clippie," as he is affectionately known, has now sired Ch. Sungold's Calypso Gal and the sensational Ch. Sungold's Darling Spectacular.

I quote their experience at length because I have for so long advocated to beginners that the only way to quick and sure success is through a good bitch bred to an outstanding stud with the females from such a litter, if at all promising, kept as basic brood stock.

Bill Auer will soon retire. With the resulting leisure, this is a kennel to watch in the future. Really great Poms can only come out of such a kennel.

Mary E. McCoy of Mar-Bi-Lea Poms, Bloomington, Indiana, is of an "exhibiting" family. Daughter Vicki, now 12, has been showing Poms since she was 9. Husband Bill is a professional handler. They began in Poms in 1958 with a pet, but within two weeks had purchased a show specimen and were shopping for foundation stock. They have about 20 of Ch. Great Elm's Little Timstopper's descendants. Their Ch. Mar-Bi-Lea's Jackie Boy was BOS at Westminster in 1963, 1964 and 1965. Their Ch. Mar-Bi-Lea's Gay Cinderella, half-sister to Jackie, was BOS at Chicago International in 1964 and 1965 and at New York Specialty in 1964. "Muffie" has won 20 BB's under 13 different judges and, with Edna Voyles handling, was never defeated in her own sex.

Ann Cowie is a professional handler. Formerly with large dogs only, her first contact with a Pomeranian turned her into an enthusiastic Pom breeder. Her kennel name of Nanjo is well known. Her first Champion was Nanjo Fire Dancer, bred by Anne Blair; her second Ch. Nanjo Flame was bred by Thelcolyn Kennels. Both Fire Dancer and Flame finished their titles quickly, Flame finishing at "the Garden."

Ch. Blair's Solitaire and Ch. Nanjo Fire Dancer are sired by Thelma Gunter's famous Showstopper and most of the several champions owned by this kennel have Thelcolyn and Blair background. Ann has long been known in show rings as a top handler and she and Showstopper made unforgettable and formidable competition. Ch. Thelcolyn's Showstopper produced 16 champions with Ann Cowie handling 14 of them.

Ina Kniffin of Staatsburg, New York, is one of the newer breeders but her stock is real competition in any ring. She has been producing Poms for 7 years and showing for only four but she has finished 5 champions in this time. Her Ch. Leader's Little Buckaroo at the age of 10 months won a Group I and to date has 28 BB's, 3 Group I's and one BIS.

Ina has 17 Pomeranians in her home but plans a kennel to house 50. She has Ch. Little Bambi's Delight and Ch. Kniffin's Mollie B as background material on the maternal side and Ch. Scotia Cavalier's Leader, a son of Ch. Sungold's Gay Cavalier, on the sire's side, a combination hard to beat.

Mrs. Maria Wieters of Ashboro, North Carolina, is not only a Pom lover but a lover of "pets" in the larger sense. Her pet family includes several Poms, 4 horses, 6 ponies, 3 Siamese cats, 2 Cocker Spaniels, 1 Doberman Pinscher, 2 Poodles, a Parakeet, all on friendly terms and running at large on her farm. A former teacher in Government Indian Schools, she says she was "hooked" on Poms in 1951 and now has 15 broods from Ruth Beam's Great Elm's Kennels.

Mrs. James K. Lee of "The Populars," Greenville, Pennsylvania, is a new breeder who has made a flying start with Lee's Mystic Gold Bug out of Ch. Evening Star's Mystic Memento, who, at the age of 9 months, has 12 points. A Sungold dam is daughter of Ch. Rhapsody of Hadley, a BIS winner.

Nelson's Best Bred Pomeranians of La Mesa, California, owned by Mae Nelson, is a small kennel of fine quality stock. Ch. Nelson's Hot Toddy, their top stud, made his championship with four majors, handled by Blanche Rider, after he had won BIM at Ocean City, California, handled by his owner. Toddy is a golden blonde siring quality stock.

Pom Town Kennels of Mrs. Floy M. Sledge began several years ago when Mrs. Sledge lost her husband and purchased a Pom to ease her loneliness, Sledge's Pee Wee, and carried him to a show. He won and another breeder-exhibitor was born. She now has 12 adult Pomeranians, five of which are champions: Ch. La Lyn Dainty Doll (Canadian), Ch. Surprise Box Black Eyed Susan, Ch. Richochet Triumphal March, Ch. Surprise Box Sweet Columbine, and Ch. Cynpeg Artiste Model, an English import, and seven puppies.

Wee Gold Kennels of Stella Davis, Urbana, Ohio, is steadily producing champions with Rossmoyne, Moneybox, Gold Toy, Aristic and Showstopper bloodlines. Stella now line breeds with enviable success. She has about 35 Poms most of the time and finished her first homebred champion in 1960. Her matron line goes back to her grand old Candy Girl of Pom Chee Bue, herself not a champion but an outstanding producer of fine stock. Ch. Davis Wee Gold Teena finished as a puppy and won a Group first at 10 months of age. In 1961 Ch. Davis Wee Gold Jill was finished. Both of these champions were granddaughters of "Candy."

In 1962 Ch. Puff and Ch. Wee Gold Penny, another granddaughter of "Candy," were finished. In 1963 Ch. Davis Wee Gold Boxie finished and Wee Gold Fancy Pants was streaking for his title but suffered the loss of his front teeth and was retired from the ring. His first daughter became Ch. Davis Wee Gold Fanceyetta, a 1964 titleholder. This kennel seems to have the habit of finishing one or more champions a year on limited showing.

Joy Le Compte, an administrative secretary, acquired her first Pomeranian back in 1958. Joy credits her beginning to the encouragement of Sally Cohn McGilbry, Rita La Verne and Vi Munz. Sally advised the showing of Joy's little red-orange female who became the famous Canadian and American Champion Beach's Brightest Angel, also Am. and Can. CD in obedience, a great granddaughter of the famed Ch. Dromore Bombardier.

Next came a foundation sire out of Amer., Can., Mex., Ch. Kavilla's Christmas Joy, also Am., Can. and Mex. CDX in obedience. The stud prospect became Ch. Tiralin Dark of the Moon who sired the latest champion out of this kennel, Ch. Goldpaz Wee Bonnie Laddie, who finished his title at one year of age with three majors and one Group first. Tiralin was to die an early death.

The next purchase after Tiralin was a lovely black bitch of Bombardier-Moneybox breeding. In 1961, Margo of Hadleigh, a daughter of famed English Ch. Zambo of Zanow, was purchased from Col. James Arima. The most recent purchase is another show quality bitch, an 8 months old black daughter of Ch. Rougeland's Apache Chief.

Joy is a firm believer that obedience and conformation go hand in hand, proving the true worth of a Pomeranian in possessing not only beauty but exemplary intelligence.

Bud and Margaret Coleman, although breeders and exhibitors of note, do not consider themselves as having a "kennel," in the true sense of the word, as they state that they have just "nine little spoiled pets." But this kennel houses Ch. La Rita's Stormy Knight, Ch. La Rita's Faithful One, and Ch. La Rita's Copper Doll, among others. Copper Doll was shown when 5½ years of age at a Specialty, because the Colemans wanted to show and had nothing else ready at the time. As Copper Doll was very fat they thought themselves "just among those present." To their surprise, Copper Doll went Reserve and the judge advised them to take off the fat and show her seriously, which they did, and at 7½ years of age she finished to the title. Their present champion prospect with points is La Rita's Wee Sherry, a great granddaughter of Hart's Wee Buttons, famous producer of noted champions, including "Sparky," and Ch. Topper's Little Moppit.

Schirman Oaks Kennels of Portland, Oregon, is owned by Nancy and Harry Schirman, an enterprising young couple still in their twenties. They have stated a determination that Schirman Oaks Pomeranians shall always be known and respected for preeminently top quality and they have made a flying start in that direction. This is another kennel built on a firm foundation of following expert advice, mostly from Ruth Beam, to build on top quality females bred to top quality studs. The high quality of their first two females has made them unsatisfied with anything but the best.

They began in 1961 in North Carolina with two fine females from the kennels of Ruth Beam: Great Elm's Pride and Joy and Great Elm's Little Pom Fashion, which when they reached the age of two years were linebred. Pride and Joy was bred to Ch. Great Elm's Timstopper Again and produced two fine males, Ch. Schirman Oak's Golden Timsun and Ch. Schirman Oak's Timstopper, both winners of numerous BB's and Toy Groups. Timstopper won two of his Toy Groups at the age of ten months.

Great Elm's Little Pom Fashion bred to Ch. Great Elm's Little

Buddy produced Schirman Oak's Chocolate Chip and Schirman Oak's Fashion Rebel, both now being shown and with points.

Ch. Schirman Oak's Timstopper has been sold to Mrs. J. Whitney Peterson of Greenwich, Connecticut, and is continuing his show wins. The accomplishment of the Schirmans should be proof positive that purchasing two good females from a reliable background and breeding back to a quality stud in direct line breeding is the only way to quick and sure success.

Doyle and Phyllis Nave of Valier, Illinois, are breeders who started out the wrong way, as so many of us did in the beginning. They began eight years ago in Poms with a mediocre female and for four years produced "mostly pet stock" as they state.

Then, they write, "the show bug bit us." They purchased a male from Bertha Disher, and shortly he was Ch. Tepees Lucky Jim Dandy. They purchased six females from Bertha and recently acquired a male out of Ch. Mu-Ra-Jo's Dream Girl and by Ch. Great Elm's Timstopper Again, with a final addition to their breeding stock of a daughter of Ch. Aristic Little Pepper Pod. On the right track now, they nevertheless lost four years getting on the proper course. Thanks to not being "kennel blind" as to the quality of their own stock, they righted their course and now are strong contenders for top honors.

Paul and Clara Garrett of Ottawa, Kansas, are new breeders with Golden Glow, Moneybox, and Aristic bloodlines. Their kennel and grounds was recently badly damaged by a tornado but their plans for breeding good stock has not diminished.

Dan Mercer of Big Springs, Nebraska, is a newcomer from whom we can expect top Poms in the future. At the age of twenty-three Dan has made a most promising start, searching out genetic and bloodline information and buying fine breeding stock from well-known breeders of top Pomeranians in the country. He has Latham, Julo Wee Wonder and Moneybox in one line and Ch. Gold Toy's Gay Flame, Ch. Gold Toy's Gay Starette, Aristic, and the famous International Champion Pixietown Serenade of Hadleigh on hand, and with Great Elm's on order.

Norma Creider purchased her first pair of Poms from Gold Toy Kennels when in 1953 she married, moved near Tulsa, Oklahoma, and established Toy Town Kennels. The first pair of

145

Poms quickly were known as Ch. Gold Toy's May King Model and Ch. Gold Toy's Gay Starette. The kennel foundation was provided by these two fine Poms. Norma stayed mostly with Gold Toy lines but recently made an outcross by breeding one of her best matrons to Int. Ch. Pixietown Serenade of Hadleigh. This outcross produced a male that has gone BIS in Bermuda, among other honors. He is Int. Ch. Creider's T-Town Serenade, sold as a youngster to Maybelle Allen.

The litter sister to T-Town Serenade was of equal quality but has not been shown due to maternal duties which Norma considers of more importance than titles. The litter sister has already whelped a bitch that has finished her title and two sons are closing in on their titles. Mrs. Creider has kept her kennel small, aiming only at producing the best, not the most.

Phyllis Picksley has been showing Poms a good many years and is a charter member of the Northern California Pomeranian Club. Her foundation stock comes from Fa-Rob's Red Buttons, a beautiful red son of Int. Ch. Golden Glow Dandy. He in turn is the sire of Ch. Golden Glow Sally and Ch. Sacramento's Inn Keeper, litter brother and sister. Pom Ador's Scarlett, Fa-Rob's Red Buttons' last puppy, was WB last January at the Northern California Pomeranian Club Specialty show over 22 bitches. Ch. Pom-Ador's Sparkling Doll was BB at the same specialty in 1964. Ch. Pom Ador's Pride and Joy, great-granddaughter of Fa-Rob is now mother of a son of Ch. Pom Ador's King, a son of Fa-Rob and is expected to be their next champion. Both Fa-Rob's Red Buttons and his son Ch. Pom Ador's King, were taken out of the kennel and shown for the first time at the ages of seven years. "Buzzie," as Fa-Rob is known, was shown at a match of a Pomeranian Specialty Club and went BIM over 45 Poms. Poms that can start their show careers at the age of seven years and score outstanding wins are few and far between.

Rita La Verne, of Milwaukee, Oregon, owner of La Rita's Poms, is a breeder of undeniable standing both as to the quality of her Poms and as a person. She is known and loved throughout dogdom on the West Coast and is seen at most of the important shows. She never fails to give aid, advice, and encouragement to newcomers as well as those well along toward stardom. She has been breeding and exhibiting fine Pomeranians for more than

12 years, but it is only since the advent of *Pomeranian Review* that she has become well known in the mid-west and east as the important link in the Pomeranian breeder chain of ever-finer Poms that she really is.

Friends and professional handlers alike praise her highly for her acumen in exhibiting, her fine Poms, and her unfailing courtesy. She has one of the largest Pom kennels on the west coast and many of the top Poms shown there are of her breeding or have La Rita's Poms in their background.

Joy Le Compte, another leader in Poms on the west coast tells many interesting stories of Rita's help to others. Rita is most critical of hereditary faults in dogs and carries on a constant watch over her own stock and that of others to have breeders eliminate all breeding stock that carries a prominent hereditary fault, especially orchidism, large ears, undershot mouths, and dysplasia or other hip joint weaknesses.

At present she is carrying on research into the history and background of Latham Pomeranians of long ago fame, as she personally was acquainted with Marvin Latham. She has much of his bloodlines in her own Poms' background and her early struggles to produce fine Poms was aided and abetted by Latham. She also has much of the "Hart" line and only recently lost her Hart's Wee Buttons at the age of 15 years, and Buttons' daughter, Ch. Toppers Little Moppit, age 13 years. Moppit was a litter sister to Ch. Topper's Little Corkie who sired two all-time greats, Ch. Rider's Sparklin' Gold Nugget and Ch. Reddy Teddy.

Sally (Cohen) McGilbry, another of the old-timers in Pom greats still active as a breeder, also played a big part in Rita's early struggles. It was Sally who told Rita that Blanche Rider of California was offering for sale her Topper's Little Moppit who was later finished as a champion by Rita. Moppit was ten months old at the time and was in whelp to her half-brother, Ch. Sungold's Wee Desire, owned by Anna La Fortune. Since Moppit was out of Hart's Wee Buttons and sired by Int. Ch. Teeco's Little Topper, Rita purchased Moppit sight unseen. The background was too good for any enterprising breeder and exhibitor to pass up.

Moppit was a lovely orange with short back, high tail set, perfect head and sweet expression with tiny ears and she had that

147

high-stepping gait so adorable in a good Pom. The breeding she brought to La Rita Poms was tops and to the day of her death she never let her new owner down.

The list of La Rita champions from this beginning is far too long to name here, but among the greats are Chs. La Rita's Golden Rhapsody, La Rita's Faithful One, La Rita's Angel Mia II, La Rita's Stormy Knight, La Rita's Copper Doll; and Goldpaz Wee Bonnie Laddie, sired by a La Rita stud.

Another of the older breeders to whom many champions are credited and who has done much in importation of fine blood from England, is Mrs. Norris McCamey of Bettendorf, Iowa. I have seen several of Mrs. McCamey's dogs and they are in the upper echelons of perfection of coat, type, and showmanship.

Mrs. McCamey began with an orange granddaughter of Ch. Aristic Moneybox Paycheck and never again was satisfied with lesser quality than that of the top Aristic Pomeranians. She later purchased several from Aristic kennels, among them the beautiful Aristic Sunbeau who later was made a champion.

She then imported from the Preservenes line in England and purchased offspring of the famous Preservenes Live Wire and later bred one of the daughters to Mrs. Tankesley's Ch. Little Tim's Sunburst. From this union came two beautiful champions, Ch. McCamey's Sundawn Enchanting and Ch. McCamey's Margaret Rose. I once had Margaret Rose in the ring and carried her to a major win. She was most beautiful and good.

Marie Morlan, Mrs. McCamey's agent and handler, cannot praise Sundawn dogs high enough and their wins are impressive. Among recent champions are McCamey's Sundawn Gold Nina, McCamey's Sundawn Enchanting, McCamey's Sunbeau's Just Me, McCamey's Sundawn Just Gold, McCamey's Sunbeau's Beauty, and McCamey's Sundawn Perfection.

There is much that has not been said here and many top breeders of quality stock that have not been named, but space is limited and time and another book will be needed to do full justice to "The Pomeranian Story."

Am. & Can. Ch. Golden Glow Dandy, bred by Laura Burwell and owned by Elva (Cohen) McGilbry.

Eng. Ch. Wilmscote Wee Caress, bred by Mr. Robert Flavell, Eng., and owned by Mr. and Mrs. James Arima.

Ch. Wilmscote Wee Conquest
Bred by R. Flavell
Owned by Mrs. Ellis

Ch. Rider's Sparklin' Gold Nugget
Breeder, Lee Johnson
Owners, Mr. & Mrs. P. Washington

Ch. Great Elms Little Timstopper,
sire of 18 champions.
Breeder-Owner, Ruth Beam

Am. & Can. Ch. Dromore Bombardier
Breeder, Earnest Sharland
Owner, Elva McGilbry

Ch. Blair's Solitaire, owned
by Mrs. Ann Cowie.

Lou-Lan's Token of
Friendship, owned by
Louise Lanouette.

Ch. Aristic Wee Pepper Pod, Breeder-Owner, Mrs. I. Schoenberg

Ch. Aristic Little Pepper Pod, Breeder, Mrs. I.
Schoenberg, Owners, Mr. & Mrs. C. D. Cloninger

Ch. Sungold's Gay Cavalier
Owner, Edna E. Girardot, R.N.

Ch. Sealand Moneybox (imported from England), sire of 27
champions. Owner, Mrs. Vincent Matta.

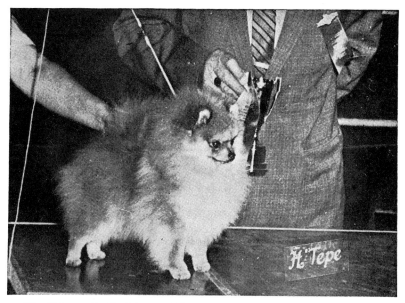

Ch. Edward's Reddy Teddy, BOW at the Chicago International with Maxine Beam as handler. Owner, Edd Bivin.

Ch. Toppers Little Corkie, BIS winner and sire of a number of champions, including the sire of the famous Ch. Rider's Sparklin' Gold Nugget. Owners, Jack and Shirley Woodall.

U.S., Can. & Mex. Ch. Kavilla's Christmas Joy, U.S., Can. & Mex. C.D., C.D.X. Bred by Mrs. V. G. Munz and owned by Mrs. Margaret Carlos.

Int. Ch. Sungold's Wee Desire, a BIS winner, bred and owned by Anna La Fortune.

Chs. Goldpaz Wee Bonnie Lassie and Goldpaz Wee Bonnie
Laddie, litter mates with their dam, Goldpaz Golden Trinket.

Ch. Great Elm's Timstopper Again, sire of 7 chs., bred and
owned by Ruth Beam.

Ch. Miss Spice-O-Life
Breeder-Owner, Robert Goodrich

Ch. Gold Toy's Gay Toy
Breeder, Joyce Brown
Owners, Eleanor & Ken Miller

Pom-Ador's Scarlett, bred and
owned by Phyllis A. Picksley.
Record-Times Photo by Giles

Ch. Creider's Lemon Chiffon,
bred-owned by Mrs. N. Creider.
Dan's Photography

El-O-C's Sir Johnny, bred and
owned by El-O-C Kennels.

Ch. Boxwink's Little Wee One, bred by
Marguerite Dolan and owned by W.
W. Steinhauer.

Ch. Millamor's Music Man, bred and owned
by Eleanor and Ken Miller.

Int. Ch. Bonner's Prettytune Petit, American, Canadian and
Bermudan titles, bred by Dorothy Bonner, owned by Dorothy
Guild. *Bill Francis*

Ch. La Rita's Stormy Knight, bred by
Rita La Verne and owned by Mr. and
Mrs. L. E. Coleman.
Bennet Associates

Ch. Leader's Little Buck A Roo,
owned by Ina Kniffin.   *Shafer*

Ch. Eve-Ron's Toy Ba Bee, bred
and owned by Evelyn Schaeffer.
Sho-Foto

Ch. Surprise Box Black Eyed Susan,
owned by Mrs. Floy Sledge.
Alexander Photo

Part II

GENERAL CARE AND TRAINING OF YOUR DOG

by

Elsworth S. Howell

Milo G. Denlinger

A. C. Merrick, D.V.M.

Introduction

THE normal care and training of dogs involve no great mysteries. The application of common sense and good judgment is required, however. The pages that follow distill the combined experience and knowledge of three authorities who have devoted most of their lives to dogs.

Milo Denlinger wrote many books out of his rich and varied experience as a breeder, exhibitor and owner of a commercial kennel. Elsworth Howell has been a fancier since young boyhood and claims intimate knowledge of 25 different breeds; he is an American Kennel Club delegate and judge of the sporting breeds. Dr. A. C. Merrick is a leading veterinarian with a wide practice.

The chapter on "Training and Simple Obedience" covers the basic behavior and performance every dog should have to be accepted by your friends, relatives, neighbors and strangers. The good manners and exercises described will avoid costly bills for damage to the owner's or neighbor's property and will prevent heartbreaking accidents to the dog and to the people he meets. The instructions are given in simple, clear language so that a child may easily follow them.

"The Exhibition of Dogs" describes the kinds of dog shows, their classes and how an owner may enter his dog and show it. If one practices good sportsmanship, shows can be enjoyable.

The chapter on feeding offers sound advice on feeding puppies,

3

adult dogs, the stud dog and the brood bitch. The values of proteins, carbohydrates, fats, minerals and vitamins in the dog's diet are thoroughly covered. Specific diets and quantities are not given because of the many variations among dogs, even of the same breed or size, in their individual needs, likes, dislikes, allergies, etc.

"The Breeding of Dogs" contains the fundamental precepts everyone who wishes to raise puppies should know. Suggestions for choosing a stud dog are given. The differences among outcrossing, inbreeding and line breeding are clearly explained. Care tips for the pregnant and whelping bitch will be found most helpful.

The material on "External Vermin and Parasites" gives specific treatments for removing and preventing fleas, lice, ticks and flies. With today's wonder insecticides and with proper management there is no excuse for a dog to be infested with any of these pests which often cause secondary problems.

"Intestinal Parasites and Their Control" supplies the knowledge dog owners must have of the kinds of worms that invade dogs and the symptoms they cause. While drugs used for the removal of these debilitating dog enemies are discussed, dosages are not given because it is the authors' and publisher's belief that such treatment is best left in the hands of the veterinarian. These drugs are powerful and dangerous in inexperienced hands.

The chapter on "Skin Troubles" supplies the information and treatments needed to recognize and cure these diseases. The hints appearing on coat care will do much to prevent skin problems.

One of the most valuable sections in this book is the "instant" advice on "FIRST AID" appearing on pages 95-98. The publisher strongly urges the reader to commit this section to memory. It may save a pet's life.

The information on diseases will help the dog owner to diagnose symptoms. Some dog owners rush their dogs to the veterinarian for the slightest, transitory upsets.

Finally, the chapters on "Housing for Dogs" and "Care of the Old Dog" round out this highly useful guide for all dog lovers.

Training and Simple Obedience

E VERY DOG that is mentally and physically sound can be taught good manners and simple obedience by any normal man, woman, or child over eight years old.

Certain requirements must be met by the dog, trainer and the environment if the training is to be enjoyable and effective. The dog must be rested and calm. The trainer must be rested, calm, gentle, firm, patient and persistent. The training site should be dry, comfortable and, except for certain exercises, devoid of distractions.

Proper techniques can achieve quick and sure results. Always use short, strong words for commands and always use the *same* word or words for the same command. Speak with authority; never scream or yell. Teach one command or exercise at a time and make sure the dog understands it and performs it perfectly before you proceed to the next step. Demand the dog's undivided attention; if he wavers or wanders, speak his name or pat him smartly or jerk his leash. Use pats and praise plentifully; avoid tidbit training if at all possible because tidbits may not always be available in an emergency and the dog will learn better without them. Keep lessons short; when the dog begins to show boredom, stop and do not resume in less than two hours. One or two ten-minute lessons a day should be ample, especially for a young puppy. Dogs have their good and bad days; if your well dog seems unduly lazy, tired, bored or off-color, put off the lesson until tomorrow. Try to make lessons a joy, a happy time both for you and the dog, but do demand and get the desired action. Whenever correction or punishment is needed, use ways and devices that the dog does not connect with you; some of these means are given in the following instructions. Use painful punishment only as a last resort.

"NO!"

The most useful and easily understood command is "NO!" spoken in a sharp, disapproving tone and accompanied with a shaking finger. At first, speak the dog's name following with "NO!" until the meaning of the word—your displeasure—is clear.

"COME!"

Indoors or out, let the dog go ten or more feet away from you. Speak his name following at once with "COME!" Crouch, clap your hands, pick up a stick, throw a ball up and catch it, or create any other diversion which will lure the dog to you. When he comes, praise and pat effusively. As with all commands and exercises repeat the lesson, until the dog *always* comes to you.

THE FIRST NIGHTS

Puppies left alone will bark, moan and whine. If your dog is not to have the run of the house, put him in a room where he can do the least damage. Give him a Nylabone and a strip of beef hide (both available in supermarkets or pet shops and excellent as teething pacifiers). A very young puppy may appreciate a loud-ticking clock which, some dog trainers say, simulates the heart-beat of his former litter mates. Beyond providing these diversions, grit your teeth and steel your heart. If in pity you go to the howling puppy, he will howl every time you leave him. Suffer one night, two nights or possibly three, and you'll have it made.

The greatest boon to dog training and management is the wooden or wire crate. Any two-handed man can make a ⅜" plywood crate. It needs only four sides, a top, a bottom, a door on hinges and

6

with a strong hasp, and a fitting burlap bag stuffed with shredded newspaper, cedar shavings or 2″ foam rubber. Feed dealers or seed stores should give you burlap bags; be sure to wash them thoroughly to remove any chemical or allergy-causing material. The crate should be as long, as high and three times as wide as the dog will be full grown. The crate will become as much a sanctuary to your dog as a cave was to his prehistoric ancestor; it will also help immeasurably in housebreaking.

HOUSEBREAKING

The secret to housebreaking a healthy normal dog is simple: take him out every hour if he is from two to six months old when you get him; or the first thing in the morning, immediately after every meal, and the last thing at night if he is over six months.

For very young puppies, the paper break is indicated. Lay eight or ten layers of newspapers in a room corner most remote from the puppy's bed. By four months of age or after two weeks in a new home if older, a healthy puppy should not need the paper *IF* it is exercised outdoors often and *IF* no liquid (including milk) is given after 5 P.M. and *IF* it is taken out not earlier than 10 P.M. at night and not later than 7 A.M. the next morning.

When the dog does what it should when and where it should, praise, praise and praise some more. Be patient outdoors: keep the dog out until action occurs. Take the dog to the same general area always; its own traces and those of other dogs thus drawn to the spot will help to inspire the desired action.

In extreme cases where frequent exercising outdoors fails, try to catch the dog in the act and throw a chain or a closed tin can with pebbles in it near the dog but not on him; say "NO!" loudly as the chain or can lands. In the most extreme case, a full 30-second spanking with a light strap may be indicated but be sure you catch the miscreant *in the act*. Dog memories are short.

Remember the crate discussed under "THE FIRST NIGHTS." If you give the dog a fair chance, he will NOT soil his crate.

Do not rub his nose in "it." Dogs have dignity and pride. It is permissible to lead him to his error as soon as he commits it and to remonstrate forcefully with "NO!"

7

COLLAR AND LEASH TRAINING

Put on a collar tight enough not to slip over the head. Leave it on for lengthening periods from a few minutes to a few hours over several days. A flat collar for shorthaired breeds; a round or rolled collar for longhairs. For collar breaking, do NOT use a choke collar; it may catch on a branch or other jutting object and strangle the dog.

After a few days' lessons with the collar, attach a heavy cord or rope to it without a loop or knot at the end (to avoid snagging or catching on a stump or other object). Allow the dog to run free with collar and cord attached a few moments at a time for several days. Do not allow dog to chew cord!

When the dog appears to be accustomed to the free-riding cord, pick up end of the cord, loop it around your hand and take your dog for a walk (not the other way around!). DON'T STOP WALKING if the dog pulls, balks or screams bloody murder. Keep going and make encouraging noises. If dog leaps ahead of you, turn sharply left or right whichever is *away* from dog's direction— AND KEEP MOVING! The biggest mistake in leash training is stopping when the dog stops, or going the way the dog goes when the dog goes wrong. You're the leader; make the dog aware of it. This is one lesson you should continue until the dog realizes who is boss. If the dog gets the upper leg now, you will find it difficult to resume your rightful position as master. Brutality, no; firmness, yes!

If the dog pulls ahead, jerk the cord—or by now, the leash— backward. Do not pull. Jerk or snap the leash only!

JUMPING ON PEOPLE

Nip this annoying habit at once by bumping the dog with your knee on his chest or stepping with authority on his rear feet. A sharp "NO!" at the same time helps. Don't permit this action when you're in your work clothes and ban it only when dressed in glad rags. The dog is not Beau Brummel, and it is cruel to expect him to distinguish between denim and silk.

8

THE "PROBLEM" DOG

The following corrections are indicated when softer methods fail. Remember that it's better to rehabilitate than to destroy.

Biting. For the puppy habit of mouthing or teething on the owner's hand, a sharp rap with a folded newspaper on the nose, or snapping the middle finger off the thumb against the dog's nose, will usually discourage nibbling tactics. For the biter that means it, truly drastic corrections may be preferable to destroying the dog. If your dog is approaching one year of age and is biting in earnest, take him to a professional dog trainer and don't quibble with his methods unless you would rather see the dog dead.

Chewing. For teething puppies, provide a Nylabone (trade mark) and beef hide strips (see "THE FIRST NIGHTS" above). Every time the puppy attacks a chair, a rug, your hand, or any other chewable object, snap your finger or rap a newspaper on his nose, or throw the chain or a covered pebble-laden tin can near him, say "NO!" and hand him the bone or beef hide. If he persists, put him in his crate with the bone and hide. For incorrigible chewers, check diet for deficiencies first. William Koehler, trainer of many movie dogs including *The Thin Man's* Asta, recommends in his book, *The Koehler Method of Dog Training,* that the chewed object or part of it be taped crosswise in the dog's mouth until he develops a hearty distaste for it.

Digging. While he is in the act, throw the chain or noisy tin can and call out "NO!" For the real delinquent Koehler recommends filling the dug hole with water, forcing the dog's nose into it until the dog thinks he's drowning—and he'll never dig again. Drastic perhaps, but better than the bullet from an angry neighbor's gun, or a surreptitious poisoning.

The Runaway. If your dog wanders while walking with you, throw the chain or tin can and call "COME!" to him. If he persists, have a friend or neighbor cooperate in chasing him home. A very long line, perhaps 25 feet or more, can be effective if you permit the dog to run its length and then snap it sharply to remind him not to get too far from you.

Car Chasing. Your dog will certainly live longer if you make him car-wise; in fact, deathly afraid of anything on wheels. Ask a friend or neighbor to drive you in *his* car. Lie below the windows and as your dog chases the car throw the chain or tin can while your neighbor or friend says "GO HOME!" sharply. Another method is to shoot a water pistol filled with highly diluted ammonia at the dog. If your dog runs after children on bicycles, the latter device is especially effective but may turn the dog against children.

The Possessive Dog. If a dog displays overly protective habits, berate him in no uncertain terms. The chain, the noisy can, the rolled newspaper, or light strap sharply applied, may convince him that, while he loves you, there's no percentage in overdoing it.

The Cat Chaser. Again, the chain, the can, the newspaper, the strap—or the cat's claws if all else fails, but only as the last resort.

The Defiant, or Revengeful, Wetter. Some dogs seem to resent being left alone. Some are jealous when their owners play with another dog or animal. Get a friend or neighbor in this case to heave the chain or noisy tin can when the dog relieves himself in sheer spite.

For other canine delinquencies, you will find *The Koehler Method of Dog Training* effective. William Koehler's techniques have been certified as extremely successful by directors of motion pictures featuring dogs and by officers of dog obedience clubs.

OBEDIENCE EXERCISES

A well-mannered dog saves its owner money, embarrassment and possible heartbreak. The destruction of property by canine delinquents, avoidable accidents to dogs and children, and other unnecessary disadvantages to dog ownership can be eliminated by simple obedience training. The elementary exercises of heeling, sitting, staying and lying down can keep the dog out of trouble in most situations.

The only tools needed for basic obedience training are a slip collar made of chain link, leather or nylon and a strong six-foot leather leash with a good spring snap. Reviewing the requirements and basic techniques given earlier, let's proceed with the dog's schooling.

Heeling. Keep your dog on your left side, with the leash in your left hand. Start straight ahead in a brisk walk. If your dog pulls ahead, jerk (do not pull) the leash and say "Heel" firmly. If the dog persists in pulling ahead, stop, turn right or left and go on for several yards, saying "Heel" each time you change direction.

If your dog balks, fix leash *under* his throat and coax him forward by repeating his name and tapping your hip.

Whatever you do, don't stop walking! If the dog jumps up or "fights" the leash, just keep moving briskly. Sooner than later he will catch on and with the repetition of "Heel" on every correction, you will have him trotting by your side with style and respect.

Sit. Keeping your dog on leash, hold his neck up and push his rump down while repeating "Sit." If he resists, "spank" him lightly several times on his rump. Be firm, but not cruel. Repeat this lesson often until it is learned perfectly. When the dog knows the command, test him at a distance without the leash. Return to him every time he fails to sit and repeat the exercise.

Stay. If you have properly trained your dog to "Sit," the "Stay" is simple. Take his leash off and repeat "Stay" holding your hand up, palm toward dog, and move away. If dog moves toward you, you must repeat the "sit" lesson until properly learned. After your

11

dog "stays" while you are in sight, move out of his sight and keep repeating "Stay." Once he has learned to "stay" even while you are out of his sight, you can test him under various conditions, such as when another dog is near, a child is playing close to him, or a car appears on the road. (Warning: do not tax your dog's patience on the "stay" until he has learned the performance perfectly.)

Down. For this lesson, keep your dog on leash. First tell him to "sit." When he has sat for a minute, place your shoe over his leash between the heel and sole. Slowly pull on the leash and repeat "Down" while you push his head down with your other hand. Do this exercise very quietly so that dog does not become excited and uncontrollable. In fact, this performance is best trained when the dog is rather quiet. Later, after the dog has learned the voice signal perfectly, you can command the "Down" with a hand signal, sweeping your hand from an upright position to a downward motion with your palm toward the dog. Be sure to say "Down" with the hand signal.

For more advanced obedience the following guides by Blanche Saunders are recommended:

The Complete Novice Obedience Course
The Complete Open Obedience Course
The Complete Utility Obedience Course (with Tracking)
Dog Training for Boys and Girls (includes simple tricks.)
All are published by Howell Book House at $3.00 each.

OBEDIENCE TRIALS

Booklets covering the rules and regulations of Obedience Trials may be obtained from The American Kennel Club, 51 Madison Avenue, New York, N.Y. 10010. In Canada, write The Canadian Kennel Club, 667 Yonge Street, Toronto, Ontario.

Both these national clubs can give you the names and locations of local and regional dog clubs that conduct training classes in obedience and run Obedience Trials in which trained dogs compete for degrees as follow: CD (Companion Dog), CDX (Companion Dog Excellent), UD (Utility Dog), TD (Tracking Dog) and UDT (Utility Dog, Tracking.)

The Exhibition
of Dogs

NOBODY should exhibit a dog in the shows unless he can win without gloating and can lose without rancor. The showing of dogs is first of all a sport, and it is to be approached in a sportsmanlike spirit. It is not always so approached. That there are so many wretched losers and so many supercilious winners among the exhibitors in dog shows is the reason for this warning.

The confidence that one's dog is of exhibition excellence is all that prompts one to enter him in the show, but, if he fails in comparison with his competitors, nobody is harmed. It is no personal disgrace to have a dog beaten. It may be due to the dog's fundamental faults, to its condition, or to inexpert handling. One way to avoid such hazards is to turn the dog over to a good professional handler. Such a man with a flourishing established business will not accept an inferior dog, one that is not worth exhibiting. He will put the dog in the best possible condition before he goes into the ring with him, and he knows all the tricks of getting out of a dog all he has to give. Good handlers come high, however. Fees for taking a dog into the ring will range from ten to twenty-five dollars, plus any cash prizes the dog may win, and plus a bonus for wins made in the group.

Handlers do not win all the prizes, despite the gossip that they do, but good handlers choose only good dogs and they usually

13

finish at or near the top of their classes. It is a mistake to assume that this is due to any favoritism or any connivance with the judges; the handlers have simply chosen the best dogs, conditioned them well, and so maneuvered them in the ring as to bring out their best points.

The services of a professional handler are not essential, however. Many an amateur shows his dogs as well, but the exhibitor without previous experience is ordinarily at something of a disadvantage. If the dog is good enough, he may be expected to win.

The premium list of the show, setting forth the prizes to be offered, giving the names of the judges, containing the entry form, and describing the conditions under which the show is to be held, are usually mailed out to prospective exhibitors about a month before the show is scheduled to be held. Any show superintendent is glad to add names of interested persons to the mailing list.

Entries for a Licensed show close at a stated date, usually about two weeks before the show opens, and under the rules no entry may be accepted after the advertised date of closing. It behooves the exhibitor to make his entries promptly. The exhibitor is responsible for all errors he may make on the entry form of his dog; such errors cannot be rectified and may result in the disqualification of the exhibit. It therefore is wise for the owner to double check all data submitted with an entry. The cost of making an entry, which is stated in the premium list, is usually from six to eight dollars. An unregistered dog may be shown at three shows, after which he must be registered or a statement must be made to the American Kennel Club that he is ineligible for registry and why, with a request for permission to continue to exhibit the dog. Such permission is seldom denied. The listing fee for an unregistered dog is twenty-five cents, which must be added to the entry fee.

Match or Sanctioned shows are excellent training and experience for regular bench shows. Entry fees are low, usually ranging from fifty cents to a dollar, and are made at the show instead of in advance. Sanctioned shows are unbenched, informal affairs where the puppy may follow his owner about on the leash and become accustomed to strange dogs, to behaving himself in the ring, and to being handled by a judge. For the novice exhibitor, too, Sanctioned shows will provide valuable experience, for ring procedure is similar to that at regular bench shows.

14

The classes open at most shows and usually divided by sex are as follows: Puppy Class (often Junior Puppy for dogs 6 to 9 months old, and Senior Puppy for dogs 9 to 12 months); Novice Class, for dogs that have never won first in any except the Puppy Class; Bred-by-Exhibitor Class, for dogs of which the breeder and owner are the same person or persons; the American-bred Class, for dogs whose parents were mated in America; and the Open Class, which is open to all comers. The respective first prize winners of these various classes compete in what is known as the Winners Class for points toward championship. No entry can be made in the Winners Class, which is open without additional charge to the winners of the earlier classes, all of which are obligated to compete.

A dog eligible to more than one class can be entered in each of them, but it is usually wiser to enter him in only one. A puppy should, unless unusually precocious and mature, be placed in the Puppy Class, and it is unfair to so young a dog to expect him to defeat older dogs, although an exceptional puppy may receive an award in the Winners Class. The exhibitor who is satisfied merely that his dog may win the class in which he is entered is advised to place him in the lowest class to which he is eligible, but the exhibitor with confidence in his dog and shooting for high honors should enter the dog in the Open Class, where the competition is usually the toughest. The winner of the Open Class usually (but by no means always) is also the top of the Winners Class; the runner-up to this dog is named Reserve Winners.

The winner of the Winners Class for dogs competes with the Winners Bitch for Best of Winners, after competing for Best of Breed or Best of Variety with any Champions of Record which may be entered for Specials Only. In the closing hours of the show, the Best of Breed or Best of Variety is eligible to compete in the respective Variety Group to which his breed belongs. And if, perchance, he should win his Variety Group, he is obligated to compete for Best Dog in Show. This is a major honor which few inexperienced exhibitors attain and to which they seldom aspire.

Duly entered, the dog should be brought into the best possible condition for his exhibition in the show and taught to move and to pose at his best. He should be equipped with a neat, strong collar without ornaments or spikes, a show lead of the proper length, width and material for his size and coat, and a nickel bench chain of strong links with which to fasten him to his bench. Food such as the dog is used to, a bottle of the water he is accustomed to drink, and all grooming equipment should be assembled in a bag the night before departure for the show. The exhibitor's pass, on which the dog is assigned a stall number, is sent by mail by the show superintendent and should not be left behind, since it is difficult to have the pass duplicated and it enables the dog's care-taker to leave and return to the show at will.

The time of the opening of the show is stated in the premium list, and it is wise to have one's dog at the show promptly. Late arrivals are subject to disqualification if they are protested.

Sometimes examination is made by the veterinarian at the en-trance of the show, and healthy dogs are quickly passed along. Once admitted to the show, if it is a "benched" show, it is wise to find one's bench, the number of which is on the exhibitor's ticket, to affix one's dog to the bench, and not to remove him from it except for exercising or until he is to be taken into the ring to be judged. A familiar blanket or cushion for the bench makes a dog feel at home there. It is contrary to the rules to remove dogs from their benches and to keep them in crates during show hours, and these rules are strictly enforced. Many outdoor shows are not "benched," and you provide your own crate or place for your dog.

At bench shows some exhibitors choose to sit by their dog's bench, but if he is securely chained he is likely to be safe in his owner's absence. Dogs have been stolen from their benches and others allegedly poisoned in the shows, but such incidents are rare indeed. The greater danger is that the dog may grow nervous and insecure, and it is best that the owner return now and again to the bench to reassure the dog of his security.

The advertised program of the show permits exhibitors to know the approximate hour of the judging of their respective breeds. Although that time may be somewhat delayed, it may be de-pended upon that judging will not begin before the stated hour. The dog should have been groomed and made ready for his ap-pearance in the show ring. When his class is called the dog should be taken unhurriedly to the entrance of the ring, where the handler will receive an arm band with the dog's number.

When the class is assembled and the judge asks that the dogs be paraded before him, the handler should fall into the counter-clock-wise line and walk his dog until the signal to stop is given. In moving in a circle, the dog should be kept on the inside so that he may be readily seen by the judge, who stands in the center of the ring. In stopping the line, there is no advantage to be gained in maneuvering one's dog to the premier position, since the judge will change the position of the dogs as he sees fit.

Keep the dog alert and facing toward the judge at all times. When summoned to the center of the ring for examination, go briskly but not brashly. It is unwise to enter into conversation with the judge, except briefly to reply to any questions he may ask. Do not call his attention to any excellences the dog may possess or excuse any shortcomings; the judge is presumed to evaluate the exhibit's merits as he sees them.

If asked to move the dog, he should be led directly away from the judge and again toward the judge. A brisk but not too rapid trot is the gait the judge wishes to see, unless he declares otherwise. He may ask that the movement be repeated, with which request the handler should respond with alacrity. It is best not to choke a dog in moving him, but rather to move him on a loose lead. The judge will assign or signal a dog to his position, which should be assumed without quibble.

Fig. 1

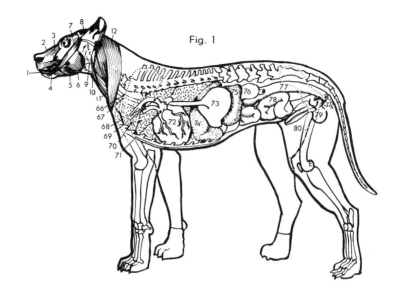

Fig. 2

Fig. 1

1 Orbicularis oris.
2 Levator nasolabialis.
3 Levator labii superioris proprius (levator of upper lip).
4 Dilator naris lateralis.
5 Zygomaticus.
6 Masseter (large and well developed in the dog).
7 Scutularis.
8 Parotid Gland.
9 Submaxillary Gland.
10 Parotido-auricularis.
11 Sterno-hyoideus.
12 Brachio-cephalicus.

(Between figures 8 and 12 on top the Elevator and Depressor muscles of the ear are to be seen.)

66 Œsophagus (gullet).
67 Trachea (wind pipe).
68 Left Carotid Artery.
69 Anterior Aorta.
70 Lungs.
71 Posterior Aorta.
72 Heart.
73 Stomach.

74 Liver. (The line in front of Liver shows the Diaphragm separating Thoracic from Abdominal cavity.)
75 Spleen.
76 Kidney (left).
77 Rectum.
77A Anal Glands (position) just inside rectum.
78 Intestine.
79 Testicle.
80 Penis.
(Midway between 76 and 79 is the seat of the Bladder and behind this the seat of the Prostate gland in males, uterus in females.)

Fig. 2

Section of Head and Neck.
1 Nasal septum.
2 Tongue.
3 Cerebrum.
4 Cerebellum.
5 Medulla oblongata.
6 Spinal Cord.
7 Œsophagus (gullet).
8 Trachea (wind pipe).
9 Hard palate.
10 Soft palate.
11 Larynx, containing vocal cords.

18

The Feeding of Dogs, Constitutional Vigor

I N selecting a new dog, it is quite as essential that he shall be of sound constitution as that he shall be of the correct type of his own particular breed. The animal that is thoroughly typical of his breed is likely to be vigorous, with a will and a body to surmount diseases and ill treatment, but the converse of this statement is not always true. A dog may have constitutional vigor without breed type. We want both.

Half of the care and effort of rearing a dog is saved by choosing at the outset a puppy of sound constitution, one with a will and an ability to survive and flourish in spite of such adversity and neglect as he may encounter in life. This does not mean that the reader has any intention of obtaining a healthy dog and ill treating it, trusting its good constitution to bring it through whatever crises may beset it. It only means that he will save himself work, expense, and disappointment if only he will exercise care in the first place to obtain a healthy dog, one bred from sound and vigorous parents and one which has received adequate care and good food.

The first warning is not to economize too much in buying a dog. Never accept a cull of the litter at any price. The difference in first cost between a fragile, ill nourished, weedy, and unhealthy puppy and a sound, vigorous one, with adequate substance and the will to survive, may be ten dollars or it may be fifty dollars. But whatever it may be, it is worthwhile. A dog is an investment and it

19

is not the cost but the upkeep that makes the difference. We may save fifty dollars on the first price of a dog, only to lay out twice or five times that sum for veterinary fees over and above what it would cost to rear a dog of sound fundamental constitution and structure.

The vital, desirable dog, the one that is easy to rear and worth the care bestowed upon him, is active, inquisitive, and happy. He is sleek, his eyes free from pus or tears, his coat shining and alive, his flesh adequate and firm. He is not necessarily fat, but a small amount of surplus flesh, especially in puppyhood, is not undesirable. He is free from rachitic knobs on his joints or from crooked bones resultant from rickets. His teeth are firm and white and even. His breath is sweet to the smell. Above all, he is playful and responsive. Puppies, like babies, are much given to sleep, but when they are awake the sturdy ones do not mope lethargically around.

An adult dog that is too thin may often be fattened; if he is too fat he may be reduced. But it is essential that he shall be sound and healthy with a good normal appetite and that he be active and full of the joy of being alive. He must have had the benefit of a good heredity and a good start in life.

A dog without a fundamental inheritance of good vitality, or one that has been neglected throughout his growing period is seldom worth his feed. We must face these facts at the very beginning. Buy only from an owner who is willing to guarantee the soundness of his stock, and before consummating the purchase, have the dog, whether puppy or adult, examined by a veterinarian in order to determine the state of the dog's health.

If the dog to be cared for has been already acquired, there is nothing to do but to make the best of whatever weaknesses or frailties he may possess. But, when it is decided to replace him with another, let us make sure that he has constitutional vigor.

THE FEEDING AND NUTRITION OF
THE ADULT DOG

The dog is a carnivore, an eater of meat. This is a truism that cannot be repeated too often. Dog keepers know it but are prone to disregard it, although they do so at their peril and the peril of their dogs. Despite all the old-wives' tales to the contrary, meat does not cause a dog to be vicious, it does not give him worms nor cause him to have fits. It is his food. This is by no means all that is needed to know about food for the dog, but it is the essential knowledge. Give a dog enough sound meat and he will not be ill fed.

The dog is believed to have been the first of the animals that was brought under domestication. In his feral state he was almost exclusively an eater of meat. In his long association with man, however, his metabolism has adjusted itself somewhat to the consumption of human diet until he now can eat, even if he cannot flourish upon, whatever his master chooses to share with him, be it caviar or corn pone. It is not to be denied that a mature dog can survive without ill effects upon an exclusive diet of rice for a considerable period, but it is not to be recommended that he should be forced to do so.

Even if we had no empirical evidence that dogs thrive best upon foods of animal origin, and we possess conclusive proof of that fact, the anatomy and physiology of the dog would convince us of it. An observation of the structure of the dog's alimentary canal, superimposed upon many trial and error methods of feeding, leads us to the conclusion that a diet with meat predominating is the best food we can give a dog.

To begin with, the dental formation of the dog is typical of the carnivores. His teeth are designed for tearing rather than for mastication. He bolts his food and swallows it with a minimum of chewing. It is harmless that he should do this. No digestion takes place in the dog's mouth.

The capacity of the dog's stomach is great in comparison with the size of his body and with the capacity of his intestines. The amounts of carbohydrates and of fats digested in the stomach are minimal. The chief function of the dog's stomach is the digestion of proteins. In the dog as in the other carnivores, carbohydrates

21

and fats are digested for the most part in the small intestine, and absorption of food materials is largely from the small intestine. The enzymes necessary for the completion of the digestion of proteins which have not been fully digested in the stomach and for the digestion of sugars, starches, and fats are present in the pancreatic and intestinal juices. The capacity of the small intestine in the dog is not great and for that reason digestion that takes place there must be rapid.

The so-called large intestine (although in the dog it is really not "large" at all) is short and of small capacity in comparison with that of animals adapted by nature to subsist wholly or largely upon plant foods. In the dog, the large gut is designed to serve chiefly for storage of a limited and compact bulk of waste materials, which are later to be discharged as feces. Some absorption of water occurs there, but there is little if any absorption there of the products of digestion.

It will be readily seen that the short digestive tract of the dog is best adapted to a concentrated diet, which can be quickly digested and which leaves a small residue. Foods of animal origin (flesh, fish, milk, and eggs) are therefore suited to the digestive physiology of the dog because of the ease and completeness with which they are digested as compared with plant foods, which contain considerable amounts of indigestible structural material. The dog is best fed with a concentrated diet with a minimum of roughage.

This means meat. Flesh, milk, and eggs are, in effect, vegetation partly predigested. The steer or horse eats grain and herbage, from which its long digestive tract enables it to extract the food value and eliminate the indigestible material. The carnivore eats the flesh of the herbivore, thus obtaining his grain and grass in a concentrated form suitable for digestion in his short alimentary tract. Thus it is seen that meat is the ideal as a chief ingredient of the dog's ration.

Like that of all other animals, the dog's diet must be made up of proteins, carbohydrates, fats, minerals, vitamins, and water. None of these substances may be excluded if the dog is to survive. If he fails to obtain any of them from one source, it must come from another. It may be argued that before minerals were artificially supplied in the dog's diet and before we were aware of the existence of the various vitamins, we had dogs and they (some of them) appeared to thrive. However, they obtained such substances in their foods, although we were not aware of it. It is very likely that few dogs obtained much more than their very minimum of requirements of the minerals and vitamins. It is known that rickets were more prevalent before we learned to supply our dogs with ample calcium, and black tongue, now almost unknown, was a common canine disease before we supplied in the dog's diet that fraction of the vitamin B complex known as nicotinic acid. There is no way for us to know how large a portion of our dogs died for want of some particular food element before we learned to supply all the necessary ones. The dogs that survived received somewhere in their diet some of all of these compounds.

PROTEIN

The various proteins are the nitrogenous part of the food. They are composed of the amino acids, singly or in combination. There are at least twenty-two of these amino acids known to the nutritional scientists, ten of which are regarded as dietary essentials, the others of which, if not supplied in the diet, can be compounded in the body, which requires an adequate supply of all twenty-two. When any one of the essential ten amino acids is withdrawn from the diet of any animal, growth ceases or is greatly retarded. Thus, a high protein content in any food is not an assurance of its food value if taken alone; it may be lacking in one or more of the essential ten amino acids. When the absent essential amino acids are added to it in sufficient quantities or included separately in the diet, the protein may be complete and fully assimilated.

Proteins, as such, are ingested and in the digestive tract are broken down into the separate amino acids of which they are composed. These amino acids have been likened to building stones, since they are taken up by the blood stream and conveyed to the various parts of the animal as they may be required, where they are deposited and re-united with other complementary amino acids again to form bone and muscles in the resumed form of protein.

To correct amino acid deficiencies in the diet, it is not necessary to add the required units in pure form. The same object may be accomplished more efficiently by employing proteins which contain the required amino acids.

Foods of animal origin—meat, fish, eggs, and milk—supply proteins of high nutritive value, both from the standpoint of digestibility and amino acid content. Gelatin is an exception to that statement, since gelatin is very incomplete.

Even foods of animal origin vary among themselves in their protein content and amino acid balance. The protein of muscle meat does not rank quite as high as that of eggs or milk. The glandular tissues—such as liver, kidneys, sweetbreads or pancreas—contain proteins of exceptionally high nutritive value, and these organs should be added to the dog's diet whenever it is possible to do so. Each pint of milk contains two-thirds of an ounce (dry weight) of particularly high class protein, in addition to minerals, vitamins, carbohydrates, and fats. (The only dietary necessity absent

24

from milk is iron.) Animal proteins have a high content of dietary-essential amino acids, which makes them very effective in supplementing many proteins of vegetable origin. The whites of eggs, while somewhat inferior to the yolks, contain excellent proteins. The lysine of milk can be destroyed by excessive heat and the growth promoting value of its protein so destroyed. Evaporated tinned milk has not been subjected to enough heat to injure its proteins.

Thus we can readily see why meat with its concentrated, balanced, and easily assimilated proteins should form the major part of dry weight of a dog's ration.

It has never been determined how much protein the dog requires in his diet. It may be assumed to vary as to the size, age, and breed of the dog under consideration; as to the individual dog, some assimilating protein better, or utilizing more of it than others; as to the activity or inactivity of the subject; and as to the amino acid content of the protein employed. When wheat protein gliadin is fed as the sole protein, three times as much of it is required as of the milk protein, lactalbumin. It has been estimated that approximately twenty to twenty-five percent of animal protein (dry weight) in a dog's diet is adequate for maintenance in good health, although no final conclusion has been reached and probably never can be.

Our purpose, however, is not to feed the dog the minimum ration with which he can survive or even the minimum ration with which he can flourish. It is rather to give him the maximum food in quantity and balance which he can digest and enjoy without developing a paunch. Who wants to live on the minimum diet necessary for adequate sustenance? We all enjoy a full belly of good food, and so do our dogs.

Roy G. Daggs found from experimentation that milk production in the dog was influenced by the different kinds of proteins fed to it. He has pointed out that relatively high protein diets stimulate lactation and that, in the bitch, animal proteins are better suited to the synthesis of milk than plant proteins. He concluded that liver was a better source of protein for lactation than eggs or round steak.

THE CARBOHYDRATES

The carbohydrates include all the starches, the sugars, and the cellulose and hemicellulose, which last two, known as fiber, are the chief constituents of wood, of the stalks and leaves of plants, and of the coverings of seeds. There remains considerable controversy as to the amount of carbohydrates required or desirable in canine nutrition. It has been shown experimentally that the dog is able to digest large quantities of cornstarch, either raw or cooked. Rice fed to mature dogs in amounts sufficient to satisfy total energy requirements has been found to be 95 percent digested. We know that the various commercial biscuits and meals which are marketed as food for dogs are well tolerated, especially if they are supplemented by the addition of fresh meat. There seems to be no reason why they should not be included in the dog's ration.

Carbohydrates are a cheap source of energy for the dog, both in their initial cost and in the work required of the organism for their metabolism. Since there exists ample evidence that the dog has no difficulty in digesting and utilizing considerable amounts of starches and sugars for the production of energy, there is no reason why they should be excluded from his diet. Some carbohydrate is necessary for the metabolism of fats. The only danger from the employment of carbohydrates is that, being cheap, they may be employed to the exclusion of proteins and other essential elements of the dog's diet. It should be noted that meat and milk contain a measure of carbohydrates as well as of proteins.

Thoroughly cooked rice or oatmeal in moderate quantities may well be used to supplement and cheapen a meat diet for a dog without harm to him, as may crushed dog biscuit or shredded wheat waste or the waste from manufacture of other cereal foods. They are not required but may be used without harm.

Sugar and candy, of which dogs are inordinately fond, used also to be *verboten*. They are an excellent source of energy—and harmless. They should be fed in only moderate quantities.

FATS

In the dog as in man, body fat is found in largest amounts under the skin, between the muscles and around the internal organs. The fat so stored serves as a reserve source of heat and energy when the caloric value of the food is insufficient, or for temporary periods when no food is eaten. The accumulation of a certain amount of fat around vital organs provides considerable protection against cold and injury.

Before fats can be carried to the body cells by means of the circulating blood, it is necessary for them to be digested in the intestines with the aid of enzymes. Fats require a longer time for digestion than carbohydrates or proteins. For this reason, they are of special importance in delaying the sensations of hunger. This property of fats is frequently referred to as "staying power."

It is easily possible for some dogs to accumulate too much fat, making them unattractive, ungainly, and vaguely uncomfortable. This should be avoided by withholding an excess of fats and carbo-hydrates from the diets of such dogs whenever obesity threatens them. There is greater danger, however, that dogs may through inadequacy of their diets be permitted to become too thin.

Carbohydrates can in part be transformed to fats within the an-imal body. The ratio between fats and carbohydrates can therefore be varied within wide limits in the dog's ration so long as the requirements for proteins, vitamins, and minerals are adequately met. Some dogs have been known to tolerate as much as forty per-cent of fat in their diets over prolonged periods, but so much is not to be recommended as a general practice. Perhaps fifteen to twenty percent of fat is adequate without being too much.

Fat is a heat producing food, and the amount given a dog should be stepped up in the colder parts of the year and reduced in the summer months. In a ration low in fat it is particularly important that a good source of the fat-soluble vitamins be included or that such vitamins be artificially supplied. Weight for weight, fat has more than twice the food value of the other organic food groups—carbohydrates and proteins. The use of fat tends to decrease the amount of food required to supply caloric needs. The fats offer a means of increasing or decreasing the total sum of energy in the diet with the least change in the volume of food intake.

27

It is far less important that the dog receive more than a minimum amount of fats, however, than that his ration contain an adequate amount and quality balance of proteins. Lean meat in adequate quantities will provide him with such proteins, and fats may be added to it in the form of fat meat, suet, or lard. Small quantities of dog biscuits, cooked rice, or other cereals in the diet will supply the needed carbohydrates. However, cellulose or other roughage is not required in the diet of the carnivore. It serves only to engorge the dog's colon, which is not capacious, and to increase the volume of feces, which is supererogatory.

MINERALS

At least eleven minerals are present in the normal dog, and there are probably others occurring in quantities so minute that they have not as yet been discovered. The eleven are as follows: Calcium (lime), sodium chloride (table salt), copper, iron, magnesium, manganese, phosphorus, zinc, potassium, and iodine.

Of many of these only a trace in the daily ration is required and that trace is adequately found in meat or in almost any other normal diet. There are a few that we should be at pains to add to the diet. The others we shall ignore.

Sodium chloride (salt) is present in sufficient quantities in most meats, although, more to improve the flavor of the food than to contribute to the animal's nutrition, a small amount of salt may be added to the ration. The exact amount makes no material difference, since the unutilized portions are eliminated, largely in the urine. If the brand of salt used is iodized, it will meet the iodine requirements, which are very small. Iodine deficiency in dogs is rare, but food crops and meats grown in certain areas contain little or no iodine, and it is well to be safe by using iodized salt.

Sufficient iron is usually found in meat and milk, but if the dog appears anemic or listless the trace of iron needed can be supplied with one of the iron salts—ferric sulphate, or oxide, or ferrous gluconate. Iron is utilized in the bone marrow in the synthesis of hemoglobin in the blood corpuscles. It is used over and over; when a corpuscle is worn out and is to be replaced, it surrenders its iron before being eliminated.

When more iron is ingested than can be utilized, some is stored in the liver, after which further surplus is excreted. The liver of the newborn puppy contains enough iron to supply the organism up until weaning time. No iron is present in milk, which otherwise provides a completely balanced ration.

A diet with a reasonable content of red meat, especially of liver or kidney, is likely to be adequate in respect to its iron. However, bitches in whelp require more iron than a dog on mere maintenance. It is recommended that the liver content of bitches' diets be increased for the duration of pregnancy.

Iron requires the presence of a minute trace of copper for its

29

utilization, but there is enough copper in well nigh any diet to supply the requirements.

Calcium and phosphorous are the only minerals of which an insufficiency is a warranted source of anxiety. This statement may not be true of adult dogs not employed for breeding purposes, but it does apply to brood bitches and to growing puppies. The entire skeleton and teeth are made largely from calcium and phosphorus, and it is essential that the organism have enough of those minerals.

If additional calcium is not supplied to a bitch in her diet, her own bone structure is depleted to provide her puppies with their share of calcium. Moreover, in giving birth to her puppies or shortly afterward she is likely to go into eclampsia as a result of calcium depletion.

The situation, however, is easily avoided. The addition of a small amount of calcium phosphate diabasic to the ration precludes any possible calcium deficiency. Calcium phosphate diabasic is an inexpensive substance and quite tasteless. It may be sprinkled in or over the food, especially that given to brood bitches and puppies. It is the source of strong bones and vigorous teeth of ivory whiteness.

But it must be mentioned that calcium cannot be assimilated into the bone structure, no matter how much of it is fed or otherwise administered, except in the presence of vitamin D. That is D's function, to facilitate the absorption of calcium and phosphorus. This will be elaborated upon in the following discussion of the vitamins and their functions.

VITAMINS

Vitamins have in the past been largely described by diseases resulting from their absence. It is recognized more and more that many of the subacute symptoms of general unfitness of dogs may be attributable to an inadequate supply in the diet of one or more of these essential food factors. It is to be emphasized that vitamins are to be considered a part of the dog's food, essential to his health and well being. They are not to be considered as medication. Often the morbid conditions resultant from their absence in the diet may be remedied by the addition of the particular needed vitamin.

The requirements of vitamins, as food, not as medication, in the diet cannot be too strongly emphasized. These vitamins may be in the food itself, or they may better be added to it as a supplement to insure an adequate supply. Except for vitamin D, of which it is remotely possible (though unlikely) to supply too much, a surplus of the vitamin substances in the ration is harmless. They are somewhat expensive and we have no disposition to waste them, but if too much of them are fed they are simply eliminated with no subsequent ill effect.

It must be realized that vitamins are various substances, each of which has a separate function. It is definitely not safe to add to a dog's (or a child's) diet something out of a bottle or box indefinitely labeled "Vitamins," as is the practice of so many persons. We must know which vitamins we are giving, what purpose each is designed to serve, and the potency of the preparation of the brand of each one we are using.

Any one of the "shotgun" vitamin preparations is probably adequate if administered in large enough dosages. Such a method may be wasteful, however; to be sure of enough of one substance, the surplus of the others is wasted. It is much better to buy a product that contains an adequate amount of each of the needed vitamins and a wasteful surplus of none. Such a procedure is cheaper in the long run.

There follows a brief description of each of the various vitamins so far discovered and a statement of what purpose in the diet they are respectively intended to serve:

Vitamin A—This vitamin in some form is an absolute requisite for good health, even for enduring life itself. Symptoms of ad-

31

vanced deficiency of vitamin A in dogs are an eye disease with resulting impaired vision, inflammation of the conjunctiva or mucous membranes which line the eyelid, and injury to the mucous membranes of the body. Less easily recognized symptoms are an apparent lowered resistance to bacterial infection, especially of the upper respiratory tract, retarded growth, and loss of weight. Diseases due to vitamin A deficiency may be well established while the dog is still gaining in weight. Lack of muscular coordination and paralysis have been observed in dogs and degeneration of the nervous system. Some young dogs deprived of vitamin A become wholly or partially deaf.

The potency of vitamin A is usually calculated in International Units, of which it has been estimated that the dog requires about 35 per day for each pound of his body weight. Such parts as are not utilized are not lost, but are stored in the liver for future use in time of shortage. A dog well fortified with this particular vitamin can well go a month or more without harm with none of it in his diet. At such times he draws upon his liver for its surplus.

It is for its content of vitamins A and D that cod-liver oil (and the oils from the livers of other fish) is fed to puppies and growing children. Fish liver oils are an excellent source of vitamin A, and if a small amount of them is included in the diet no anxiety about deficiency of vitamin A need be entertained. In buying cod-liver oil, it pays to obtain the best grade. The number of International Units it contains per teaspoonful is stated on most labels. The vitamin content of cod-liver oil is impaired by exposure to heat, light, and air. It should be kept in a dark, cool place and the bottle should be firmly stopped.

Another source of vitamin A is found in carrots but it is almost impossible to get enough carrots in a dog to do him any good. It is better and easier to use a preparation known as carotene, three drops of which contains almost the vitamin A in a bushel of carrots.

Other natural sources of vitamin A are liver, kidney, heart, cheese, egg yolks, butter and milk. If these foods, or any one of them, are generously included in the adult dog's maintenance ration, all other sources of vitamin A may be dispensed with. The ration for all puppies, however, and for pregnant and lactating bitches should be copiously fortified either with fish liver oil or with tablets containing vitamin A.

Vitamin B. What was formerly known as a single vitamin B has now been found to be a complex of many different factors. Some of them are, in minute quantities, very important parts of the diets of any kind of animals. The various factors of this complex, each a separate vitamin, are designated by the letter B followed by an inferior number, as B_1, B_2, or B_6.

The absence or insufficiency in the diet of Vitamin B_1, otherwise known as thiamin, has been blamed for retarded growth, loss of weight, decreased fertility, loss of appetite, and impaired digestion. A prolonged shortage of B_1 may result in paralysis, the accumulation of fluid in the tissues, and finally in death, apparently from heart failure.

It is not easy to estimate just how much B_1 a dog requires per pound of body weight, since dogs as individuals vary in their needs, and the activity of an animal rapidly depletes the thiamin in his body. The feeding of 50 International Units per day per pound of body weight is probably wasteful but harmless. That is at least enough.

Thiamin is not stored in the system for any length of time and requires a daily dosage. It is destroyed in part by heat above the boiling point. It is found in yeast (especially in brewer's yeast), liver, wheat germ, milk, eggs, and in the coloring matter of vegetables. However, few dogs or persons obtain an optimum supply of B_1 from their daily diet, and it is recommended that it be supplied to the dog daily.

Brewer's yeast, either in powdered or tablet form affords a cheap and rather efficient way to supply the average daily requirements. An overdose of yeast is likely to cause gas in the dog's stomach.

Another factor of the vitamin B complex, riboflavin, affects particularly the skin and hair. Animals fed a diet in which it is deficient are prone to develop a scruffy dryness of the skin, especially about the eyes and mouth, and the hair becomes dull and dry, finally falling out, leaving the skin rough and dry. In experiments with rats deprived of riboflavin the toes have fallen off.

Riboflavin is present in minute quantities in so many foods that a serious shortage in any well balanced diet is unlikely. It is especially to be found in whey, which is the explanation of the smooth skin and lively hair of so many dogs whose ration contains cottage cheese.

33

While few dogs manifest any positive shortage of riboflavin, experiments on various animals have shown that successively more liberal amounts of it in their diets, up to about four times as much as is needed to prevent the first signs of deficiency, result in increased positive health.

Riboflavin deteriorates with exposure to heat and light. Most vitamin products contain it in ample measure.

Dogs were immediately responsible for the discovery of the existence of vitamin B_2, or nicotinic acid, formerly known as vitamin G. The canine disease of black tongue is analogous with the human disease called pellagra, both of which are prevented and cured by sufficient amounts of nicotinic acid in the diet. Black tongue is not a threat for any dog that eats a diet which contains even a reasonable quantity of lean meat, but it used to be prevalent among dogs fed exclusively upon corn bread or corn-meal mush, as many were.

No definite optimum dosage has been established. However, many cases of vaguely irritated skin, deadness of coat, and soft, spongy, or bleeding gums have been reported to be remedied by administration of nicotinic acid.

It has been demonstrated that niacin is essential if a good sound healthy appetite is to be maintained. Pantothenic acid is essential to good nerve health. Pyridoxin influences proper gastro-intestinal functions. Vitamin B_{12}, the "animal protein factor," is essential for proper growth and health in early life. And the water soluble B factor affects the production of milk.

Vitamin C, the so-called anti-scorbutic vitamin, is presumed to be synthesized by the dog in his own body. The dog is believed not to be subject to true scurvy. Vitamin C, then, can well be ignored as pertains to the dog. It is the most expensive of the vitamins, and, its presence in the vitamin mixture for the dog will probably do no good.

Vitamin D, the anti-rachitic vitamin, is necessary to promote the assimilation of calcium and phosphorus into the skeletal structure. One may feed all of those minerals one will, but without vitamin D they will pass out of the system unused. It is impossible to develop sound bones and teeth without its presence. Exposure to sunshine unimpeded by glass enables the animal to manufacture vitamin D in his system, but sunshine is not to be depended upon for an entire supply.

Vitamin D is abundant in cod-liver oil and in the liver oils of some other fish, or it may be obtained in a dry form in combination with other vitamins. One International Unit per pound of body weight per day is sufficient to protect a dog from rickets. From a teaspoonful to a tablespoonful of cod-liver oil a day will serve well instead for any dog.

This is the only one of the vitamins with which overdosage is possible and harmful. While a dog will not suffer from several times the amount stated and an excess dosage is unlikely, it is only fair to warn the reader that it is at least theoretically possible.

Vitamin E is the so-called fertility vitamin. Whether it is required for dogs has not as yet been determined. Rats fed upon a ration from which vitamin E was wholly excluded became permanently sterile, but the finding is not believed to pertain to all animals. Some dog keepers, however, declare that the feeding of wheat germ oil, the most abundant source of vitamin E, has prevented early abortions of their bitches, has resulted in larger and more vigorous litters of puppies, has increased the fertility of stud dogs, has improved the coats of their dogs and furthered the betterment of their general health. Whether vitamin E or some other factor or factors in the wheat germ oil is responsible for these alleged benefits is impossible to say.

Vitamin E is so widely found in small quantities in well nigh all foods that the hazard of its omission from any normal diet is small.

Numerous other vitamins have been discovered and isolated in recent years, and there are suspected to be still others as yet unknown. The ones here discussed are the only ones that warrant the use of care to include them in the dog's daily ration. It is well to reiterate that vitamins are not medicine, but are food, a required part of the diet. Any person interested in the complete nutrition of his dog will not neglect them.

It should go without saying that a dog should have access to clean, fresh, pure drinking water at all times, of which he should be permitted to drink as much or as little as he chooses. The demands of his system for drinking water will depend in part upon the moisture content of his food. Fed upon dry dog biscuits, he will probably drink considerable water to moisten it; with a diet which contains much milk or soup, he will need little additional water.

That he chooses to drink water immediately after a meal is harmless. The only times his water should be limited (but not entirely withheld from him) is after violent exercise or excitement, at which times his thirst should be satisfied only gradually.

The quantities of food required daily by dogs are influenced and determined by a number of factors: the age, size, individuality, and physical condition of the animal; the kind, quality, character, and proportions of the various foods in the ration; the climate, environment and methods of management; and the type and amount of work done, or the degree of exercise. Of these considerations, the age and size of the dog and the kind and amount of work are particularly important in determining food requirements. During early puppyhood a dog may require two or three (or even more) times as much food per pound of body weight as the same dog will require at maturity.

Any statement we should make here about the food requirements of a dog as to weight or volume would be subject to modification. Dogs vary in their metabolism. One dog might stay fat and sleek on a given amount of a given ration, whereas his litter brother in an adjoining kennel might require twice or only half as much of the same ration to maintain him in the same state of flesh.

The only sound determiners of how much to feed a dog are his appetite and his condition. As a general rule, a dog should have as much food for maintenance as he will readily clean up in five or ten minutes, unless he tends to lay on unwanted fat, in which case his intake of food should be reduced, especially its content of fats and carbohydrates. A thin dog should have his ration increased and be urged to eat it. The fats in his ration should be increased, and he may be fattened with a dessert of candy, sugar, or sweet cake following his main meal. These should never be used before a meal, lest they impair the appetite, and they should not be given to a fat dog at all. Rightly employed, they are useful and harmless, contrary to the prevalent belief.

Growing puppies require frequent meals, as will be discussed later. Pregnant and lactating bitches and frequently used stud dogs should have at least two meals, and better three, each day. For the mere maintenance of healthy adult dogs, one large meal a day appears to suffice as well as more smaller ones. Many tenderhearted dog keepers choose to divide the ration into two parts and to feed their dogs twice each day. There can be no objection offered to such a program except that it involves additional work for the keeper. Whether one meal or two, they should be given at regular hours, to which dogs soon adjust and expect their dinner at a given time.

It is better to determine upon an adequate ration, with plenty of meat in it, and feed it day after day, than to vary the diet in the assumption that a dog tires of eating the same thing. There is no evidence that he does, and it is a burden upon his carnivorous digestion to be making constant adjustments and readjustments to a new diet.

Today there are available for dogs many brands of canned foods, some good and others not so good. But it is safe to feed your dog exclusively—if you do not object to the cost—a canned dog food which has been produced by a reliable concern. Many of the producers of canned dog foods are subject to Federal inspection because they also process meat and meat products for human consumption. The Federal regulations prohibit the use of diseased or unsuitable by-products in the preparation of dog food. Some of the canned dog foods on the market are mostly cereal. A glance at the analysis chart on the label will tell you whether a particular product is a good food for your dog.

If fish is fed, it should be boned—thoroughly. The same is true of fowl and rabbit meats. Small bones may be caught in the dog's throat or may puncture the stomach or intestines. Large, raw shank bones of beef may be given to the dog with impunity, but they should be renewed at frequent intervals before they spoil. A dog obtains much amusement from gnawing a raw bone, and some nutrition. Harm does not accrue from his swallowing of bone fragments, which are dissolved by the hydrochloric acid in his stomach. If the dog is fed an excessive amount of bones, constipation may result. When this occurs, the best way to relieve the condition is by the use of the enema bag. Medicinal purges of laxatives given at this time may cause irreparable damage.

Meat for dogs may be fed raw, or may be roasted, broiled, or boiled. It is not advisable to feed fried foods to dogs. All soups, gravies and juices from cooked meat must be conserved and included in the food, since they contain some of the minerals and vitamins extracted from the meat.

37

A well-known German physician selected a medium sized, strong, healthy bitch, and after she had been mated, he fed her on chopped horse meat from which the salts were to a large extent extracted by boiling for two hours in distilled water. In addition to this she was given each day a certain quantity of fried fat. As drink she had only distilled water. She gave birth to six healthy puppies, one of which was killed immediately, and its bones found to be strong and well built and free from abnormalities. The other puppies did not thrive, but remained weak, and could scarcely walk at the end of a month, when four died from excessive feebleness. And the sixth was killed two weeks· later. The mother in the meantime had become very lean but was tolerably lively and had a fair appetite. She was killed one hundred and twenty-six days after the beginning of the experiment, and it was then found that the bones of her spine and pelvis were softened—a condition known to physicians as osteomalacia.

The results of this experiment are highly interesting and instructive, showing clearly as they do that the nursing mother sends out to her young, in her milk, a part of her store of lime, which is absolutely essential to their welfare. They show also that if proper food is denied her, when in whelp and when nursing, not only her puppies but she as well must suffer greatly in consequence. And in the light of these facts is uncovered one of the most potential causes of rickets, so common among large breeds.

It may therefore be accepted that bitches in whelp must have goodly quantities of meat; moreover, that while cooking may be the rule if the broth is utilized, it is a wise plan to give the food occasionally in the raw state.

There is little choice among the varieties of meat, except that pork is seldom relished by dogs, usually contains too much fat, and should be cooked to improve its digestibility when it is used at all. Beef, mutton, lamb, goat, and horse flesh are equally valuable. The choice should be made upon the basis of their comparative cost and their availability in the particular community. A dog suddenly changed from another diet to horse flesh may develop a harmless and temporary diarrhea, which can be ignored. Horse flesh is likely to be deficient in fats, which may be added in the form of suet, lard or pure corn oil.

The particular cuts of whatever meat is used is of little consequence. Liver and kidney are especially valuable and when it is possible they should be included as part of the meat used. As the only meat in the ration, liver and kidney tend to loosen the bowels. It is better to include them as a part of each day's ration than to permit them to serve as the sole meat content one or two days a week.

It makes no difference whether meat is ground or is fed to the dog in large or medium sized pieces. He is able to digest pieces of meat as large as he can swallow. The advantage of grinding meat is that it can be better mixed with whatever else it is wished to include in the ration, the dog being unable to pick out the meat and reject the rest. There is little harm in his doing so, except for the waste, since it is the meat upon which we must depend for the most part for his nutrition.

Fresh ground meat can be kept four or five days under ordinary refrigeration without spoiling. It may be kept indefinitely if solidly frozen. Frozen ground horse meat for dogs is available in many markets, is low in price, and is entirely satisfactory for the purpose intended.

A suggested ration is made as follows: Two-thirds to three-quarters by weight of ground meat including ten to twenty percent of fat and a portion of liver or kidney, with the remainder thoroughly cooked rice or oatmeal, or shredded wheat, or dog biscuit, or wheat germ, with a sprinkling of calcium phosphate diabasic. Vitamins may be added, or given separately.

If it is desired to offer the dog a second meal, it may be of shredded wheat or other breakfast cereal with plenty of milk, with or without one or more soft boiled eggs. Evaporated canned milk or powdered milk is just as good food for the dog as fresh milk. Cottage cheese is excellent for this second meal.

These are not the only possible rations for the dog, but they will prove adequate. Leavings from the owner's table can be added to either ration, but can hardly be depended upon for the entire nourishment of the dog.

The dog's food should be at approximately body heat, tepid but never hot.

Little consideration is here given to the costs of the various foods. Economies in rations and feeding practices are admittedly desirable, but not if they are made at the expense of the dog's health.

SOME BRIEF PRECEPTS ABOUT FEEDING

Many dogs are overfed. Others do not receive adequate rations. Both extremes should be avoided, but particularly overfeeding of grown dogs. Coupled with lack of exercise, overfeeding usually produces excessive body weight and laziness, and it may result in illness and sterility. Prolonged undernourishment causes loss of weight, listlessness, dull coats, sickness, and death.

An adequate ration will keep most mature dogs at a uniform body weight and in a thrifty, moderately lean condition. Observation of condition is the best guide in determining the correct amount of food.

The axiom, "One man's meat is another man's poison," is applicable to dogs also. Foods that are not tolerated by the dog or those that cause digestive and other disturbances should be discontinued. The use of moldy, spoiled, or rotten food is never good practice. Food should be protected from fouling by rats or mice, especially because rats are vectors of leptospirosis. The excessive use of food of low energy content and low biological values will often result in poor condition and may cause loss of weight and paunchiness.

All feeding and drinking utensils must be kept scrupulously clean. They should be washed after each using.

It is usually desirable to reduce the food allotment somewhat during hot weather. Dogs should be fed at regular intervals, and the best results may be expected when regular feeding is accompanied by regular, but not exhausting, exercise.

Most dogs do not thrive on a ration containing large amounts of sloppy foods, and excessive bulk is to be avoided especially for hardworking dogs, puppies, and pregnant or lactating bitches. If the ration is known to be adequate and the dog is losing weight or is not in good condition, the presence of intestinal parasites is to be suspected. However, dogs sometimes go "off feed" for a day or two. This is cause for no immediate anxiety, but if it lasts more than two or three days, a veterinarian should be consulted.

FOOD FOR THE STUD DOG

The stud dog that is used for breeding only at infrequent intervals requires only the food needed for his maintenance in good health, as set forth in the foregoing pages. He should be well fed with ample meat in his diet, moderately exercised to keep his flesh firm and hard, and not permitted to become too thin or too fat.

More care is required for the adequate nutrition of the dog offered at public stud and frequently employed for breeding. A vigorous stud dog may very handily serve two bitches a week over a long period without a serious tax upon his health and strength if he is fully nourished and adequately but not excessively exercised. Such a dog should have at least two meals a day, and they should consist of even more meat, milk (canned is as good as fresh), eggs, cottage cheese, and other foods of animal origin than is used in most maintenance rations. Liver and some fat should be included, and the vitamins especially are not to be forgotten. In volume this will be only a little more than the basic maintenance diet, the difference being in its richness and concentration.

An interval of an hour or two should intervene between a dog's meal and his employment for breeding. He may be fed, but only lightly, immediately after he has been used for breeding.

The immediate reason that a stud dog should be adequately fed and exercised is the maintenance of his strength and virility. The secondary reason is that a popular stud dog is on exhibition at all times, between the shows as well as at the shows. Clients with bitches to be bred appear without notice to examine a dog at public stud, and the dog should be presented to them in the best possible condition—clean, hard, in exactly the most becoming state of flesh, and with a gleaming, lively coat. These all depend largely upon the highly nutritious diet the dog receives.

FOOD FOR THE BROOD BITCH

Often a well fed bitch comes through the ordeal of rearing a large litter of puppies without any impairment of her vitality and flesh. In such case she may be returned to a good maintenance ration until she is ready to be bred again. About the time she weans her puppies her coat will be dead and ready to drop out, but if she is healthy and well fed a new and vigorous coat will grow in, and she will be no worse off for her maternal ordeal. Some bitches, either from a deficient nutrition or a constitutional disposition to contribute too much of their own strength and substance to the nutrition of the puppies, are thin and exhausted at the time of weaning. Such a bitch needs the continuance of at least two good and especially nutritious meals a day for a month or more until her flesh and strength are restored before she is returned to her routine maintenance ration, upon which she may be kept until time comes to breed her again.

At breeding time a bitch's flesh should be hard, and she should be on the lean side rather than too fat. No change in her regular maintenance diet need be made until about the fourth or fifth week of her pregnancy. The growth of the fetus is small up until the middle of the pregnancy, after which it becomes rapid.

The bitch usually begins to "show in whelp" in four to six weeks after breeding, and her food consumption should be then gradually stepped up. If she has been having only one meal a day, she should be given two; if she has had two, both should be larger. Henceforth until her puppies are weaned, she must eat not merely for two, as is said of the pregnant woman, but for four or five, possibly for ten or twelve. She is not to be encouraged to grow fat. Especial emphasis should be laid upon her ration's content of meat, including liver, milk, calcium phosphate, and vitamins A and D, both of which are found in cod-liver oil.

Some breeders destroy all but a limited number of puppies in a litter in the belief that a bitch will be unable adequately to nourish all the puppies she has whelped. In some extreme cases it may be necessary to do this or to obtain a foster mother or wet nurse to share the burden of rearing the puppies. However, the healthy bitch with normal metabolism can usually generate enough milk to feed adequately all the puppies she has produced, provided she is well enough fed and provided the puppies are fed additionally as soon as they are able to eat.

After whelping until the puppies are weaned, throughout the lactating period, the bitch should have all the nourishing food she can be induced to eat—up to four or five meals a day. These should consist largely of meat and liver, some fat, a small amount of cereals, milk, eggs, cottage cheese, calcium phosphate, and vitamins, with especial reference to vitamins A and D. At that time it is hardly possible to feed a bitch too much or to keep her too fat. The growth of the puppies is much more rapid after they are born than was their growth in the dam's uterus, and the large amount of food needed to maintain that rapid growth must pass through the bitch and be transformed to milk, while at the same time she must maintain her own body.

THE FEEDING OF PUPPIES

If the number of puppies in a litter is small, if the mother is vigorous, healthy, and a good milker, the youngsters up until their weaning time may require no additional food over and above the milk they suck from their dam's breasts. If the puppies are numerous or if the dam's milk is deficient in quality or quantity, it is wise to begin feeding the puppies artificially as soon as they are able and willing to accept food. This is earlier than used to be realized.

It is for the sake of the puppies' vigor rather than for the sake of their ultimate size that their growth is to be promoted as rapidly as possible. Vigorous and healthy puppies attain early maturity if they are given the right amounts of the right quality of food. The ultimate size of the dog at maturity is laid down in his germ plasm, and he can be stunted or dwarfed, if at all, only at the expense of his type. If one tries to prevent the full growth of a dog by withholding from him the food he needs, one will wind up with a rachitic, cowhocked dog, one with a delicate digestive apparatus, a sterile one, one with all of these shortcomings combined, or even a dead dog.

Growth may be slowed with improper food, sometimes without serious harm, but the dog is in all ways better off if he is forced along with the best food and encouraged to attain his full size at an early age. Dogs of the smaller breeds usually reach their full maturity several months earlier than those of the larger breeds. A well grown dog reaches his sexual maturity and can be safely used for limited breeding at one year of age.

As soon as teeth can be felt with the finger in a puppy's mouth, which is usually at about seventeen or eighteen days of age, it is safe to begin to feed him. His first food (except for his mother's milk) should be of scraped raw beef at body temperature. The first day he may have 1/4 to 2 teaspoonfuls, according to size. He will not need to learn to eat this meat; he will seize upon it avidly and lick his chops for more. The second day he may have 1/3 to 3 teaspoonfuls, according to size, with two feedings 12 hours apart. Thereafter, the amount and frequency of this feeding may be rapidly increased. By the twenty-fifth day the meat need not be scraped, but only finely ground. This process of the early feeding of raw meat to puppies not only gives them a good start in life, but

44

it also relieves their mother of a part of her burden of providing milk for them.

At about the fourth week, some cereal (thoroughly cooked oatmeal, shredded wheat, or dried bread) may be either moistened and mixed with the meat or be served to the puppies with milk, fresh or canned. It may be necessary to immerse their noses into such a mixture to teach them to eat it. Calcium phosphate and a small amount of cod-liver oil should be added to such a mixture, both of which substances the puppies should have every day until their maturity. At the fourth week, while they are still at the dam's breast, they may be fed three or four times a day upon this extra ration, or something similar, such as cottage cheese or soft boiled egg. By the sixth week their dam will be trying to wean them, and they may have four or five meals daily. One of these may be finely broken dog biscuit thoroughly soaked in milk. One or two of the meals should consist largely or entirely of meat with liver.

The old advice about feeding puppies "little and often" should be altered to "much and often." Each puppy at each meal should have all the food he will readily clean up. Food should not be left in front of the puppies. They should be fed and after two or three minutes the receptacle should be taken away. Young puppies should be roly-poly fat, and kept so up to at least five or six months of age. Thereafter they should be slightly on the fat side, but not pudgy, until maturity.

The varied diet of six-week-old puppies may be continued, but at eight or nine weeks the number of meals may be reduced to four, and at three months, to three large rations per day. After six months the meals may be safely reduced again to two a day, but they must be generous meals with meat, liver, milk, cod-liver oil, and calcium phosphate. At full maturity, one meal a day suffices, or two may be continued.

The secret of turning good puppies into fine, vigorous dogs is to keep them growing through the entire period of their maturation. The most important item in the rearing of puppies is adequate and frequent meals of highly nourishing foods. Growth requires two or three times as much food as maintenance. Time between meals should be allowed for digestion, but puppies should never be permitted to become really hungry. Water in a shallow dish should be available to puppies at all times after they are able to walk.

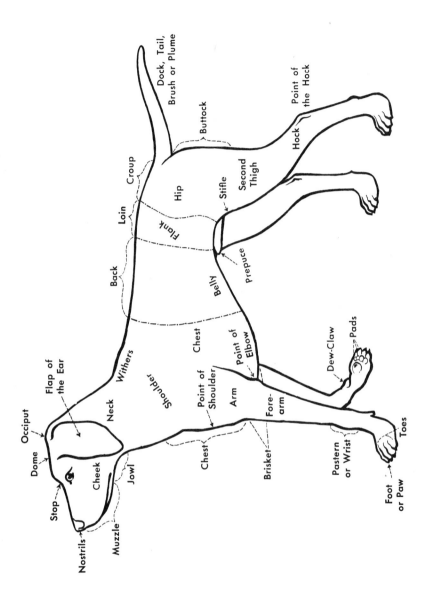

Dock, Tail, Brush or Plume
Point of the Hock
Buttock
Hock
Second Thigh
Stifle
Hip
Croup
Loin
Flank
Back
Prepuce
Belly
Chest
Point of Elbow
Pads
Dew-Claw
Occiput
Flap of the Ear
Withers
Neck
Shoulder
Point of Shoulder
Arm
Fore-arm
Dome
Cheek
Jowl
Chest
Brisket
Pastern or Wrist
Toes
Foot or Paw
Stop
Muzzle
Nostrils

46

The Breeding
of Dogs

H ERE, if anywhere in the entire process of the care and management of dogs, the exercise of good judgment is involved. Upon the choice of the two dogs, male and female, to be mated together depends the future success or failure of one's dogs. If the two to be mated are ill chosen, either individually or as pertains to their fitness as mates, one to the other, all the painstaking care to feed and rear the resultant puppies correctly is wasted. The mating together of two dogs is the drafting of the blueprints and the writing of the specifications of what the puppies are to be like. The plans, it is true, require to be executed; the puppies, when they arrive, must be adequately fed and cared for in order to develop them into the kinds of dogs they are in their germ plasm designed to become. However, if the plans as determined in the mating are defective, just so will the puppies that result from them be defective, in spite of all the good raising one can give them.

The element of luck in the breeding of dogs cannot be discounted, for it exists. The mating which on paper appears to be the best possible may result in puppies that are poor and untypical of their breed. Even less frequently, a good puppy may result from a chance mating together of two ill chosen parents. These results are fortuitous and unusual, however. The best dogs as a lot come from parents carefully chosen as to their individual excellences and as to their suitability as mates for each other. It is as unwise as

47

it is unnecessary to trust to luck in the breeding of dogs. Careful planning pays off in the long run, and few truly excellent dogs are produced without it.

Some breeders without any knowledge of genetics have been successful, without knowing exactly why they succeeded. Some of them have adhered to beliefs in old wives' tales and to traditional concepts that science has long since exploded and abandoned. Such as have succeeded have done so in spite of their lack of knowledge and not because of it.

There is insufficient space at our disposal in this book to discuss in detail the science of genetics and the application of that science to the breeding of dogs. Whole books have been written about the subject. One of the best, clearest, and easiest for the layman to understand is *The New Art of Breeding Better Dogs,* by Philip Onstott, which may be obtained from Howell Book House, the publisher. In it and in other books upon the subject of genetics will be found more data about the practical application of science to the breeding of livestock than can be included here.

The most that can be done here is to offer some advice soundly based upon the genetic laws. Every feature a dog may or can possess is determined by the genes carried in the two reproductive cells, one from each parent, from the union of which he was developed. There are thousands of pairs of these determiners in the life plan of every puppy, and often a complex of many genes is required to produce a single recognizable attribute of the dog.

These genes function in pairs, one member of each pair being contributed by the father and the other member of the pair coming from the mother. The parents obtained these genes they hand on from their parents, and it is merely fortuitous which half of any pair of genes present in a dog's or a bitch's germ plasm may be passed on to any one of the progeny. Of any pair of its own genes, a dog or a bitch may contribute one member to one puppy and the other member to another puppy in the same litter or in different litters. The unknown number of pairs of genes is so great that there is an infinite number of combinations of them, which accounts for the differences we find between two full brothers or two full sisters. In fact, it depends upon the genes received whether a dog be a male or a female.

We know that the male dog contributes one and the bitch the

other of every pair of genes that unite to determine what the puppy will be like and what he will grow into. Thus, the parents make exactly equal contributions to the germ plasm or zygote from which every puppy is developed. It was long believed that the male dog was so much more important than the bitch in any mating that the excellence or shortcomings of the bitch might be disregarded. This theory was subsequently reversed and breeders considered the bitch to be more important than the dog. We now know that their contribution in every mating and in every individual puppy is exactly equal, and neither is to be considered more than the other.

There are two kinds of genes—the recessive genes and the dominant. And there are three kinds of pairs of genes: a recessive from the sire plus a recessive from the dam; a dominant from the sire plus a dominant from the dam; and a dominant from one parent plus a recessive from the other. It is the last combination that is the source of our trouble in breeding. When both members of a pair of genes are recessive, the result is a recessive attribute in the animal that carries them; when both members of the pair are dominant, the result is a pure dominant attribute; but when one member of the pair is recessive and the other member dominant, the result will be a wholly or only partially dominant attribute, which will breed true only half of the time. This explains why a dog or a bitch may fail to produce progeny that looks at all like itself.

If all the pairs of a dog's genes were purely dominant, we could expect him to produce puppies that resembled himself in all particulars, no matter what kind of mate he was bred to. Or if all his genes were recessive and he were mated to a bitch with all recessive genes, the puppies might be expected to look quite like the parents. However, a dog with mixed pairs of genes bred to a bitch with mixed pairs of genes may produce anything at all, puppies that bear no resemblance to either parent.

Long before the Mendelian laws were discovered, some dogs were known to be "prepotent" to produce certain characters, that is the characters would show up in their puppies irrespective of what their mates might be like. For instance, some dogs, themselves with dark eyes, might be depended upon never to produce a puppy with light eyes, no matter how light eyed the mate to which he was

49

bred. This was true despite the fact that the dog's litter brother which had equally dark eyes, when bred to a light eyed bitch might produce a large percentage of puppies with light eyes.

Before it is decided to breed a bitch, it is well to consider whether she is worth breeding, whether she is good enough as an individual and whether she came from a good enough family to warrant the expectations that she will produce puppies worth the expense and trouble of raising. It is to be remembered that the bitch contributes exactly half the genes to each of her puppies; if she has not good genes to contribute, the time and money involved in breeding her and rearing her puppies will be wasted.

It is conceded that a bad or mediocre bitch when bred to an excellent dog will probably produce puppies better than herself. But while one is "grading up" from mediocre stock, other breeders are also grading upward from better stock and they will keep just so far ahead of one's efforts that one can never catch up with them. A merely pretty good bitch is no good at all for breeding. It is better to dispose of a mediocre bitch or to relegate her to the position of a family pet than to breed from her. It is difficult enough, with all the care and judgment one is able to muster, to obtain superlative puppies even from a fine bitch, without cluttering the earth with inferior puppies from just any old bitch.

If one will go into the market and buy the best possible bitch from the best possible family one's purse can afford and breed her sensibly to the best and most suitable stud dog one can find, success is reasonably sure. Even if for economy's sake, the bitch is but a promising puppy backed up by the best possible pedigree, it will require only a few months until she is old enough to be bred. From such a bitch, one may expect first-rate puppies at the first try, whereas in starting with an inferior bitch one is merely lucky if in two or three generations he obtains a semblance of the kind of dog he is trying to produce.

Assuming it is decided that the bitch is adequate to serve as a brood bitch, it becomes necessary to choose for her a mate in collaboration with which she may realize the ultimate of her possibilities. It is never wise to utilize for stud the family pet or the neighbor's pet just because he happens to be registered in the studbook or because his service costs nothing. Any dog short of the best and most suitable (wherever he may be and whoever may own him) is an extravagance. If the bitch is worth breeding at all, she is worth shipping clear across the continent, if need be, to obtain for her a mate to enable her to realize her possibilities. Stud fees may range from fifty to one hundred dollars or even more. The average value of each puppy, if well reared, should at the time of weaning approximate the legitimate stud fee of its sire. With a good bitch it is therefore profitable to lay out as much as may be required to obtain the services of the best and most suitable stud dog—always assuming that he is worth the price asked. However, it is never wise to choose an inferior or unsuitable dog just because he is well ballyhooed and commands an exorbitant stud fee.

There are three considerations by which to evaluate the merits of a stud dog—his outstanding excellence as an individual, his pedigree and the family from which he derived, and the excellence or inferiority of the progeny he is known to have produced.

As an individual a good stud dog may be expected to be bold and aggressive (not vicious) and structurally typical of his breed, but without any freakish exaggerations of type. He must be sound, a free and true mover, possess fineness and quality, and be a gentleman of his own breed. Accidentally acquired scars or injuries such as broken legs should not be held against him, because he can transmit only his genes to his puppies and no such accidents impair his genes.

A dog's pedigree may mean much or little. One of two litter brothers, with pedigrees exactly alike, may prove to be a superlative show and stud dog, and the other worth exactly nothing for either purpose. The pedigree especially is not to be judged on its length, since three generations is at most all that is required, although further extension of the pedigree may prove interesting to a curious owner. No matter how well-bred his pedigree may show a dog to be, if he is not a good dog the ink required to write the pedigree was wasted.

The chief value of a pedigree is to enable us to know from which of a dog's parents, grandparents, or great-grandparents, he derived his merits, and from which his faults. In choosing a mate for him (or for her, as the case may be) one seeks to reinforce the one and to avoid the other. Let us assume that one of the grandmothers was upright in shoulder, whereas the shoulder should be well laid back; we can avoid as a mate for such a dog one with any

51

tendency to straight shoulders or one from straight shouldered ancestry. The same principle would apply to an uneven mouth, a light eye, a soft back, splayed feet, cowhocks, or to any other inherited fault. Suppose, on the other hand, that the dog himself, the parents, and all the grandparents are particularly nice in regard to their fronts; in a mate for such a dog, one desires as good a front as is obtainable, but if she, or some of her ancestors are not too good in respect to their fronts, one may take a chance anyway and trust to the good fronted dog with his good fronted ancestry to correct the fault. That then is the purpose of the pedigree as a guide to breeding.

A stud dog can best be judged, however, by the excellence of the progeny he is known to have produced, if it is possible to obtain all the data to enable the breeder to evaluate that record. A complete comparative evaluation is perhaps impossible to make, but one close enough to justify conclusions is available. Not only the number but the quality of the bitches to which the dog has been bred must enter into the consideration. A young dog may not have had the opportunity to prove his prowess in the stud. He may have been bred to few bitches and those few of indifferent merits, or his get may not be old enough as yet to hit the shows and establish a record for themselves or for their sire. Allowance may be made for such a dog.

On the other hand, a dog may have proved himself to be phenomenal in the show ring, or may have been made to seem phenomenal by means of the owner's ballyhoo and exploitation. Half of the top bitches in the entire country may have been bred to him upon the strength of his winning record. Merely from the laws of probability such a dog, if he is not too bad, will produce some creditable progeny. It is necessary to take into consideration the opportunities a dog has had in relation to the fine progeny he has produced.

That, however, is the chief criterion by which a good stud dog may be recognized. A dog which can sire two or three excellent puppies in every litter from a reasonably good bitch may be considered as an acceptable stud. If he has in his lifetime sired one or two champions each year, and especially if one or two of the lot are superlative champions, top members of their breed, he is a great stud dog. Ordinarily and without other considerations, such a dog is to be preferred to one of his unproved sons, even though the son be as good or better an individual. In this way one employs genes one knows to produce what one wants. The son may be only hybrid dominant for his excellent qualities.

In the choice of a stud dog no attention whatever need be paid to claims that he sires numerically big litters. Unless the sire is deficient in sperm, the number of puppies in the litter, provided there are any puppies at all, depends entirely upon the bitch. At one service, a dog deposits enough spermatozoa to produce a million puppies, if there were so many ova to be fertilized. In any event, the major purpose should be to obtain good puppies, not large numbers of them.

There are three methods of breeding employed by experienced breeders—outcrossing, inbreeding, and line breeding. By outcrossing is meant the breeding together of mates of which no blood relationship can be traced. It is much favored by novice breeders, who feel that the breeding together of blood relatives is likely to result in imbecility, constitutional weakness, or some other kind of degeneration. Inbreeding is the mating together of closely related animals—father to daughter, mother to son, brother to sister, half brother to half sister. Some of the best animals ever produced have been bred from some such incestuous mating, and the danger from such practices, if they are carried out by persons who know what they are about, is minimal. Line breeding is the mating together of animals related one to another, but less closely—such as first cousins, grandsire to granddaughter, granddam to grandson, uncle to niece, or aunt to nephew.

Absolute outcrossing is usually impossible, since all the good dogs in any breed are more or less related—descended from some common ancestor in the fifth or sixth or seventh generation of their pedigrees. In any event, it is seldom to be recommended, since the results from it in the first generation of progeny are usually not satisfactory. It may be undertaken by some far-sighted and experienced breeder for the purpose of bringing into his strain some particular merit lacking in it and present in the strain of the unrelated dog. While dogs so bred may obtain an added vigor from what is known in genetics as *heterosis,* they are likely to manifest a coarseness and a lack of uniformity in the litter which is not to be found in more closely bred puppies. Good breeders never outcross if it is possible to obtain the virtues they want by sticking to their own strain. And when they do outcross, it is for the purpose of utilizing the outcrossed product for further breeding. It is not an end in itself.

Inbreeding (or incest breeding, as it is sometimes called) involves no such hazards as are and in the past have been attributed to it. It produces some very excellent dogs when correctly employed, some very bad ones even when correctly employed, and all bad ones when carelessly used. All the standard breeds of dogs were established as uniform breeds through intense inbreeding and culling over many generations. Inbreeding brings into manifestation undesirable recessive genes, the bearers of which can be discarded and the strain can thus be purged of its bad recessives.

Dogs of great soundness and excellence, from excellent parents and grandparents, all of them much alike, may be safely mated together, no matter how closely they may be related, with reasonable hope that most of the progeny will be sound and typical with a close resemblance to all the members of their ancestry. However, two such superlative and well-bred dogs are seldom to be found. It is the way to make progress rapidly and to establish a strain of dogs much alike and which breeds true. The amateur with the boldness and courage to try such a mating in the belief that his dogs are good enough for it is not to be discouraged. But if his judgment is not justified by the results, let him not complain that he has not been warned.

Line breeding is the safest course between the Scylla of outcrossing and the Charybdis of inbreeding for the inexperienced navigator in the sea of breeding. It, too, is to be used with care, because when it succeeds it partakes much of the nature of inbreeding. At any rate, its purpose is the pairing of like genes.

Here the pedigrees come into use. We examine the pedigree of the bitch to be bred. We hope that all the dogs named in it are magnificent dogs, but we look them over and choose the best of the four grandparents. We check this grandparent's breeding and find it good, as it probably is if it is itself a dog or bitch of great excellence. We shall assume that this best dog in the bitch's pedigree is the maternal grandsire. Then our bitch may be bred back to this particular grandsire, to his full brother if he has one of equal excellence, to his best son or best grandson. In such a fashion we compound the genes of this grandsire, and hope to obtain some puppies with his excellences intensified.

The best name in the pedigree may be some other dog or bitch, in which case it is his or her germ plasm that is to be doubled to serve for the foundation of the pedigrees of the puppies of the projected litter.

In making a mating, it is never wise to employ two dogs with the same positive fault. It is wise to use two dogs with as many of the same positive virtues as it is possible to obtain. Neither should faults balance each other, as one with a front too wide, the other with a front too narrow; one with a sway back, the other roach backed. Rather, one member of the mating should be right where the other is wrong. We cannot trust to obtain the intermediate, if we overcompensate the fault of one mate with a fault of the other.

NEGOTIATIONS TO USE THE STUD DOG

Plans to use a stud dog should be laid far enough in advance to enable one to make sure that the services of the dog will be available when they are required. Most men with a dog at public stud publish "stud cards," on which are printed the dog's pedigree and pertinent data pertaining to its record. These should be requested for all the dogs one contemplates using. Most such owners reserve the right to refuse to breed their dogs to bitches they deem unsuitable for them; they wish to safeguard their dog's reputation as a producer of superior puppies, by choosing the bitches to which he shall be bred. Therefore, it is advisable to submit a description of the bitch, with or without a picture of her, and her pedigree to the stud dog's owner at the time the application to use him is made.

Notification should be sent to the owner of the dog as soon as the bitch begins to show in heat, and she should be taken or sent by air or by railway express to the dog's owner about the time she is first recognized to be in full heat and ready to breed. The stud dog's owner should be advised by telegram or telephone just how she has been sent and just when she may be expected, and instruction should be given about how she is to be returned.

Extreme care should be used in securely crating a bitch for shipment when she is in heat. Such bitches are prone to chew their way out of insecure boxes and escape to be bred by some vagrant mongrel. A card containing a statement of the bitch's condition should be attached to the crate as a warning to the carrier to assure her greater security.

MATING

The only time the bitch may become pregnant is during her period of oestruation, a time also variously referred to as the "oestrus," "the season," and as being in "heat." A bitch's first season usually occurs when she is between six and nine months of age, with the average age being eight months. In rare instances it may occur as early as five months or as late as thirteen months of age. After the first season, oestrus usually recurs at intervals of approximately six months, though this too is subject to variation. Also, the bitch's cycle may be influenced by factors such as a change of environment or a change of climate, and her cycle will, of course, be changed if it is interrupted by pregnancy. Most bitches again come in season four to six months after whelping.

There is a decided controversy among breeders as to the wisdom of breeding a bitch during her first season. Some believe a really fine bitch should be bred during her first season in order that she may produce as many puppies as possible during the fertile years of her life span. Others feel that definite physical harm results from breeding a bitch at her first season. Since a normal healthy bitch can safely produce puppies until she is about nine years old, she can comfortably yield eight to ten litters with rests between them in her life. Any breeder should be satisfied with this production from one animal. It seems wiser, therefore, to avoid the risk of any harm and pass her first season. Bitches vary in temperament and in the ages at which they reach sufficient maturity for motherhood and its responsibilities. As with the human animal, stability comes with age and a dam is much more likely to be a good mother if she is out of the puppy phase herself. If the bitch is of show quality, she might become a champion between her first and second heats if not bred.

Usually, oestruation continues for a period of approximately three weeks, but this too is subject to variation. Prior to the beginning of the oestrus, there may be changes in the bitch's actions and demeanor; she may appear restless, or she may become increasingly affectionate. Often there is increased frequency of urination and the bitch may be inclined to lick her external parts. The breeder should be alert for any signs of the approach of oestrus since the bitch must be confined and protected at this time in order to preclude the possibility of the occurrence of a mating with any but the selected stud.

The first physical sign of oestrus is a bloody discharge of watery consistency. The mucous membrane lining the vulva becomes congested, enlarged, and reddened, and the external parts become puffy and swollen. The color of the discharge gradually deepens during the first day or two until it is a rich red color; then it gradually becomes lighter until by the tenth to twelfth day it has only a slightly reddish, or straw-colored, tinge. During the next day or so it becomes almost clear. During this same period, the swelling and hardness of the external parts gradually subside, and by the time the discharge has lost most of its color, the parts are softened and spongy. It is at this time that ovulation, the production of ripened ova (or eggs), takes place, although physical manifestations of oestrus may continue for another week.

A normal bitch has two ovaries which contain her ova. All the eggs she will produce during her lifetime are present in the ovaries at birth. Ordinarily, some of the ova ripen each time the bitch comes in season. Should a bitch fail to ovulate (produce ripened ova), she cannot, of course, become pregnant. Actually, only one ovary is necessary for ovulation, and loss of or damage to one ovary without impairment of the other will not prevent the bitch from producing puppies.

If fertilization does not occur, the ova (and this is also true of the sperm of the male) live only a short time—probably a couple of days at the most. Therefore, if mating takes place too long before or after ovulation, a bitch will not conceive, and the unfertilized ova will pass through the uterus into the vagina. Eventually they will either be absorbed or will pass out through the vulva by the same opening through which urination takes place. If fertilization does occur, the fertilized eggs become implanted on the inner surface of the uterus and grow to maturity.

Obviously, the breeder must exercise great care in determining when the dog and the bitch should be put together. Because the length of time between the beginning of the oestrus and the time of ovulation varies in different bitches, no hard and fast rule can be established, although the twelfth to fourteenth day is in most cases the correct time. The wise breeder will keep a daily record of the changes in the bitch's condition and will arrange to put the bitch and dog together when the discharge has become almost clear and the external parts are softened and spongy. If the bitch refuses the advances of the dog, it is preferable to separate the two, wait a day, then again permit the dog to approach the bitch.

Ordinarily, if the bitch is willing to accept the dog, fertilization of the ovum will take place. Usually one good service is sufficient, although two at intervals of twenty-four to forty-eight hours are often allowed.

Male dogs have glands on the penis which swell after passing the sphincter muscle of the vagina and "tie" the two animals together. The time may last for a period of a few minutes, a half hour, or occasionally up to an hour or more, but will end naturally when the locking glands have deflated the needful amount. While tying may increase the probability of success, in many cases no tie occurs, yet the bitches become pregnant.

Sperm are produced in the dog's testicles and are stored in the epididymis, a twisting tube at the side of the testicle. The occasional male dog whose testicles are not descended (a cryptorchid) is generally conceded to be sterile, although in a few instances it has been asserted that cryptorchids were capable of begetting progeny. The sterility in cryptorchids is believed to be due to the fact that the sperm are destroyed if the testicle remains within the abdominal cavity because the temperature is much higher there than in the normally descended testicle. Thus all sperm produced by the dog may be destroyed if both testicles are undescended. A monorchid (a dog with one testicle descended, the other undescended) may be fertile. Nevertheless, it is unwise to use a monorchid for stud purposes, because monorchidism is believed to be a heritable trait, and the monorchid, as well as the cryptorchid, is ineligible for the show ring.

After breeding, a bitch should be confined for a week to ten days to avoid mismating with another dog.

WHELPING CALENDAR

Find the month and date on which your bitch was bred in one of the left-hand columns. Directly opposite that date, in the right-hand column, is her expected date of whelping, bearing in mind that 61 days is as common as 63.

Date bred	Date due to whelp	Date bred	Date due to whelp	Date bred	Date due to whelp	Date bred	Date due to whelp	Date bred	Date due to whelp	Date bred	Date due to whelp	Date bred	Date due to whelp	Date bred	Date due to whelp	Date bred	Date due to whelp	Date bred	Date due to whelp	Date bred	Date due to whelp	Date bred	Date due to whelp
January	March	February	April	March	May	April	June	May	July	June	August	July	September	August	October	September	November	October	December	November	January	December	February
1	5	1	5	1	3	1	3	1	3	1	3	1	2	1	3	1	3	1	3	1	3	1	2
2	6	2	6	2	4	2	4	2	4	2	4	2	3	2	4	2	4	2	4	2	4	2	3
3	7	3	7	3	5	3	5	3	5	3	5	3	4	3	5	3	5	3	5	3	5	3	4
4	8	4	8	4	6	4	6	4	6	4	6	4	5	4	6	4	6	4	6	4	6	4	5
5	9	5	9	5	7	5	7	5	7	5	7	5	6	5	7	5	7	5	7	5	7	5	6
6	10	6	10	6	8	6	8	6	8	6	8	6	7	6	8	6	8	6	8	6	8	6	7
7	11	7	11	7	9	7	9	7	9	7	9	7	8	7	9	7	9	7	9	7	9	7	8
8	12	8	12	8	10	8	10	8	10	8	10	8	9	8	10	8	10	8	10	8	10	8	9
9	13	9	13	9	11	9	11	9	11	9	11	9	10	9	11	9	11	9	11	9	11	9	10
10	14	10	14	10	12	10	12	10	12	10	12	10	11	10	12	10	12	10	12	10	12	10	11
11	15	11	15	11	13	11	13	11	13	11	13	11	12	11	13	11	13	11	13	11	13	11	12
12	16	12	16	12	14	12	14	12	14	12	14	12	13	12	14	12	14	12	14	12	14	12	13
13	17	13	17	13	15	13	15	13	15	13	15	13	14	13	15	13	15	13	15	13	15	13	14
14	18	14	18	14	16	14	16	14	16	14	16	14	15	14	16	14	16	14	16	14	16	14	15
15	19	15	19	15	17	15	17	15	17	15	17	15	16	15	17	15	17	15	17	15	17	15	16
16	20	16	20	16	18	16	18	16	18	16	18	16	17	16	18	16	18	16	18	16	18	16	17
17	21	17	21	17	19	17	19	17	19	17	19	17	18	17	19	17	19	17	19	17	19	17	18
18	22	18	22	18	20	18	20	18	20	18	20	18	19	18	20	18	20	18	20	18	20	18	19
19	23	19	23	19	21	19	21	19	21	19	21	19	20	19	21	19	21	19	21	19	21	19	20
20	24	20	24	20	22	20	22	20	22	20	22	20	21	20	22	20	22	20	22	20	22	20	21
21	25	21	25	21	23	21	23	21	23	21	23	21	22	21	23	21	23	21	23	21	23	21	22
22	26	22	26	22	24	22	24	22	24	22	24	22	23	22	24	22	24	22	24	22	24	22	23
23	27	23	27	23	25	23	25	23	25	23	25	23	24	23	25	23	25	23	25	23	25	23	24
24	28	24	28	24	26	24	26	24	26	24	26	24	25	24	26	24	26	24	26	24	26	24	25
25	29	25	29	25	27	25	27	25	27	25	27	25	26	25	27	25	27	25	27	25	27	25	26
26	30	26	30	26	28	26	28	26	28	26	28	26	27	26	28	26	28	26	28	26	28	26	27
27	31	27	1 (May)	27	29	27	29	27	29	27	29	27	28	27	29	27	29	27	29	27	29	27	28
28	1 (Apr.)	28	2	28	29	28	30	28	30	28	30	28	29	28	30	28	30	28	30	28	30	28	1 (Mar.)
29	2			29	31	29	1 (July)	29	31	29	31	29	30	29	31	29	1 (Dec.)	29	31	29	31	29	2
30	3			30	1 (June)	30	2	30	1 (Aug.)	30	1 (Sep.)	30	1 (Oct.)	30	1 (Nov.)	30	2	30	1 (Jan.)	30	1 (Feb.)	30	3
31	4			31	2			31	2			31	2	31	2			31	2			31	4

Reproduction by courtesy of the Gaines Dog Research Center, N.Y.C.

THE PREGNANCY AND WHELPING
OF THE BITCH

The "period of gestation" of the bitch, by which is meant the duration of her pregnancy, is usually estimated at sixty-three days. Many bitches, especially young ones, have their puppies as early as sixty days after they are bred. Cases have occurred in which strong puppies were born after only fifty-seven days, and there have been cases that required as many as sixty-six days. However, if puppies do not arrive by the sixty-fourth day, it is time to consult a veterinarian.

For the first five to six weeks of her pregnancy, the bitch requires no more than normal good care and unrestricted exercise. For that period, she needs no additional quantity of food, although her diet must contain sufficient amounts of all the food factors, as is stated in the division of this book that pertains to food. After the fifth to sixth week, the ration must be increased and the violence of exercise restricted. Normal running and walking are likely to be better for the pregnant bitch than a sedentary existence but she should not be permitted to jump, hunt, or fight during the latter half of her gestation. Violent activity may cause her to abort her puppies.

About a week before she is due to whelp, a bed should be prepared for her and she be persuaded to use it for sleeping. This bed may be a box of generous size, big enough to accommodate her with room for activity. It should be high enough to permit her to stand upright, and is better for having a hinged cover. An opening in one side will afford her ingress and egress. This box should be placed in a secluded location, away from any possible molestation by other dogs, animals, or children. The bitch must be made confident of her security in her box.

A few hours, or perhaps a day or two, before her whelping, the bitch will probably begin arranging the bedding of the box to suit herself, tearing blankets or cushions and nosing the parts into the corners. Before the whelping actually starts, however, it is best to substitute burlap sacking, securely tacked to the floor of the box. This is to provide traction for the puppies to reach the dam's breast.

The whelping may take place at night without any assistance from the owner. The box may be opened in the morning to reveal

61

the happy bitch nursing a litter of complacent puppies. But she may need some assistance in her parturition. If whelping is recognized to be in process, it is best to help the bitch.

As the puppies arrive, one by one, the enveloping membranes should be removed as quickly as possible, lest the puppies suffocate. Having removed the membrane, the umbilical cord should be severed with clean scissors some three or four inches from the puppy's belly. (The part of the cord attached to the belly will dry up and drop off in a few days.) There is no need for any medicament or dressing of the cord after it is cut.

The bitch should be permitted to eat the afterbirth if she so desires, and she normally does. If she has no assistance, she will probably remove the membrane and sever the cord with her teeth. The only dangers are that she may delay too long or may bite the cord too short. Some bitches, few of them, eat their newborn puppies (especially bitches not adequately fed during pregnancy). This unlikelihood should be guarded against.

As they arrive, it is wise to remove all the puppies except one, placing them in a box or basket lined and covered by a woolen cloth, somewhere aside or away from the whelping bed, until all have come and the bitch's activity has ceased. The purpose of this is to prevent her from walking or lying on the whelps, and to keep her from being disturbed by the puppies' whining. A single puppy should be left with the bitch to ease her anxiety.

It is best that the "midwife" be somebody with whom the bitch is on intimate terms and in whom she has confidence. Some bitches exhibit a jealous fear and even viciousness while they are whelping. Such animals are few, and most appear grateful for gentle assistance through their ordeal.

The puppies arrive at intervals of a few minutes to an hour until all are delivered. It is wise to call a veterinarian if the interval is greater than one hour. Though such service is seldom needed, an experienced veterinarian can usually be depended upon to withdraw with obstetrical forceps an abnormally presented puppy. It is possible, but unlikely, that the veterinarian will recommend a Caesarian section. This surgery in the dog is not very grave, but it should be performed only by an expert veterinarian. It is unnecessary to describe the process here, or the subsequent management of the patient, since, if a Caesarian section should be necessary, the veterinarian will provide all the needed instructions.

Some bitches, at or immediately after their whelping period, go into a convulsive paralysis, which is called *eclampsia*. This is unlikely if the bitch throughout her pregnancy has had an adequate measure of calcium in her rations. The remedy for eclampsia is the intravenous or intramuscular administration of parenteral calcium. The bitch suspected of having eclampsia should be attended by a veterinarian.

Assuming that the whelping has been normal and without untoward incident, all of the puppies are returned to the bitch, and put, one by one, to the breast, which strong puppies will accept with alacrity. The less handling of puppies for the first four or five hours of their lives, the better. However, the litter should be looked over carefully for possible defectives and discards, which should be destroyed as soon as possible. There is no virtue in rearing hare-lipped, crippled, or mismarked puppies.

It is usually unwise to destroy sound, healthy puppies just to reduce the number in the litter, since it is impossible to sort young puppies for excellence and one may be destroying the best member of the litter, a future champion. Unless a litter is extraordinarily numerous, the dam, if well fed, can probably suckle them all. If it is found that her milk is insufficient, the litter may be artificially fed or may be divided, and the surplus placed on a foster mother if it is possible to obtain one. The foster mother need not be of the same breed as the puppies, a mongrel being as good as any. She should be approximately the same size as the actual mother of the puppies, clean, healthy, and her other puppies should be of as nearly the same age as the ones she is to take over as possible. She should be removed from her own puppies (which may well be destroyed) and her breasts be permitted to fill with milk until she is somewhat uncomfortable, at which time her foster puppies can be put to her breasts and will usually be accepted without difficulty. Unless the services of the foster mother are really required, it is better not to use her.

The whelping bitch may be grateful for a warm meal even between the arrivals of her puppies. As soon as her chore is over, she should be offered food in her box. This should be of cereal and milk or of meat and broth, something sloppy. She will probably not leave her puppies to eat and her meals must be brought to her.

It is wise to give a mild laxative for her bowels, also milk of magnesia. She will be reluctant to get out of her box even to relieve herself for about two days, but she should be urged, even forced, to do so regularly. A sensible bitch will soon settle down to care for her brood and will seldom give further trouble. She should be fed often and well, all that she can be induced to eat during her entire lactation.

As a preventive for infections sometimes occurring after whelping, some experienced breeders and veterinarians recommend injecting the bitch with penicillin or another antibiotic immediately following the birth of the last puppy. Oral doses of the same drug may be given daily thereafter for the first week. It is best to consult your veterinarian about this treatment.

ACID MILK

Occasionally a bitch produces early milk (colostrum) so acid that it disagrees with, sometimes kills, her puppies. The symptoms of the puppies are whining, disquiet, frequently refusal to nurse, frailty, and death. It is true that all milk is slightly acid, and it should be, turning blue litmus paper immersed in it a very light pink. However, milk harmfully on the acid side will readily turn litmus paper a vivid red. It seems that only the first two or three days milk is so affected. Milk problems come also from mastitis and other infections in the bitch.

This is not likely to occur with a bitch that throughout her pregnancy has received an adequate supply of calcium phosphate regularly in her daily ration. That is the best way to deal with the situation—to see to the bitch's correct nutrition in advance of her whelping. The owner has only himself to blame for the bitch's too acid milk, since adequate calcium in advance would have neutralized the acid.

If it is found too late that her milk is too acid, the puppies must be taken from her breast and either given to a foster mother or artificially fed from bottle or by medicine dropper. Artificial feeding of very young puppies seldom is successful. Sometimes the acidity of the dam's milk can be neutralized by giving her large doses of bicarbonate of soda (baking soda), but the puppies should not be restored to her breasts until her milk ceases to turn litmus paper red.

If it is necessary to feed the puppies artificially, "Esbilac," a commercial product, or the following orphan puppy formula, may be used.

7 oz. whole milk
1 oz. cream (top milk)
1 egg yolk
2 tbsp. corn syrup
2 tbsp. lime water

REARING THE PUPPIES

Puppies are born blind and open their eyes at approximately the ninth day thereafter. If they were whelped earlier than the full sixty-three days after the breeding from which they resulted, the difference should be added to the nine days of anticipated blindness. The early eye color of young puppies is no criterion of the color to which the eyes are likely to change, and the breeder's anxiety about his puppies' having light eyes is premature.

In breeds that require the docking of the tail, this should be done on the third day and is a surgical job for the veterinarian. Many a dog has had his tail cut off by an inexperienced person, ruining his good looks and his possibility for a win in the show ring. Dew claws should be removed at the same time. There is little else to do with normal puppies except to let them alone and permit them to grow. The most important thing about their management is their nutrition, which is discussed in another chapter. The first two or three weeks, they will thrive and grow rapidly on their mother's milk, after which they should have additional food as described.

Puppies sleep much of the time, as do other babies, and they should not be frequently awakened to be played with. They grow more and more playful as they mature.

After the second week their nails begin to grow long and sharp. The mother will be grateful if the puppies' nails are blunted with scissors from time to time so that in their pawing of the breast they do not lacerate it. Sharp nails tend to prompt the mother to wean the whelps early, and she should be encouraged to keep them with her as long as she will tolerate them. Even the small amount of milk they can drain from her after the weaning process is begun is the best food they can obtain. It supplements and makes digestible the remainder of their ration.

Many bitches, after their puppies are about four weeks of age, eat and regurgitate food, which is eaten by the puppies. This food is warmed and partly digested in the bitch's stomach. This practice, while it may appear digusting to the novice keeper of dogs, is perfectly normal and should not be discouraged. However, it renders it all the more necessary that the food of the bitch be sound, clean, and nutritious.

It is all but impossible to rear a litter of puppies without their becoming infested with roundworms. Of course, the bitch should be wormed, if she harbors such parasites, before she is bred, and her teats should be thoroughly washed with mild soap just before she whelps to free them from the eggs of roundworms. Every precaution must be taken to reduce the infestation of the puppies to a minimum. But, in spite of all it is possible to do, puppies will have roundworms. These pests hamper growth, reduce the puppies' normal resistance to disease, and may kill them outright unless the worms are eliminated. The worming of puppies is discussed in the chapter entitled "Intestinal Parasites and Their Control."

External Vermin
and Parasites

UNDER this heading the most common external parasites will be given consideration. Fleas, lice, ticks, and flies are those most commonly encountered and causing the most concern. The external parasite does not pose the problem that it used to before we had the new "miracle" insecticides. Today, with DDT, lindane, and chlordane, the course of extermination and prevention is much easier to follow. Many of the insecticide sprays have a four to six weeks residual effect. Thus the premises can be sprayed and the insect pests can be quite readily controlled.

FLEAS

Neglected dogs are too often beset by hundreds of blood-thirsty fleas, which do not always confine their attacks to the dogs but also sometimes feast upon their masters. Unchecked, they overrun kennels, homes, and playgrounds. Moreover, they are the intermediate hosts for the development of the kind of tapeworm most frequently found in dogs, as will be more fully discussed under the subject of *Intestinal Parasites*. Fleas are all-round bad actors and nuisances. Although it need hardly concern us in America, where the disease is not known to exist, fleas are the recognized and only vectors of bubonic plague.

There are numerous kinds and varieties of fleas, of which we shall discuss here only the three species often found on dogs. These are the human flea (*Pulex irritans*), the dog flea (*Ctenocephalides canis*), and the so-called chicken flea or sticktight flea (*Echidnophaga gallinacea*).

Of these the human flea prefers the blood of man to that of the dog, and unless humans are also bothered, are not likely to be found on the dog. They are small, nearly black insects, and occur mostly in the Mississippi Valley and in California. Their control is the same as for the dog flea.

The dog flea is much larger than his human counterpart, is dark brown in color and seldom bites mankind. On an infested dog these dog fleas may be found buried in the coat of any part of the anatomy, but their choicest habitat is the area of the back just forward from the tail and over the loins. On that part of a badly neglected dog, especially in summer, fleas by the hundreds will be found intermixed with their dung and with dried blood. They may cause the dog some discomfort or none. It must not be credited that because a dog is not kept in a constant or frequent agitation of scratching that he harbors no fleas. The coats of pet animals are soiled and roughened by the fleas and torn by the scratching that they sometimes induce. Fleas also appear to be connected with summer eczema of dogs; at least the diseased condition of the skin often clears up after fleas are eradicated.

Although the adults seldom remain long away from the dog's body, fleas do not reproduce themselves on the dog. Rather, their breeding haunts are the debris, dust, and sand of the kennel floor, and especially the accumulations of dropped hair, sand, and loose soil of unclean sleeping boxes. Nooks and cracks and crannies of the kennel may harbor the eggs or maggot-like larvae of immature fleas.

This debris and accumulation must be eliminated—preferably by incineration—after which all possible breeding areas should be thoroughly sprayed with a residual effect spray.

The adult dog may be combed well, then bathed in a detergent solution, rinsed thoroughly in warm water, and allowed to drip fairly dry. A solution of Pine Oil (1 oz. to a quart of water) is then used as a final rinse. This method of ridding the dog of its fleas is ideal in warm weather. The Pine Oil imparts a pleasant odor to the dog's coat and the animal will enjoy being bathed and groomed.

The same procedure may be followed for young puppies except that the Pine Oil solution should be rinsed off. When bathing is not feasible, then a good flea powder—one containing lindane—should be used.

Sticktight fleas are minute, but are to be found, if at all, in patches on the dog's head and especially on the ears. They remain quiescent and do not jump, as the dog fleas and human fleas do. Their tiny heads are buried in the dog's flesh. To force them loose from the area decapitates them and the heads remain in the skin which is prone to fester from the irritation. They may be dislodged by placing a cotton pad or thick cloth well soaked in ether or alcohol over the flea patch, which causes them immediately to relinquish their hold, after which they can be easily combed loose and destroyed.

These sticktights abound in neglected, dirty, and abandoned chicken houses, which, if the dogs have access to them, should be cleaned out thoroughly and sprayed with DDT.

Fleas, while a nuisance, are only a minor problem. They should be eliminated not only from the dog but from all the premises he inhabits. Dogs frequently are reinfested with fleas from other dogs with which they play or come in contact. Every dog should be occasionally inspected for the presence of fleas, and, if any are found, immediate means should be taken to eradicate them.

LICE

There are even more kinds of lice than of fleas, although as they pertain to dogs there is no reason to differentiate them. They do not infest dogs, except in the events of gross neglect or of unforeseen accident. Lice reproduce themselves on the body of the dog. To rid him of the adult lice is easy. The standard Pine Oil solution used to kill fleas will also kill lice. However, the eggs or "nits" are harder to remove. Weather permitting, it is sometimes best to have the dog clipped of all its hair. In heavily infested dogs this is the only sure way to cope with the situation. When the hair is clipped, most of the "nits" are removed automatically. A good commercial flea and louse powder applied to the skin will then keep the situation under control.

Rare as the occurrence of lice upon dogs may be, they must be promptly treated and eradicated. Having a dog with lice can prove to be embarrassing, for people just do not like to be around anything lousy. Furthermore, the louse may serve as the intermediate host of the tapeworm in dogs.

The dog's quarters should be thoroughly sprayed with a residual spray of the same type recommended for use in the control of fleas. The problem of disinfecting kennel and quarters is not as great as it is in the case of fleas, for the louse tends to stay on its host, not leaving the dog as the flea does.

TICKS

The terms "wood ticks" and "dog ticks," as usually employed, refer to at least eight different species, whose appearances and habits are so similar that none but entomologists are likely to know them apart. It is useless to attempt to differentiate between these various species here, except to warn the reader that the Rocky Mountain spotted fever tick (*Dermacentor andersoni*) is a vector of the human disease for which it is named, as well as of rabbit fever (tularemia), and care must be employed in removing it from dogs lest the hands be infected. Some one or more of these numerous species are to be found in well nigh every state in the Union, although there exist wide areas where wood ticks are seldom seen and are not a menace to dogs.

All the ticks must feed on blood in order to reproduce themselves. The eggs are always deposited on the ground or elsewhere after the female, engorged with blood, has dropped from the dog or other animal upon which she has fed. The eggs are laid in masses in protected places on the ground, particularly in thick clumps of grass. Each female lays only one such mass, which contains 2500 to 5000 eggs. The development of the American dog tick embraces four stages: the egg, the larva or seed tick, the nymph, and the adult. The two intermediate stages in the growth of the tick are spent on rodents, and only in the adult stage does it attach itself to the dog. Both sexes affix themselves to dogs and to other animals and feed on their blood; the males do not increase in size, although the female is tremendously enlarged as she gorges. Mating occurs while the female is feeding. After some five to thirteen days, she drops from her host, lays her eggs and dies. At no time do ticks feed on anything except the blood of animals.

The longevity and hardihood of the tick are amazing. The larvae and nymphs may live for a full year without feeding, and the adults survive for more than two years if they fail to encounter a host to which they may attach. In the Northern United States the adults are most active in the spring and summer, few being found after July. But in the warmer Southern states they may be active the year around.

Although most of the tick species require a vegetative cover and wild animal hosts to complete their development, at least one species, the brown tick (*Rhipicephalus sanguinius*), is adapted to life in the dryer environment of kennels, sheds, and houses, with the dog as its only necessary host. This tick is the vector of canine piroplasmosis, although this disease is at this time almot negligible in the United States.

This brown dog tick often infests houses in large numbers, both immature and adult ticks lurking around baseboards, window casings, furniture, the folds of curtains, and elsewhere. Thus, even dogs kept in houses are sometimes infested with hundreds of larvae, nymphs, and adults of this tick. Because of its ability to live in heated buildings, the species has become established in many Northern areas. Unlike the other tick species, the adult of the brown dog tick does not bite human beings. However, also unlike the other ticks, it is necessary not only to rid the dogs of this particular tick but also to eliminate the pests from their habitat, especially the dogs' beds and sleeping boxes. A spray with a 10% solution of DDT suffices for this purpose. Fumigation of premises seldom suffices, since not only are brown dog ticks very resistant to mere fumigation, but the ticks are prone to lurk around entry ways, porches and outbuildings, where they cannot be reached with a fumigant. The spraying with DDT may not penetrate to spots where some ticks are in hiding, and it must be repeated at intervals until all the pests are believed to be completely eradicated.

Dogs should not be permitted to run in brushy areas known to be infested with ticks, and upon their return from exercise in a place believed to harbor ticks, dogs should be carefully inspected for their presence.

If a dog's infestation is light, the ticks may be picked individually

71

from his skin. To make tick release its grip, dab with alcohol or a drop of ammonia. If the infestation is heavy, it is easier and quicker to saturate his coat with a derris solution (one ounce of soap and two ounces of derris powder dissolved in one gallon of water). The derris should be of an excellent grade containing at least 3% of rotenone. The mixture may be used and reused, since it retains its strength for about three weeks if it is kept in a dark place.

If possible, the dip should be permitted to dry on the dog's coat. It should not get into a dog's eyes. The dip will not only kill the ticks that are attached to the dog, but the powder drying in the hair will repel further infestation for two or three days and kill most if not all the boarders. These materials act slowly, requiring sometimes as much as twenty-four hours to complete the kill.

If the weather is cold or the use of the dip should be otherwise inconvenient, derris powder may be applied as a dust, care being taken that it penetrates the hair and reaches the skin. Breathing or swallowing derris may cause a dog to vomit, but he will not be harmed by it. The dust and liquid should be kept from his eyes.

Since the dog is the principal host on which the adult tick feeds and since each female lays several thousand eggs after feeding, treating the dog regularly will not only bring him immediate relief but will limit the reproduction of the ticks. Keeping underbrush, weeds, and grass closely cut tends to remove protection favorable to the ticks. Burning vegetation accomplishes the same results.

Many of the ticks in an infested area may be killed by the thorough application of a spray made as follows: Four tablespoonfuls of nicotine sulphate (40% nicotine) in three gallons of water. More permanent results may be obtained by adding to this solution four ounces of sodium fluorides, but this will injure the vegetation.

Besides the ticks that attach themselves to all parts of the dog, there is another species that infests the ear specifically. This pest, the spinose ear tick, penetrates deep into the convolutions of the ear and often causes irritation and pain, as evidenced by the dog's scratching its ears, shaking its head or holding it on one side. One part derris powder (5% rotenone) mixed with ten parts medicinal mineral oil and dropped into the ear will kill spinose ear ticks. Only a few drops of the material is required, but it is best to massage the base of the ear to make sure the remedy penetrates to the deepest part of the ear to reach all the ticks.

FLIES

Flies can play havoc with dogs in outdoor kennels, stinging them and biting the ears until they are raw. Until recently the only protection against them was the screening of the entire kennel. The breeding places of flies, which are damp filth and stagnant garbage, are in most areas now happily abated, but the chief agent for control of the pest is DDT.

A spray of a 10% solution of DDT over all surfaces of the kennel property may be trusted to destroy all the flies that light on those surfaces for from two weeks to one month. It must, of course, be repeated from time to time when it is seen that the efficacy of the former treatment begins to diminish.

Intestinal Parasites and
Their Control

THE varieties of worms that may inhabit the alimentary tract of the dog are numerous. Much misapprehension exists, even among experienced dog keepers, about the harm these parasites may cause and about the methods of getting rid of them. Some dog keepers live in terror of these worms and continually treat their dogs for them whether they are known to be present or not; others ignore the presence of worms and do nothing about them. Neither policy is justified.

Promiscuous dosing, without the certainty that the dog harbors worms or what kind he may have, is a practice fraught with danger for the well-being of the animal. All drugs for the expulsion or destruction of parasites are poisonous or irritant to a certain degree and should be administered only when it is known that the dog is infested by parasites and what kind. It is hardly necessary to say that when a dog is known to harbor worms he should be cleared of them, but in most instances there is no such urgency as is sometimes manifested.

It may be assumed that puppies at weaning time are more or less infested with intestinal roundworms or ascarids (*Toxocara canis*) and that such puppies need to be treated for worms. It is all but impossible to rear a litter of puppies to weaning age free from those parasites. Once the puppies are purged of them, it is amazing to see the spurt of their growth and the renewal of their thriftiness.

Many neglected puppies surmount the handicap of their worms and at least some of them survive. This, however, is no reason that good puppies—puppies that are worth saving—should go unwormed and neglected.

The ways to find out that a dog actually has worms are to see some of the worms themselves in the dog's droppings or to submit a sample of his feces to a veterinarian or to a biological laboratory for microscopic examination. From a report of such an examination, it is possible to know whether or not a dog is a host to intestinal parasites at all and intelligently to undertake the treatment and control of the specific kind he may harbor.

All of the vermifuges, vermicides, and anthelmintic remedies tend to expel other worms besides the kind for which they are specifically intended, but it is better to employ the remedy particularly effective against the individual kind of parasite the dog is known to have, and to refrain from worm treatment unless or until it is known to be needed.

ROUNDWORMS

The ascarids, or large intestinal roundworms, are the largest of the worm parasites occurring in the digestive tract of the dog, varying in length from 1 to 8 inches, the females being larger than the males. The name "spool worms," which is sometimes applied to them, is derived from their tendency to coil in a springlike spiral when they are expelled, either from the bowel or vomited, by their hosts. There are at least two species of them which frequently parasitize dogs: *Toxocara canis* and *Toxascaris leonina,* but they are so much alike except for some minor details in the life histories of their development that it is not practically necessary for the dog keeper to seek to distinguish between them.

Neither specie requires an intermediate host for its development. Numerous eggs are deposited in the intestinal tract of the host animal; these eggs are passed out by the dog in his feces and are swallowed by the same or another animal, and hatching takes place in its small intestine. Their development requires from twelve to sixteen days under favorable circumstances.

It has been shown that puppies before their birth may be infested by roundworms from their mother. This accounts for the occasional finding of mature or nearly mature worms in very young puppies. It cannot occur if the mother is entirely free from worms, as she should be.

These roundworms are particularly injurious to young puppies. The commonest symptoms of roundworm infestation are general unthriftiness, digestive disturbances, and bloat after feeding. The hair grows dead and lusterless, and the breath may have a peculiar sweetish odor. Large numbers of roundworms may obstruct the intestine, and many have been known to penetrate the intestinal wall. In heavy infestations the worms may wander into the bile ducts, stomach, and even into the lungs and upper respiratory passages where they may cause pneumonia, especially in very young animals.

The control of intestinal roundworms depends primarily upon prompt disposal of feces, keeping the animals in clean quarters and on clean ground, and using only clean utensils for feed and water. Dampness of the ground favors the survival of worm eggs and larvae. There is no known chemical treatment feasible for the destruction of eggs in contaminated soil, but prolonged exposure to sunlight and drying has proved effective.

Numerous remedies have been in successful use for roundworms, including turpentine, which has a recognized deleterious effect upon the kidneys; santonin, an old standby; freshly powdered betel nut and its derivative, arecoline, both of which tend to purge and sicken the patient; oil of chenopodium, made from American wormseed; carbon tetrachloride, widely used as a cleaning agent; tetrachlorethylene, closely related chemically to the former, but less toxic; and numerous other medicaments. While all of them are effective as vermifuges or vermicides, if rightly employed, to each of them some valid objection can be interposed.

In addition to the foregoing, there are other vermifuges available for treatment of roundworms. Some may be purchased without a prescription, whereas others may be procured only when prescribed by a veterinarian.

HOOKWORMS

Hookworms are the most destructive of all the parasites of dogs. There are three species of them—*Ancylostoma caninum, A. braziliense,* and *Uncinaria stenocephalia*—all to be found in dogs in some parts of the United States. The first named is the most widespread; the second found only in the warmer parts of the South and Southwest; the last named, in the North and in Canada. All are similar one to another and to the hookworm that infests mankind (*Ancylostoma uncinariasis*). For purposes of their eradication, no distinction need be made between them.

It is possible to keep dogs for many years in a dry and well drained area without an infestation with hookworms, which are contracted only on infested soils. However, unthrifty dogs shipped from infested areas are suspect until it is proved that hookworm is not the cause of their unthriftiness.

Hookworm males seldom are longer than half an inch, the females somewhat larger. The head end is curved upward, and is equipped with cutting implements, which may be called teeth, by which they attach themselves to the lining of the dog's intestine and suck his blood.

The females produce numerous eggs which pass out in the dog's feces. In two weeks or a little more these eggs hatch, the worms pass through various larval stages, and reach their infective stage. Infection of the dog may take place through his swallowing the organism, or by its penetration of his skin through some lesion. In the latter case the worms enter the circulation, reach the lungs, are coughed up, swallowed, and reach the intestine where their final development occurs. Eggs appear in the dog's feces from three to six weeks after infestation.

Puppies are sometimes born with hookworms already well developed in their intestines, the infection taking place before their birth. Eggs of the hookworm are sometimes found in the feces of puppies only thirteen days old. Assumption is not to be made that all puppies are born with hookworms or even that they are likely to become infested, but in hookworm areas the possibility of either justifies precautions that neither shall happen.

Hookworm infestation in puppies and young dogs brings about a condition often called kennel anemia. There may be digestive

78

disturbances and blood streaked diarrhea. In severe cases the feces may be almost pure blood. Infested puppies fail to grow, often lose weight, and the eyes are sunken and dull. The loss of blood results in an anemia with pale mucous membranes of the mouth and eyes. This anemia is caused by the consumption of the dog's blood by the worms and the bleeding that follows the bites. The worms are not believed to secrete a poison or to cause damage to the dog except loss of blood.

There is an admitted risk in worming young puppies before weaning time, but it is risk that must be run if the puppies are known to harbor hookworms. The worms, if permitted to persist, will ruin the puppies and likely kill them. No such immediacy is needful for the treatment of older puppies and adult dogs, although hookworm infestation will grow steadily worse until it is curbed. It should not be delayed and neglected in the belief or hope that the dog can cure himself.

If treatment is attempted at home, there are available three fairly efficacious and safe drugs that may be used: normal butyl chloride, hexaresorcinal, and methyl benzine.

If a dog is visibly sick and a diagnosis of hookworm infestation has been made, treatment had best be under professional guidance.

Brine made by stirring common salt (sodium chloride) into boiling water, a pound and a half of salt to the gallon of water, will destroy hookworm infestation in the soil. A gallon of brine should be sufficient to treat eight square feet of soil surface. One treatment of the soil is sufficient unless it is reinfested.

TAPEWORMS

The numerous species of tapeworm which infest the dog may, for practical purposes, be divided into two general groups, the armed forms and the unarmed forms. Species of both groups resemble each other in their possession of a head and neck and a chain of segments. They are, however, different in their life histories, and the best manner to deal with each type varies. This is unfortunately not well understood, since to most persons a tapeworm is a tapeworm.

The armed varieties are again divided into the single pored forms of the genera *Taenia, Multiceps,* and *Echinococcus,* and the double pored tapeworm, of which the most widespread and prevalent among dogs in the United States is the so-called dog tapeworm, *Dipylidium caninum.* This is the variety with segments shaped like cucumber-seeds. The adult rarely exceeds a foot in length, and the head is armed with four or five tiny hooks. For the person with well cared for and protected dogs, this is the only tapeworm of which it is necessary to take particular cognizance.

The dog tapeworm requires but a single intermediate host for its development, which in most cases is the dog flea or the biting louse. Thus, by keeping dogs free from fleas and lice the major danger of tapeworm infestation is obviated.

The tapeworm is bi-sexual and requires the intermediate host in order to complete its life cycle. Segments containing the eggs of the tapeworm pass out with the stool, or the detached proglottid may emerge by its own motile power and attach itself to the contiguous hair. The flea then lays its eggs on this segment, thus affording sustenance for the larva. The head of the tapeworm develops in the lung chamber of the baby flea. Thus, such a flea, when it develops and finds its way back to a dog, is the potential carrier of tapeworm. Of course, the cycle is complete when the flea bites the dog and the dog, in biting the area to relieve the itching sensation, swallows the flea.

Since the egg of the tapeworm is secreted in the segment that breaks off and passes with the stool, microscopic examination of the feces is of no avail in attempting to determine whether tapeworms infest a dog. It is well to be suspicious of a finicky eater— a dog that refuses all but the choicest meat and shows very little appetite. The injury produced by this armed tapeworm to the dog that harbors it is not well understood. Frequently it produces no symptoms at all, and it is likely that it is not the actual cause of many of the symptoms attributed to it. At least, it is known that a dog may have one or many of these worms over a long period of time and apparently be no worse for their presence. Nervous symptoms or skin eruptions, or both, are often charged to the presence of tapeworm, which may or may not be the cause of the morbid condition.

Tapeworm-infested dogs sometimes involuntarily pass segments of worms and so soil floors, rugs, furniture, or bedding. The passage by dogs of a segment or a chain of segments via the anus is a frequent cause of the dog's itching, which he seeks to allay by sitting and dragging himself on the floor by his haunches. The segments or chains are sometimes mistakenly called pinworms, but pinworms are a kind of roundworm to which dogs are not subject.

Despite that they may do no harm, few dogs owners care to tolerate tapeworms in their dogs. These worms, it has been definitely established, are not transmissible from dog to dog or to man. Without the flea or the louse, it is impossible for the adult dog tapeworm to reproduce itself, and by keeping dogs free from fleas and lice it is possible to keep them also free from dog tapeworm.

The various unarmed species of tapeworm find their intermediate hosts in the flesh and other parts of various animals, fish, crustacians and crayfish. Dogs not permitted to eat raw meats which have not been officially inspected, never have these worms, and it is needless here to discuss them at length. Hares and rabbits are the intermediate hosts to some of these worms and dogs should not be encouraged to feed upon those animals.

Little is known of the effects upon dogs of infestations of the unarmed tapeworms, but they are believed to be similar to the effects (if any) of the armed species.

The prevention of tapeworm infestation may be epitomized by saying: Do not permit dogs to swallow fleas or lice nor to feed upon uninspected raw meats. It is difficult to protect dogs from such contacts if they are permitted to run at large, but it is to be presumed that persons interested enough in caring for dogs to read this book will keep their dogs at home and protect them.

The several species of tapeworm occurring in dogs are not all removable by the same treatment. The most effective treatment for the removal of the armed species, which is the one most frequently found in the dogs, is arecoline hydrobromide. This drug is a drastic purgative and acts from fifteen to forty-five minutes after its administration. The treatment should be given in the morning after the dog has fasted overnight, and food should be withheld for some three hours after dosing.

Arecoline is not so effective against the double-pored tapeworm as against the other armed species, and it may be necessary to repeat the dose after a few days waiting, since some of the tapeworm heads may not be removed by the first treatment and regeneration of the tapeworm may occur in a few weeks. The estimatedly correct dosage is not stated here, since the drug is so toxic that the dosage should be estimated for the individual dog by a competent veterinarian, and it is better that he should be permitted to administer the remedy and control the treatment.

WHIPWORMS

The dog whipworm (*Trichuris vulpis*) is so called from its fancied resemblance to a tiny blacksnake whip, the front part being slender and hairlike and the hinder part relatively thick. It rarely exceeds three inches in its total length. Whipworms in dogs exist more or less generally throughout the world, but few dogs in the United States are known to harbor them. They are for the most part confined to the caecum, from which they are hard to dislodge, but sometimes spill over into the colon, whence they are easy to dislodge.

The complete life history of the whipworm is not well established, but it is known that no intermediate host is required for its development. The eggs appear to develop in much the same way as the eggs of the large roundworm, but slower, requiring from two weeks to several months for the organisms to reach maturity.

It has not as yet been definitely established that whipworms are the true causes of all the ills of which they are accused. In many instances they appear to cause little damage, even in heavy infestations. A great variety of symptoms of an indefinite sort have been ascribed to whipworms, including digestive disturbances, diarrhea, loss of weight, nervousness, convulsions, and general unthriftiness, but it remains to be proved that whipworms were responsible.

To be effective in its removal of whipworms, a drug must enter the caecum and come into direct contact with them; but the entry of the drug into this organ is somewhat fortuitous, and to increase the chances of its happening, large doses of a drug essentially harmless to the dog must be used. Normal butyl chloride meets this requirement, but it must be given in large doses. Even then, complete clearance of whipworms from the caecum may not be expected; the best to be hoped is that their numbers will be reduced and the morbid symptoms will subside.

Before treatment the dog should be fasted for some eighteen hours, although he may be fed two hours after being treated. It is wise to follow the normal butyl chloride in one hour with a purgative dose of castor oil. This treatment, since it is not expected to be wholly effective, may be repeated at monthly intervals.

The only known means of the complete clearance of whipworms from the dog is the surgical removal of the caecum, which of course should be undertaken only by a veterinary surgeon.

HEART WORMS

Heart worms (*Dirofilaria immitis*) in dogs are rare. They occur largely in the South and Southeast, but their incidence appears to be increasing and cases have been reported along the Atlantic Seaboard as far north as New York. The various species of mosquitoes are known to be vectors of heart worms, although the flea is also accused of spreading them.

The symptoms of heart worm infestation are somewhat vague, and include coughing, shortness of breath and collapse. In advanced cases, dropsy may develop. Nervous symptoms, fixity of vision, fear of light, and convulsions may develop. However, all such symptoms may occur from other causes and it must not be assumed because a dog manifests some of these conditions that he has heart worms. The only way to be sure is a microscopic examination of the blood and the presence or absence of the larvae. Even in some cases where larvae have been found in the blood, post mortem examinations have failed to reveal heart worms in the heart.

Both the diagnosis and treatment of heart worm are functions of the veterinarian. They are beyond the province of the amateur. The drug used is a derivative from antimony known as fuadin, and many dogs are peculiarly susceptible to antimony poisoning. If proper treatment is used by a trained veterinarian, a large preponderance of cases make a complete recovery. But even the most expert of veterinarians may be expected to fail in the successful treatment of a percentage of heart worm infestations. The death of some of the victims is to be anticipated.

LESS FREQUENTLY FOUND WORMS

Besides the intestinal worms that have been enumerated, there exist in some dogs numerous other varieties and species of worms which are of so infrequent occurrence that they require no discussion in a book for the general dog keeper. These include, esophageal worms, lungworms, kidney worms, and eye worms. They are in North America, indeed, so rare as to be negligible.

COCCIDIA

Coccidia are protozoic, microscopic organisms. The forms to which the dog is a host are *Isospora rivolta, I. bigeminia* and *I. felis.* Coccidia eggs, called *oocysts,* can be carried by flies and are picked up by dogs as they lick themselves or eat their stools.

These parasides attack the intestinal wall and cause diarrhea. They are particularly harmful to younger puppies that have been weaned, bringing on fever, running eyes, poor appetite and debilitation as well as the loose stools.

The best prevention is scrupulous cleanliness of the puppy or dog, its surroundings and its playmates whether canine or human. Flies should be eliminated as described in the preceding chapter and stools removed promptly where the dog cannot touch it.

Infection can be confirmed by microscopic examination of the stool. Treatment consists of providing nourishing food, which should be force-fed if necessary, and whatever drug the veterinarian recommends. Puppies usually recover, though occasionally their teeth may be pitted as in distemper.

A dog infected once by one form develops immunity to that form but may be infected by another form.

Skin Troubles

THERE is a tendency on the part of the amateur dog keeper to consider any lesion of the dog's skin to be mange. Mange is an unusual condition in clean, well fed, and well cared for dogs. Eczema occurs much more frequently and is often more difficult to control.

MANGE OR SCABIES

There are at least two kinds of mange that effect dogs—sarcoptic mange and demodectic or red mange, the latter rare indeed and difficult to cure.

Sarcoptic mange is caused by a tiny spider-like mite (*Sarcoptes scabiei canis*) which is similar to the mite that causes human scabies or "itch." Indeed, the mange is almost identical with scabies and is transmissible from dog to man. The mite is approximately 1/100th of an inch in length and without magnification is just visible to acute human sight.

Only the female mites are the cause of the skin irritation. They burrow into the upper layers of the skin, where each lays twenty to forty eggs, which in three to seven days hatch into larvae. These larvae in turn develop into nymphs which later grow into adults. The entire life cycle requires from fourteen to twenty-one days for completion. The larvae, nymphs, and males do not burrow into the skin, but live under crusts and scabs on the surface.

The disease may make its first appearance on any part of the dog's body, although it is usually first seen on the head and muzzle, around the eyes, or at the base of the ears. Sometimes it is first noticed in the armpits, the inner parts of the thighs, the lower abdomen or on the front of the chest. If not promptly treated it may cover the whole body and an extremely bad infestation may cause the death of the dog after a few months.

Red points which soon develop into small blisters are the first signs of the disease. These are most easily seen on the unpigmented parts of the skin, such as the abdomen. As the female mites burrow into the skin, there is an exudation of serum which dries and scabs. The affected parts soon are covered with bran-like scales followed with grayish crusts. The itching is intense, especially in hot weather or after exercise. The rubbing and scratching favor secondary bacterial infections and the formation of sores. The hair may grow matted and fall out, leaving bare spots. The exuded serum decomposes and gives rise to a peculiar mousy odor which increases as the disease develops and which is especially characteristic.

Sarcoptic mange is often confused with demodectic (red) mange, ringworm, or with simple eczema. If there is any doubt about the diagnosis, a microscopic examination of the scrapings of the lesions will reveal the true facts.

It is easy to control sarcoptic mange if it is recognized in its earlier stages and treatment is begun immediately. Neglected, it may be very difficult to eradicate. If it is considered how rapidly the causative mites reproduce themselves, the necessity for early treatment becomes apparent. That treatment consists not only of medication of the dog but also of sterilization of his bedding, all tools and implements used on him, and the whole premises upon which he has been confined. Sarcoptic mange is easily and quickly transmissible from dog to dog, from area to area on the same dog, and even from dog to human.

In some manner which is not entirely understood, an inadequate or unbalanced diet appears to predispose a dog to sarcoptic mange, and few dogs adequately fed and cared for ever contract it. Once a dog has contracted mange, however, improvement in the amount of quality of his food seems not to hasten his recovery.

There are various medications recommended for sarcoptic mange, sulphur ointment being the old standby. However, it is messy, difficult to use, and not always effective. For the treatment of sar-coptic mange, there are available today such insecticides as lindane, chlordane, and DDT. The use of these chemicals greatly facilitates treatment and cure of the dogs affected with mange and those ex-posed to it.

A bath made by dissolving four ounces of derris powder (contain-ing at least 5% rotenone) and one ounce of soap in one gallon of water has proved effective, especially if large areas of the surface of the dog's skin are involved. All crusts and scabs should be re-moved before its application. The solution must be well scrubbed into the skin with a moderately stiff brush and the whole animal thoroughly soaked. Only the surplus liquid should be taken off with a towel and the remainder must be permitted to dry on the dog. This bath should be repeated at intervals of five days until all signs of mange have disappeared. Three such baths will usually suffice.

The advantage of such all over treatment is that it protects un-infected areas from infection. It is also a precautionary measure to bathe in this solution uninfected dogs which have been in contact with the infected one.

Isolated mange spots may be treated with oil of lavender. Roll a woolen cloth into a swab with which the oil of lavender can be applied and rubbed in thoroughly for about five minutes. This destroys all mites with which the oil of lavender comes into contact.

Even after a cure is believed to be accomplished, vigilance must be maintained to prevent fresh infestations and to treat new spots immediately if they appear.

DEMODECTIC OR RED MANGE

Demodectic mange, caused by the wormlike mite *Demodex canis,* which lives in the hair follicles and the sebaceous glands of the skin, is difficult to cure. It is a baffling malady of which the prognosis is not favorable. The life cycle of the causative organism is not well understood, the time required from the egg to maturity being so far unknown. The female lays eggs which hatch into young of appearance similar to that of the adult, except that they are smaller and have but three pairs of legs instead of four.

One peculiar feature about demodectic mange is that some dogs appear to be genetically predisposed to it while others do not contract it whatever their contact with infected animals may be. Young animals seem to be especially prone to it, particularly those with short hair. The first evidence of its presence is the falling out of the hair on certain areas of the dog. The spots may be somewhat reddened, and they commonly occur near the eyes, on the hocks, elbows, or toes, although they may be on any part of the dog's body. No itching occurs at the malady's inception, and it never grows so intense as in sarcoptic mange.

In the course of time, the hairless areas enlarge, and the skin attains a copper hue; in severe cases it may appear blue or leadish gray. During this period the mites multiply and small pustules develop. Secondary invasions may occur to complicate the situation. Poisons are formed by the bacteria in the pustules, and the absorption of toxic materials deranges the body functions and eventually affects the whole general health of the dog, leading to emaciation, weakness, and the development of an acrid, unpleasant odor.

This disease is slow and subtle in its development, runs a casual course, and frequently extends over a period of two or even three years. Unless it is treated, it usually terminates in death, although spontaneous recovery occasionally occurs, especially if the dog has been kept on a nourishing diet. As in other skin diseases, correct nutrition plays a major part in recovery from demodectic mange, as it plays an even larger part in its prevention.

It is possible to confuse demodectic mange with sarcoptic mange, fungus infection, acne, or eczema. A definite diagnosis is possible only from microscopic examination of skin scrapings and of material from the pustules. The possibility of demodectic mange, particularly in its earlier stages, is not negated by the failure to find the mites under the microscope, and several examinations may be necessary to arrive at a definite diagnosis.

The prognosis is not entirely favorable. It may appear that the mange is cured and a new and healthy coat may be re-established only to have the disease manifest itself in a new area, and the whole process of treatment must be undertaken afresh.

In the treatment of demodectic mange, the best results have been obtained by the persistent use of benzine hexachloride, chlordane, rotenone, and 2-mercapto benzothiazole. Perseverance is necessary, but even then failure is possible.

EAR MITES OR EAR MANGE

The mites responsible for ear mange (*Ododectes cynotis*) are considerably larger than the ones which cause sarcoptic mange. They inhabit the external auditory canal and are visible to the unaided eye as minute, slowly moving, white objects. Their life history is not known, but is probably similar to that of the mite that causes sarcoptic mange.

These mites do not burrow into the skin, but are found deep in the ear canal, near the eardrum. Considerable irritation results from their presence, and the normal secretions of the ear are interfered with. The ear canal is filled with inflammatory products, modified ear wax, and mites, causing the dog to scratch and rub its ears and to shake its head. While ear mange is not caused by incomplete washing or inefficient drying of the ears, it is encouraged by such negligence.

The ear mange infestation is purely local and is no cause for anxiety. An ointment containing benzine hexachloride is very effective in correcting this condition. The ear should be treated every third or fourth day.

ECZEMA

Eczema is probably the most common of all ailments seen in the dog. Oftentimes it is mistaken for mange or ringworm, although there is no actual relationship between the conditions. Eczema is variously referred to by such names as "hot spots," "fungitch," and "kennel itch."

Some years ago there was near-unanimity of opinion among dog people that the food of the animal was the major contributing factor of eczema. Needless to say, the manufacturers of commercial dog foods were besieged with complaints. Some research on the cause of eczema placed most of the blame on outside environmental factors, and with some help from other sources it was found that a vegetative organism was the causative agent in a great majority of the cases.

Some dogs do show an allergic skin reaction to certain types of protein given to them as food, but this is generally referred to as the "foreign protein" type of dermatitis. It manifests itself by raising numerous welts on the skin, and occasionally the head, face, and ears will become alarmingly swollen. This condition can be controlled by the injection of antihistamine products and subsequent dosage with antihistaminic tablets or capsules such as chlortrimenton or benedryl. Whether "foreign protein" dermatitis is due to an allergy or whether it is due to some toxin manufactured and elaborated by the individual dog is a disputed point.

Most cases of eczema start with reddening of the skin in certain parts. The areas most affected seem to be the region along the spine and at the base of the tail. In house dogs this may have its inception from enlarged and plugged anal glands. The glands when full and not naturally expressed are a source of irritation. The dog will rub his hind parts on the grass in order to alleviate the itching sensation. Fleas, lice, and ticks may be inciting factors, causing the dog to rub and roll in the grass in an attempt to scratch the itchy parts.

In hunting dogs, it is believed that the vegetative cover through which the dogs hunt causes the dermatitis. In this class of dogs the skin becomes irritated and inflamed in the armpits, the inner surfaces of the thighs, and along the belly. Some hunting dogs are bedded down in straw or hay, and such dogs invariably show a

91

general reddening of the skin and a tendency to scratch.

As a general rule, the difference between moist and dry eczema lies in the degree to which the dog scratches the skin with his feet or chews it with his teeth. The inflammation ranges from a simple reddening of the skin to the development of papules, vesicles, and pustules with a discharge. Crusts and scabs like dandruff may form, and if the condition is not treated, it will become chronic and then next to impossible to treat with any success. In such cases the skin becomes thickened and may be pigmented. The hair follicles become infected, and the lesions are constantly inflamed and exuding pus.

When inflammation occurs between the toes and on the pads of the feet, it closely resembles "athletes foot" in the human. Such inflammation generally causes the hair in the region to turn a reddish brown. The ears, when they are affected, emit a peculiar moldy odor and exude a brownish black substance. It is thought that most cases of canker of the ear are due to a primary invasion of the ear canal by a vegetative fungus. If there is a pustular discharge, it is due to the secondary pus-forming bacteria that gain a foothold after the resistance of the parts is lowered by the fungi.

Some breeds of dogs are more susceptible to skin ailments than are others. However, all breeds of dogs are likely to show some degree of dermatitis if they are exposed to causative factors.

Most cases of dermatitis are seen in the summer time, which probably accounts for their being referred to as "summer itch" or "hot spots." The warm moist days of summer seem to promote the growth and development of both fleas and fungi. When the fleas bite the dog, the resulting irritation causes the dog to scratch or bite to alleviate the itch. The area thus becomes moist and makes a perfect place for fungi spores to propagate. That the fungi are the cause of the trouble seems evident, because most cases respond when treated externally with a good fungicide. Moreover, the use of a powder containing both an insecticide and a fungicide tends to prevent skin irritation. Simply dusting the dog once or twice a week with a good powder of the type mentioned is sound procedure in the practice of preventive medicine.

(Editor's note: I have had some success with hydrogen peroxide in treating mild skin troubles. Saturate a cotton pad with a mixture of 2 parts 3% hydrogen peroxide to 1 part boiled water. Apply, but do NOT rub, to affected skin. Let dry naturally and when *completely* dry apply an antiseptic talcum powder like Johnson & Johnson's Medicated Powder. When this treatment was suggested to my veterinarian, he confirmed that he had had success with it. If the skin irritation is not noticeably better after two of these treatments, once daily, the case should be referred to a veterinarian.)

RINGWORM

Ringworm is a communicable disease of the skin of dogs, readily transmissible to man and to other dogs and animals. The disease is caused by specific fungi, which are somewhat similar to ordinary molds. The lesions caused by ringworm usually first appear on the face, head, or legs of the dog, but they may occur on any part of the surface of his body.

The disease in dogs is characterized by small, circular areas of dirty gray or brownish-yellow crusts or scabs partially devoid of hair, the size of a dime. As the disease progresses, the lesions increase both in size and in number and merge to form larger patches covered with crusts containing broken off hair. A raw, bleeding surface may appear when crusts are broken or removed by scratching or rubbing to relieve itching. In some cases, however, little or no itching is manifested. Microscopic examination and culture tests are necessary for accurate diagnosis.

If treatment of affected dogs is started early, the progress of the disease can be immediately arrested. Treatment consists of clipping the hair from around the infected spots, removing the scabs and painting the spots with tincture of iodine, five percent salicylic acid solution, or other fungicide two or three times weekly until recovery takes place. In applying these remedies it is well to cover the periphery of the circular lesion as well as its center, since the spots tend to expand outward from their centers. Scabs, hair, and debris removed from the dog during his treatments should be burned to destroy the causative organisms and to prevent reinfection. Precautions in the handling of animals affected with ringworm should be observed to preclude transmission to man and other animals. Isolation of affected dogs is not necessary if the treatment is thorough.

93

COAT CARE

Skin troubles can often be checked and materially alleviated by proper grooming. Every dog is entitled to the minimum of weekly attention to coat, skin and ears; ideally, a daily stint with brush and comb is highly recommended. Frequent examination may catch skin disease in its early stages and provide a better chance for a quick cure.

The outer or "guard" hairs of a dog's coat should glint in the sunlight. There should be no mats or dead hair in the coat. Wax in the outer ear should be kept at a minimum.

It is helpful to stand the dog on a flat, rigid surface off the floor at a height convenient to the groomer. Start at the head and ears brushing briskly *with* the lay of short hair, *against* the lay of long hair at first then with it. After brushing, use a fine comb with short teeth on fine, short hair and a coarse comb with long teeth on coarse or long hair. If mats cannot be readily removed with brush or comb, use barber's thinning shears and cut into the matted area several times until mat pulls free easily. Some mats can be removed with the fingers if one has the patience to separate the hair a bit at a time.

After brushing and combing, run your palms over the dog's coat from head to tail. Natural oils in your skin will impart sheen to your dog's coat.

The ears of some dogs secrete and exude great amounts of wax. Frequent examination will determine when your dog's ears need cleaning. A thin coating of clean, clear wax is not harmful. But a heavy accumulation of dirty, dark wax needs removal by cotton pads soaked in diluted hydrogen peroxide (3% cut in half with boiled water), or alcohol or plain boiled water if wax is not too thick.

There are sprays, "dry" bath preparations and other commercial products for maintaining your dog's coat health. Test them first, and if they are successful, you may find them beneficial time-savers in managing your dog's coat.

First Aid

J OHN STEINBECK, the Nobel Prize winning author, in *Travels with Charley in Search of America* bemoans the lack of a good, comprehensive book of home dog medicine. Charley is the aged Poodle that accompanies his illustrious author-owner on a motor tour of the U.S.A.

As in human medicine, most treatment and dosing of dogs are better left in the experienced, trained hands and mind of a professional—in this case, the veterinarian. However, there are times and situations when professional aid is not immediately available and an owner's prompt action may save a life or avoid permanent injury. To this purpose, the following suggestions are given.

The First Aid Kit

For instruments keep on hand a pair of tweezers, a pair of pliers, straight scissors, a rectal thermometer, a teaspoon, a tablespoon, and swabs for cotton.

For dressings, buy a container of cotton balls, a roll of cotton and a roll of 2″ gauze. Strips of clean, old sheets may come in handy.

For medicines, stock ammonia, aspirin, brandy, 3% hydrogen peroxide, bicarbonate of soda, milk of bismuth, mineral oil, salt, tea, vaseline, kaopectate, baby oil and baby talcum powder.

Handling the Dog for Treatment

Approach any injured or sick dog calmly with reassuring voice and gentle, steady hands. If the dog is in pain, slip a gauze or sheet strip noose over its muzzle tying the ends first under the throat and then back of the neck. Make sure the dog's lips are not caught between his teeth, but make noose around muzzle *tight*.

If the dog needs to be moved, grasp the loose skin on the back of the neck with one hand and support chest with the other hand. If the dog is too large to move in this manner, slide him on a large towel, blanket or folded sheet which may serve as a stretcher for two to carry.

If a pill or liquid is to be administered, back the dog in a corner in a sitting position. For a pill, pry back of jaws apart with thumb and forefinger of one hand and with the same fingers of your other hand place pill as far back in dog's throat as possible; close and hold jaws, rubbing throat to cause swallowing. If dog does not gulp, hold one hand over nostrils briefly; he will gulp for air and swallow pill. For liquids, lift the back of the upper lip and tip spoon into the natural pocket formed in the rear of the lower lip; it may be necessary to pull this pocket out with forefinger. Do not give liquids by pouring directly down the dog's throat; this might choke him or make the fluid go down the wrong way.

After treatment keep dog quiet, preferably in his bed or a room where he cannot injure himself or objects.

Bites and Wounds

Clip hair from area. Wash gently with pure soap and water or hydrogen peroxide. If profuse bleeding continues, apply sheet strip or gauze tourniquet between wound and heart but nearest the wound. Release tourniquet briefly at ten-minute intervals. Cold water compresses may stop milder bleeding.

For insect bites and stings, try to remove stinger with tweezers or a dab of cotton, and apply a few drops of ammonia. If dog is in pain, give aspirin at one grain per 10 pounds. (An aspirin tablet is usually 5 grains.)

Burns

Clip hair from area. Apply strong, lukewarm tea (for its tannic acid content) on a sheet strip compress. Vaseline may be used for slight burns. Give aspirin as recommended if dog is in pain. Keep him warm if he seems to be in shock.

Constipation

Give mineral oil: one-quarter teaspoon up to 10 pounds; half teaspoon from 10 to 25 pounds; full teaspoon from 25 to 75 pounds; three-quarters tablespoon over 75 pounds.

Diarrhea

Give kaopectate in same doses by size as indicated for mineral oil above, but repeat within four and eight hours.

Fighting

Do not try forcibly to separate dogs. If available throw a pail of cold water on them. A sharp rap on the rump of each combatant with a strap or stick may help. A heavy towel or blanket dropped over the head of the aggressor, or a newspaper twisted into a torch, lighted and held near them, may discourage the fighters. If a lighted newspaper is used, be careful that sparks do not fall or blow on dogs.

Fits

Try to get the dog into a room where he cannot injure himself. If possible, cover him with a towel or blanket. When the fit ends, give aspirin one grain for every 10 pounds.

Nervousness

Remove cause or remove the dog from the site of the cause. Give the recommended dose of aspirin. Aspirin acts as a tranquilizer.

97

Poisoning

If container of the poison is handy, use recommended antidote printed thereon. Otherwise, make a strong solution of household salt in water and force as much as possible into the dog's throat using the lip pocket method. Minutes count with several poisons; if veterinarian cannot be reached immediately, try to get dog to an MD or registered nurse.

Shock

If dog has chewed electric cord, protect hand with rubber glove or thick dry towel and pull cord from socket. If dog has collapsed, hold ammonia under its nose or apply artificial respiration as follows: place dog on side with its head low, press on abdomen and rib cage, releasing pressure at one- or two-second intervals. Keep dog warm.

Stomach Upsets

For mild stomach disorders, milk of bismuth in same doses as recommended for mineral oil under *Constipation* will be effective. For more severe cases brandy in the same doses but diluted with an equal volume of water may be helpful.

Swallowing Foreign Objects

If object is still in mouth or throat, reach in and remove it. If swallowed, give strong salt solution as for *Poisoning*. Some objects that are small, smooth or soft may not give trouble.

Porcupines and Skunks

Using tweezers or pliers, twist quills one full turn and pull out. Apply hydrogen peroxide to bleeding wounds. For skunk spray, wash dog in tomato juice.

WARNING! Get your dog to a veterinarian *soonest* for severe bites, wounds, burns, poisoning, fits and shock.

98

Internal Canine Diseases
and Their Management

THE word *management* is employed in this chapter heading rather than *treatment*, since the treatment of disease in the dog is the function of the veterinarian, and the best counsel it is possible to give the solicitous owner of a sick dog is to submit the case to the best veterinarian available and to follow his instructions implicitly. In general, it may be said, the earlier in any disease the veterinarian is consulted, the more rapid is the sick animal's recovery and the lower the outlay of money for the services of the veterinarian and for the medicine he prescribes.

Herein are presented some hints for the prevention of the various canine maladies and for their recognition when they occur. In kennel husbandry, disease is a minor problem, and, if preventive methods are employed, it is one that need not be anticipated.

DISTEMPER

Distemper, the traditional bugbear of keeping dogs, the veritable scourge of dog-kind, has at long last been well conquered. Compared with some years ago when "over distemper" was one of the best recommendations for the purchase of a dog, the incidence of distemper in well-bred and adequately cared for dogs is now minimal.

99

The difference between then and now is that we now have available preventive sera, vaccines, and viruses, which may be employed to forestall distemper before it ever appears. There are valid differences of opinion about which of these measures is best to use and at what age of the dog they are variously indicated. About the choice of preventive measures and the technique of administering them, the reader is advised to consult his veterinarian and to accept his advice. There can be no doubt, however, that any person with a valued or loved young dog should have him immunized.

For many years most veterinarians used the so-called "three-shot" method of serum, vaccine and virus, spaced two weeks apart after the puppy was three or four months old, for permanent immunization. For temporary immunization lasting up to a year, some veterinarians used only vaccine; this was repeated annually if the owner wished, though since a dog was considered most susceptible to distemper in the first year of his life, the annual injection was often discontinued. Under both these methods, serum was used at two-week intervals from weaning to the age when permanent or annual immunization was given.

Until 1950 living virus, produced by the methods then known to and used by laboratories, was considered too dangerous to inject without the preparation of the dog for it by prior use of serum or vaccine (killed virus). Then, researchers in distemper developed an attenuated or weakened live virus by injecting strong virus into egg embryos and other intermediate hosts. The weakened virus is now often used for permanent, one-shot distemper immunization of puppies as young as eight weeks.

Today certain researchers believe that the temporary immunity given by the bitch to her young depends on her own degree of immunity. If she has none, her puppies have none; if she has maximum immunity, her puppies may be immune up to the age of 12 weeks or more. By testing the degree of the bitch's immunity early in her pregnancy, these researchers believe they can determine the proper age at which her puppies should receive their shots.

The veterinarian is best qualified to determine the method of distemper immunization and the age to give it.

Canine distemper is an acute, highly contagious, febrile disease caused by a filterable virus. It is characterized by a catarrhal inflammation of all the mucous membranes of the body, frequently

100

accompanied by nervous symptoms and pustular eruptions of the skin. Its human counterpart is influenza, which, though not identical with distemper, is very similar to it in many respects. Distemper is so serious and complicated a disease as to require expert attention; when a dog is suspected of having it, a veterinarian should be consulted immediately. It is the purpose of this discussion of the malady rather to describe it that its recognition may be possible than to suggest medication for it or means of treating it.

Distemper is known in all countries and all parts of the United States in all seasons of the year, but it is most prevalent during the winter months and in the cold, damp weather of early spring and late autumn. No breed of dogs is immune. Puppies of low constitutional vigor, pampered, overfed, unexercised dogs, and those kept in overheated, unventilated quarters contract the infection more readily and suffer more from it than hardy animals, properly fed and living in a more natural environment. Devitalizing influences which decrease the resistance of the dog, such as rickets, parasitic infestations, unsanitary quarters, and especially an insufficient or unbalanced diet, are factors predisposing to distemper.

While puppies as young as ten days or two weeks have been known to have true cases of distemper, and very old dogs in rare instances, the usual subjects of distemper are between two months (after weaning) and full maturity at about eighteen months. The teething period of four to six months is highly critical. It is believed that some degree of temporary protection from distemper is passed on to a nursing litter through the milk of the mother.

As was first demonstrated by Carré in 1905 and finally established by Laidlaw and Duncan in their work for the Field Distemper Fund in 1926 to 1928, the primary causative agent of distemper is a filterable virus. The clinical course of the disease may be divided into two parts, produced respectively by the primary Carré filterable virus and by a secondary invasion of bacterial organisms which produce serious complicating conditions usually associated with the disease. It is seldom true that uncomplicated Carré distemper would cause more than a fever with malaise and indisposition if the secondary bacterial invasion could be avoided. The primary disease but prepares the ground for the secondary invasion which produces the havoc and all too often kills the patient.

Although it is often impossible to ascertain the source of infection

101

in outbreaks of distemper, it is known that the infection may spread from affected to susceptible dogs by either direct or indirect contact. The disease, while highly infectious throughout its course, is especially easy to communicate in its earliest stages, even before clinical symptoms are manifested. The virus is readily destroyed by heat and by most of the common disinfectants in a few hours, but it resists drying and low temperatures for several days, and has been known to survive freezing for months.

The period of incubation (the time between exposure to infection and the development of the first symptoms) is variable. It has been reported to be as short as three days and as long as two weeks. The usual period is approximately one week. The usual course of the disease is about four weeks, but seriously complicated cases may prolong themselves to twelve weeks.

The early symptoms of distemper, as a rule, are so mild and subtle as to escape the notice of any but the most acute observer. These first symptoms may be a rise in temperature, a watery discharge from the eyes and nose, an impaired appetite, a throat-clearing cough, and a general sluggishness. In about a week's time the symptoms become well marked, with a discharge of mucus or pus from the eyes and nose, and complications of a more or less serious nature, such as broncho-pneumonia, hemorrhagic inflammation of the gastro-intestinal tract, and disturbances of the brain and spinal cord, which may cause convulsions. In the early stages of distemper the body temperature may suddenly rise from the normal 101°F. to 103°. Shivering, dryness of the nostrils, a slight dry cough, increased thirst, a drowsy look, reluctance to eat, and a desire to sleep may follow. Later, diarrhea (frequently streaked with blood or wholly of blood), pneumonia, convulsions, paralysis, or chorea (a persistent twitching condition) may develop. An inflammation of the membranes of the eye may ensue; this may impair or destroy the sight through ulceration or opacity of the cornea. Extreme weakness and great loss of body weight occur in advanced stages.

All, any, or none of these symptoms may be noticeable. It is believed that many dogs experience distemper in so mild a form as to escape the owner's observation. Because of its protean and obscure nature and its strong similarity to other catarrhal affections, the diagnosis of distemper, especially in its early stages, is difficult. In young dogs that are known to have been exposed to the disease,

102

a rise of body temperature, together with shivering, sneezing, loss of appetite, eye and nasal discharge, sluggishness, and diarrhea (all or any of these symptoms), are indicative of trouble.

There is little specific that can be done for a dog with primary distemper. The treatment is largely concerned with alleviating the symptoms. No drug or combination of drugs is known at this time that has any specific action on the disease. Distemper runs a definite course, no matter what is done to try to cure it.

Homologous anti-distemper serum, administered subcutaneously or intravenously by the veterinarian, is of value in lessening the severity of the attack. The veterinarian may see fit to treat the secondary pneumonia with penicillin or one of the sulpha drugs, or to allay the secondary intestinal infection with medication. It is best to permit him to manage the case in his own way. The dog is more prone to respond to care in his own home and with his own people, if suitable quarters and adequate nursing are available to him. Otherwise, he is best off in a veterinary hospital.

The dog affected with distemper should be provided with clean, dry, warm but not hot, well ventilated quarters. It should be given moderate quantities of nourishing, easily digested food—milk, soft boiled eggs, cottage cheese, and scraped lean beef. The sick dog should not be disturbed by children or other dogs. Discharges from eyes and nose should be wiped away. The eyes may be bathed with boric acid solution, and irritation of the nose allayed with greasy substances such as petrolatum. The dog should not be permitted to get wet or chilled, and he should have such medication as the veterinarian prescribes and no other.

When signs of improvement are apparent, the dog must not be given an undue amount of food at one meal, although he may be fed at frequent intervals. The convalescing dog should be permitted to exercise only very moderately until complete recovery is assured.

In the control of distemper, affected animals should be promptly isolated from susceptible dogs. After the disease has run its course, whether it end in recovery or death, the premises where the patient has been kept during the illness should be thoroughly cleaned and disinfected, as should all combs, brushes, or other utensils used on the dog, before other susceptible dogs are brought in. After an apparent recovery has been made in the patient, the germs are present for about four weeks and can be transmitted to susceptible dogs.

CHOREA OR ST. VITUS DANCE

A frequent sequela of distemper is chorea, which is characterized by a more or less pronounced and frequent twitching of a muscle or muscles. There is no known remedy for the condition. It does not impair the usefulness of a good dog for breeding, and having a litter of puppies often betters or cures chorea in the bitch. Chorea is considered a form of unsoundness and is penalized in the show ring. The condition generally becomes worse.

ECLAMPSIA OR WHELPING TETANY

Convulsions of bitches before, during, or shortly after their whelping are called eclampsia. It seldom occurs to a bitch receiving a sufficient amount of calcium and vitamin D in her diet during her pregnancy. The symptoms vary in their severity for nervousness and mild convulsions to severe attacks which may terminate in coma and death. The demands of the nursing litter for calcium frequently depletes the supply in the bitch's system.

Eclampsia can be controlled by the hypodermic administration of calcium gluconate. Its recurrence is prevented by the addition to the bitch's ration of readily utilized calcium and vitamin D.

RICKETS, OR RACHITIS

The failure of the bones of puppies to calcify normally is termed rickets, or more technically rachitis. Perhaps more otherwise excellent puppies are killed or ruined by rickets than by any other disease. It is essentially a disease of puppies, but the malformation of the skeleton produced by rickets persists through the life of the dog.

The symptoms of rickets include lethargy, arched neck, crouched stance, knobby and deformed joints, bowed legs, and flabby muscles. The changes characteristic of defective calcification in the puppy are most marked in the growth of the long bones of the leg, and at the cartilaginous junction of the ribs. In the more advanced stages of rickets the entire bone becomes soft and easily deformed or broken. The development of the teeth is also retarded.

Rickets results from a deficiency in the diet of calcium, phos-

104

phorus, or vitamin D. It may be prevented by the inclusion of sufficient amounts of those substances in the puppy's diet. It may also be cured, if not too far advanced, by the same means, although distortions in the skeleton that have already occurred are seldom rectified. The requirements of vitamin D to be artificially supplied are greater for puppies raised indoors and with limited exposure to sunlight or to sunlight filtered through window glass.

(It is possible to give a dog too much vitamin D, but very unlikely without deliberate intent.)

Adult dogs that have had rickets in puppyhood and whose recovery is complete may be bred from without fear of their transmission to their puppies of the malformations of their skeletons produced by the disease. The same imbalance or absence from their diet that produced rickets in the parent may produce it in the progeny, but the disease in such case is reproduced and not inherited.

The requirements of adult dogs for calcium, phosphorus, and vitamin D are much less than for puppies and young dogs, but a condition called osteomalacia, or late rickets, is sometimes seen in grown dogs as the result of the same kind of nutritional deficiency that causes rickets in puppies. In such cases a softening of the bones leads to lameness and deformity. The remedy is the same as in the rickets of puppyhood, namely the addition of calcium, phosphorus, and vitamin D to the diet. It is especially essential that bitches during pregnancy and lactation have included in their diets ample amounts of these elements, both for their own nutrition and for the adequate skeletal formations of their fetuses and the development of their puppies.

BLACKTONGUE

Blacktongue (the canine analogue of pellagra in the human) is no longer to be feared in dogs fed upon an adequate diet. For many years, it was a recognized scourge among dogs, and its cause and treatment were unknown. It is now known to be caused solely by the insufficiency in the ration of vitamin B complex and specifically by an insufficiency of nicotinic acid. (Nicotinic acid is vitamin B_2, formerly known as vitamin G.)

Blacktongue may require a considerable time for its full development. It usually begins with a degree of lethargy, a lack of appetite for the kind of food the dog has been receiving, constipation, often with spells of vomiting, and particularly with a foul odor from the mouth. As the disease develops, the mucous membranes of the mouth, gums, and tongue grow red and become inflamed, with purple splotches of greater or lesser extent, especially upon the front part of the tongue, and with ulcers and pustules on the lips and the lining of the cheeks. Constipation may give way to diarrhea as the disease develops. Blacktongue is an insidious malady, since its development is so gradual.

This disease is unlikely to occur except among dogs whose owners are so unenlightened, careless, or stingy as to feed their dogs exclusively on a diet of cornmeal mush, salt pork, cowpeas, sweet potatoes, or other foodstuffs that are known to be responsible for the development of pellagra in mankind. Blacktongue is not infectious or contagious, although the same deficiency in the diet of dogs may produce the malady in all the inmates throughout a kennel.

Correct treatment involves no medication as such, but consists wholly in the alteration of the diet to include foods which are good sources of the vitamin B complex, including nicotinic acid; such food as the muscles of beef, mutton, or horse, dried yeast, wheat germ, milk, eggs, and especially fresh liver. As an emergency treatment, the hypodermic injection of nicotinic acid may be indicated. Local treatments of the mouth, its cleansing and disinfection, are usually included, although they will avail nothing without the alteration in the diet.

LEPTOSPIROSIS OR CANINE TYPHUS

Leptospirosis, often referred to as canine typhus, is believed to be identical with Weil's disease (infectious jaundice) in the human species. It is not to be confused with non-infectious jaundice in the dog, which is a mere obstruction in the bile duct which occurs in some liver and gastric disorders. Leptospirosis is a comparatively rare disease as yet, but its incidence is growing and it is becoming more widespread.

It is caused by either of two spirocheates, *Leptospira canicola* or *Leptospira icterohenorrhagiae*. These causative organisms are found in the feces or urine of infected rats, and the disease is transmitted to dogs by their ingestion of food fouled by those rodents. It is therefore wise in rat infested houses to keep all dog food in covered metal containers to which it is impossible for rats to gain access. It is also possible for an ill dog to transmit the infection to a well one, and, it is believed, to man. Such cases, however, are rare.

Symptoms of leptospirosis include a variable temperature, vomiting, loss of appetite, gastroenteritis, diarrhea, jaundice and depression. Analysis of blood and urine may be helpful toward diagnosis. The disease is one for immediate reference to the veterinarian whenever suspected.

Prognosis is not entirely favorable, especially if the disease is neglected in its earlier stages. Taken in its incipience, treatment with penicillin has produced excellent results, as has antileptospiral serum and vaccine.

Control measures include the extermination of rats in areas where the disease is known to exist, and the cleaning and disinfection of premises where infected dogs have been kept.

INFECTIOUS HEPATITIS

This is a virus disease attacking the liver. Apparently it is not the same virus that causes hepatitis in humans. Symptoms include an unusual thirst, loss of appetite, vomiting, diarrhea, pain causing the dog to moan, anemia and fever. The afflicted dog may try to hide.

The disease runs a fast course and is often fatal. A dog recovering from it may carry the virus in his urine for a long period, thus infecting other dogs months later.

Serum and vaccine are available to offer protection. A combination for distemper and hepatitis is now offered.

TURNED-IN OR TURNED-OUT EYELIDS

When the eyelid is inverted, or turned-in, it is technically termed entropion. When the eyelid is turned-out, it is referred to as extropion. Both conditions seem to be found in certain strains of dogs and are classified as being heritable. Both conditions may be corrected by competent surgery. It is possible to operate on such

107

cases and have complete recovery without scar formation. However, cognizance should be taken of either defect in a dog to be used for breeding purposes.

CONJUNCTIVITIS OR INFLAMMATION
OF THE EYE

Certain irritants, injuries or infections, and many febrile diseases, such as distemper, produce conjunctivitis, an inflammation of the membranes lining the lids of the dog's eyes. At first there is a slight reddening of the membranes and a watery discharge. As the condition progresses, the conjunctivae become more inflamed looking and the color darkens. The discharge changes consistency and color, becoming muco-purulent in character and yellow in color. The eyelids may be pasted shut and granulation of the lids may follow.

When eye infection persists for an extended period of time, the cornea sometimes becomes involved. Ulcers may develop, eventually penetrating the eyeball. When this happens, the condition becomes very painful and, even worse, often leads to the loss of vision.

Home treatment, to be used only until professional care may be had, consists of regular cleaning of the eye with a 2% boric acid solution and the application of one of the antibiotic eye ointments.

When anything happens to the dog's eye, it is always best to seek professional help and advice.

RABIES

This disease, caused by a virus, is transmissible to all warm blooded animals, and the dog seems to be the number one disseminator of the virus. However, outbreaks of rabies have been traced to wild animals—the wolf, coyote, or fox biting a dog which in turn bites people, other dogs, or other species of animals.

The virus, which is found in the saliva of the rabid animal, enters the body only through broken skin. This usually is brought about by biting and breaking the skin, or through licking an open cut on the skin. The disease manifests itself clinically in two distinct forms. One is called the "furious type" and the other the "dumb type." Both types are produced by the same strain of virus.

The disease works rather peculiarly on the dog's disposition and character. The kindly old dog may suddenly become ferocious; just the reverse may also occur, the mean, vicious dog becoming gentle and biddable. At first the infected dog wants to be near his master, wants to lick his hand or his boots; his appetite undergoes a sudden change, becoming voracious, and the animal will eat anything— stones, bits of wood, even metal. Soon there develops a sense of wanderlust, and the dog seems to wish to get as far away as possible from his owner.

In all rabid animals there is an accentuation of the defense mechanisms. In other words, the dog will bite, the cat will hiss and claw, the horse will bite and kick, and the cow will attack anything that moves.

An animal afflicted with rabies cannot swallow because there is usually a paralysis of the muscles of deglutinition. The animal, famished for a drink, tries to bite the water or whatever fluid he may be attempting to drink. The constant champing of the jaws causes the saliva to become mixed and churned with air, making it appear whipped and foamy. In the old days when a dog "frothed at the mouth," he was considered "mad." There is no doubt but what some uninfected dogs have been suspected of being rabid and shot to death simply because they exhibited these symptoms.

One of the early signs of rabies in the dog is the dropping of the lower jaw. This is a sign of rabies of the so-called "dumb type." The animal has a "faraway" look in his eyes, and his voice or bark has an odd pitch. Manifesting these symptoms, the dog is often taken to the clinic by the owner, who is sure the dog has a bone in the throat. The hind legs, and eventually the whole hindquarters, subsequently become paralyzed, and death ensues.

Many commonwealths have passed laws requiring that all dogs be vaccinated against rabies, and usually, a vaccination certificate must be presented before a dog license may be issued. The general enforcement of this law alone would go a long way toward the eradication of rabies.

Some will ask why a dog must be impounded as a biter when he has taken a little "nip" at someone and merely broken the skin— if this must be done, they cannot understand the "good" of the vaccination. But the vaccination does not give the dog the right to bite. Statistics show that rabies vaccination is effective in about 88% of the cases. All health authorities wish it were 100% effective, thus eliminating a good deal of worry from their minds. Because the vaccination is not 100% effective, we cannot take a chance on the vaccine alone. The animal must be impounded and under the daily supervision of a qualified observer, generally for a period of fourteen days. It is pretty well recognized that if the bite was provocated by rabies, the biting animal will develop clinical symptoms in that length of time; otherwise, he will be released as "clinically normal."

THE SPAYING OF BITCHES

The spaying operation, technically known as an ovariectomy, is the subject of a good deal of controversy. It is an operation that has its good and its bad points.

Spayed bitches cannot be entered in the show ring, and of course can never reproduce their kind. However, under certain circumstances, the operation is recommended by veterinarians. If the operation is to be performed, the bitch should preferably be six to eight months of age. At this age, she has pretty well reached the adolescent period; time enough has been allowed for the endocrine balance to become established and the secondary sex organs to develop.

Mechanical difficulties sometimes arise in the urinary systems of bitches that have been operated on at three or four months of age. In a very small percentage of the cases, loss of control of the sphincter muscles of the bladder is observed. But this can readily be corrected by an injection of the female hormone stilbestrol.

There are many erroneous ideas as to what may happen to the female if she is spayed. Some people argue that the disposition will be changed, that the timid dog may become ferocious, and, strangely enough, that the aggressive animal will become docile. Some breeders say that the spayed bitch will become fat, lazy, and lethargic. According to the records that have been kept on bitches following the spaying operation, such is not the case. It is unjust to accuse the spaying operation when really the dog's owner is at fault—he just feeds the dog too much.

THE CASTRATION OF DOGS

This operation consists of the complete removal of the testes. Ordinarily the operation is not encouraged. Circumstances may attenuate the judgment, however. Castration may be necessary to correct certain pathological conditions such as a tumor, chronic prostatitis, and types of perineal troubles. Promiscuous wetting is sometimes an excuse for desexing.

It must be remembered that as with the spayed bitch, the castrated dog is barred from the show ring.

ANAL GLANDS

On either side of the anus of the dog is situated an anal gland, which secretes a lubricant that better enables the dog to expel the contents of the rectum. These glands are subject to being clogged, and in them accumulates a fetid mass. This accumulation is not, strictly speaking, a disease—unless it becomes infected and purulent. Almost all dogs have it, and most of them are neglected without serious consequences. However, they are better if they are relieved. Their spirits improve, their eyes brighten, and even their coats gradually grow more lively if the putrid mass is occasionally squeezed out of the anus.

This is accomplished by seizing the tail with the left hand, encircling its base with the thumb and forefinger of the right hand, and pressing the anus firmly between thumb and finger. The process results in momentary pain to the dog and often causes him to flinch, which may be disregarded. A semi-liquid of vile odor is extruded from the anus. The operation should be repeated at intervals of from one week to one month, depending on the rapidity of glandular accumulation. No harm results from the frequency of such relief, although there may be no apparent results if the anal glands are kept free of their accumulations.

If this process of squeezing out of the glands is neglected, the glands sometimes become infected and surgery becomes necessary. This is seldom the case, but, if needful at all, it must be entrusted to a skillful veterinary surgeon.

METRITIS

Metritis is the acute or chronic inflammation of the uterus of the bitch and may result from any one of a number of things. Perhaps the most common factor, especially in eight- to twelve-year-old bitches, is pseudocyesis, or false pregnancy. Metritis often follows whelping; it may be the result of a retained placenta, or of infection of the uterus following the manual or instrument removal of a puppy.

The term pyometria is generally restricted to cases where the uterus is greatly enlarged and filled with pus. In most such cases surgery must be resorted to in order to effect a cure.

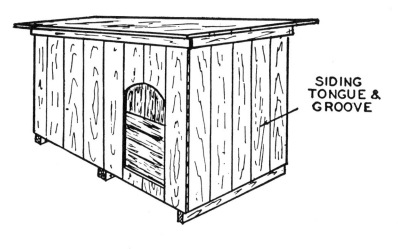

SIDING
TONGUE &
GROOVE

ASSEMBLED VIEW

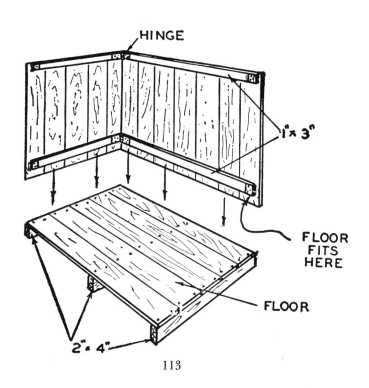

HINGE

1" x 3"

FLOOR
FITS
HERE

FLOOR

2" x 4"

113

Housing for Dogs

E VERY owner will have, and will have to solve, his own problems about providing his dog or dogs with quarters best suited to the dog's convenience. The special circumstances of each particular owner will determine what kind of home he will provide for his dogs. Here it is impossible to provide more than a few generalities upon the subject.

Little more need be said than that fit quarters for dogs must be secure, clean, dry, and warm. Consideration must be given to convenience in the care of kennel inmates by owners of a large number of dogs, but by the time one's activities enlarge to such proportions one will have formulated one's own concept of how best to house one's dogs. Here, advice will be predicated upon the maintenance of not more than three or four adult dogs with accommodations for an occasional litter of puppies.

First, let it be noted that dogs are not sensitive to aesthetic considerations in the place they are kept; they have no appreciation of the beauty of their surroundings. They do like soft beds of sufficient thickness to protect them from the coldness of the floors. These beds should be secluded and covered to conserve body heat. A box or crate of adequate size to permit the dog to lie full length in it will suffice. The cushion may be a burlap bag stuffed with shredded paper, *not straw, hay, or grass.* Paper is recommended, for its use will reduce the possibility of the dog's developing skin trouble.

Most dogs are allergic to fungi found on vegetative matter such as straw, hay, and grass. Wood shavings and excelsior may be used with impunity.

The kennel should be light, except for a retiring place; if sunshine is available at least part of the day, so much the better. Boxes in a shed or garage with secure wire runs to which the dogs have ready access suffice very well, are very inexpensive, and are easy to plan and to arrange. The runs should be made of wire fencing strong enough that the dogs are unable to tear it with their teeth and high enough that the dogs are unable to jump or climb over it. In-turning flanges of wire netting at the tops of the fences tend to obviate jumping. Boards, rocks, or cement buried around the fences forestall burrowing to freedom.

These pens need not be large, if the dogs are given frequent respites from their captivity and an opportunity to obtain needed exercise. However, they should be large enough to relieve them of the aspect of cages. Concrete floors for such pens are admittedly easy to keep clean and sanitary. However, they have no resilience, and the feet of dogs confined for long periods on concrete floors are prone to spread and their shoulders to loosen. A further objection to concrete is that it grows hot in the summer sunshine and is very cold in winter. If it is used for flooring at all, a low platform of wood, large enough to enable the dogs to sprawl out on it full length, should be provided in each pen.

A well drained soil is to be preferred to concrete, if it is available; but it must be dug out to the depth of three inches and renewed occasionally, if it is used. Otherwise, the accumulation of urine will make it sour and offensive. Agricultural limestone, applied monthly and liberally, will "sweeten" the soil.

Gates, hinges, latches, and other hardware must be trustworthy. The purpose of such quarters is to confine the dogs and to keep them from running at large; unless they serve such a purpose they are useless. One wants to know when one puts a dog in his kennel, the dog will be there when one returns. An improvised kennel of old chicken wire will not suffice for one never knows whether it will hold one's dogs or not.

Frequently two friendly bitches may be housed together, or a dog housed with a bitch. Unless one is sure of male friendships, it is seldom safe to house two adult male dogs together. It is better, if

115

possible, to provide a separate kennel for each mature dog. But, if the dogs can be housed side by side with only a wire fence between them, they can have companionship without rancor. Night barking can be controlled by confining the dogs indoors or by shutting them up in their boxes.

Adult dogs require artificial heat in only the coldest of climates, if they are provided with tight boxes placed under shelter. Puppies need heat in cold weather up until weaning time, and even thereafter if they are not permitted to sleep together. Snuggled together in a tight box with shredded paper, they can withstand much cold without discomfort. All dogs in winter without artificial heat should have an increase of their rations—especially as pertains to fat content.

Whatever artificial heat is provided for dogs should be safe, foolproof, and dog-proof. Caution should be exercised that electric wiring is not exposed, that stoves cannot be tipped over, and that it is impossible for sparks from them to ignite the premises. Many fires in kennels, the results of defective heating apparatus or careless handling of it, have brought about the deaths of the inmates. It is because of them that this seemingly unnecessary warning is given.

No better place for a dog to live can be found than the home of its owner, sharing even his bed if permitted. So is the dog happiest. There is a limit, however, to the number of dogs that can be tolerated in the house. The keeper of a small kennel can be expected to alternate his favorite dogs in his own house, thus giving them a respite to confinement in a kennel. Provision must be made for a place of exercise and relief at frequent intervals for dogs kept in the house. An enclosed dooryard will serve such a purpose, or the dog may be exercised on a lead with as much benefit to the owner as to the dog.

That the quarters of the dog shall be dry is even more important than that they shall be warm. A damp, drafty kennel is the cause of much kennel disease and indisposition. It is harmless to permit a dog to go out into inclement weather of his own choice, if he is provided with a sheltered bed to which he may retire to dry himself.

By cleanness, sanitation is meant—freedom from vermin and bacteria. A little coat of dust or a degree of disorder does not discommode the dog or impair his welfare, but the best dog keepers are orderly persons. They at least do not permit bedding and old

116

bones to accumulate in a dog's bed, and they take the trouble to spray with antiseptic or wash with soap and water their dog's house at frequent intervals. The feces in the kennel runs should be picked up and destroyed at least once, and better twice, daily. Persistent filth in kennels can be counted on as a source of illness sooner or later. This warning appears superfluous, but it isn't; the number of ailing dogs kept in dirty, unsanitary kennels is amazing. It is one of the axioms of keeping dogs that their quarters must be sanitary or disease is sure to ensue.

GOOD DOG KEEPING PRACTICES

Pride of ownership is greatly enhanced when the owner takes care to maintain his dog in the best possible condition at all times. And meticulous grooming not only will make the dog look better but also will make him feel better. As part of the regular, daily routine, the grooming of the dog will prove neither arduous nor time consuming; it will also obviate the necessity for indulging in a rigorous program designed to correct the unkempt state in which too many owners permit their dogs to appear. Certainly, spending a few minutes each day will be well worth while, for the result will be a healthier, happier, and more desirable canine companion.

THAT DOGGY ODOR

Many persons are disgusted to the point of refusal to keep a dog by what they fancy is a "doggy odor." Of course, almost everything has a characteristic odor—everyone is familiar with the smell of the rose. No one would want the dog to smell like a rose, and, conversely, the world wouldn't like it very well if the rose smelled doggy. The dog must emit a certain amount of characteristic odor or he wouldn't be a dog. That seems to be his God-given grant. However, when the odor becomes too strong and obnoxious, then it is time to look for the reason. In most cases it is the result of clogged anal glands. If this be the case, all one must do to rid the pet of his odor is to express the contents of these glands and apply to the anal region a little soap and water.

If the odor is one of putrefaction, look to his mouth for the trouble. The teeth may need scaling, or a diseased root of some

117

one or two teeth that need to be treated may be the source of the odor. In some dogs there is a fold or a crease in the lower lip near the lower canine tooth, and this may need attention. This spot is favored by fungi that cause considerable damage to the part. The smell here is somewhat akin to the odor of human feet that have been attacked by the fungus of athlete's foot.

The odor may be coming from the coat if the dog is heavily infested with fleas or lice. Too, dogs seem to enjoy the odor of dead fish and often roll on a foul smelling fish that has been cast up on the beach. The dog with a bad case of otitis can fairly "drive you out of the room" with this peculiar odor. Obviously, the way to rid the dog of odor is to find from whence it comes and then take steps to eliminate it. Some dogs have a tendency toward excessive flatulence (gas). These animals should have a complete change of diet and with the reducing of the carbohydrate content, a teaspoon of granular charcoal should be added to each feeding.

BATHING THE DOG

There is little to say about giving a bath to a dog, except that he shall be placed in a tub of warm (not hot) water and thoroughly scrubbed. He may, like a spoiled child, object to the ordeal, but if handled gently and firmly he will submit to what he knows to be inevitable.

The water must be only tepid, so as not to shock or chill the dog. A bland, unmedicated soap is best, for such soaps do not irritate the skin or dry out the hair. Even better than soap is one of the powdered detergents marketed especially for this purpose. They rinse away better and more easily than soap and do not leave the coat gummy or sticky.

It is best to begin with the face, which should be thoroughly and briskly washed with a cloth. Care should be taken that the cleaning solvent does not get into the dog's eyes, not because of the likelihood of causing permanent harm, but because such an experience is unpleasant to the dog and prone to prejudice him against future baths. The interior of the ear canals should be thoroughly cleansed until they not only look clean but also until no unpleasant odor comes from them. The head may then be rinsed and dried before proceeding to the body. Especial attention should be given to the

118

drying of the ears, inside and outside. Many ear infections arise from failure to dry the canals completely.

With the head bathed and the surplus water removed from that part, the body must be soaked thoroughly with water, either with a hose or by dipping the water from the bath and pouring it over the dog's back until he is totally wetted. Thereafter, the soap or detergent should be applied and rubbed until it lathers freely. A stiff brush is useful in penetrating the coat and cleansing the skin. It is not sufficient to wash only the back and sides—the belly, neck, legs, feet, and tail must all be scrubbed thoroughly.

If the dog is very dirty, it may be well to rinse him lightly and repeat the soaping process and scrub again. Thereafter, the dog must be rinsed with warm (tepid) water until all suds and soil come away. If a bath spray is available, the rinsing is an easy matter. If the dog must be rinsed in standing water, it will be needful to renew it two or three times.

When he is thoroughly rinsed, it is well to remove such surplus water as may be squeezed with the hand, after which he is enveloped with a turkish towel, lifted from the tub, and rubbed until he is dry. This will probably require two or three dry towels. In the process of drying the dog, it is well to return again and again to the interior of the ears.

THE DOG'S TEETH

The dog, like the human being, has two successive sets of teeth, the so-called milk teeth or baby teeth, which are shed and replaced later by the permanent teeth. The temporary teeth, which begin to emerge when the puppy is two and a half to three weeks of age, offer no difficulty. The full set of milk teeth (consisting usually of six incisors and two canines in each jaw, with four molars in the upper jaw and six molars in the lower jaw) is completed usually just before weaning time. Except for some obvious malformation, the milk teeth may be ignored and forgotten about.

At about the fourth month the baby teeth are shed and gradually replaced by the permanent teeth. This shedding and replacement process may consume some three or four months. This is about the most critical period of the dog's life—his adolescence. Some constitutionally vigorous dogs go through their teething easily, with no

119

seeming awareness that the change is taking place. Others, less vigorous, may suffer from soreness of the gums, go off in flesh, and require pampering. While they are teething, puppies should be particularly protected from exposure to infectious diseases and should be fed on nutritious foods, especially meat and milk.

The permanent teeth normally consist of 42—six incisors and two canines (fangs) in each jaw, with twelve molars in the upper jaw and fourteen in the lower jaw. Occasionally the front molars fail to emerge; this deficiency is considered by most judges to be only a minor fault, if the absence is noticed at all.

Dentition is a heritable factor in the dog, and some dogs have soft, brittle and defective permanent teeth, no matter how excellent the diet and the care given them. The teeth of those dogs which are predisposed to have excellent sound ones, however, can be ruined by an inferior diet prior to and during the period of their eruption. At this time, for the teeth to develop properly, a dog must have an adequate supply of calcium phosphate and vitamin D, besides all the protein he can consume.

Often the permanent teeth emerge before the shedding of the milk teeth, in which case the dog may have parts of both sets at the same time. The milk teeth will eventually drop out, but as long as they remain they may deflect or displace the second teeth in the process of their growth. The incisors are the teeth in which a malformation may result from the late dropping of the baby teeth. When it is realized just how important a correct "bite" may be deemed in the show ring, the hazards of permitting the baby teeth to deflect the permanent set will be understood.

The baby teeth in such a case must be dislodged and removed. The roots of the baby teeth are resorbed in the gums, and the teeth can usually be extracted by firm pressure of thumb and finger, although it may be necessary to employ forceps or to take the puppy to the veterinarian.

The permanent teeth of the puppy are usually somewhat overshot, by which is meant that the upper incisors protrude over and do not play upon the lower incisors. Maturity may be trusted to remedy this apparent defect unless it is too pronounced.

An undershot mouth in a puppy, on the other hand, tends to grow worse as the dog matures. Whether or not it has been caused by the displacement of the permanent teeth by the persistence of the milk teeth, it can sometimes be remedied (or at least bettered) by frequent hard pressure of the thumb on the lower jaw, forcing the lower teeth backward to meet the upper ones. Braces on dog teeth have seldom proved efficacious, but pressure and massage are worth trying on the bad mouth of an otherwise excellent puppy.

High and persistent fevers, especially from the fourth to the ninth month, sometimes result in discolored, pitted, and defective teeth, commonly called "distemper teeth." They often result from maladies other than distemper. There is little that can be done for them. They are unpleasant to see and are subject to penalty in the show ring, but are serviceable to the dog. Distemper teeth are not in themselves heritable, but the predisposition for their development appears to be. At least, at the teething age, the offspring from distemper toothed ancestors seem to be especially prone to fevers which impair their dentition.

Older dogs, especially those fed largely upon carbohydrates, tend to accumulate more or less tartar upon their teeth. The tartar generally starts at the gum line on the molars and extends gradually to the cusp. To rectify this condition, the dog's teeth should be scaled by a veterinarian.

The cleanliness of a dog's mouth may be brought about and the formation of tartar discouraged by the scouring of the teeth with a moist cloth dipped in a mixture of equal parts of table salt and baking soda.

A large bone given the dog to chew on or play with tends to prevent tartar from forming on the teeth. If tartar is present, the chewing and gnawing on the bone will help to remove the deposit mechanically. A bone given to puppies will act as a teething ring and aid in the cutting of the permanent teeth. So will beef hide strips you can buy in pet shops.

CARE OF THE NAILS

The nails of the dog should be kept shortened and blunted right down to the quick—never into the quick. If this is not done, the toes may spread and the foot may splay into a veritable pancake. Some dogs have naturally flat feet, which they have inherited. No pretense is made that the shortening of the nails of such a foot will obviate the fault entirely and make the foot beautiful or serviceable.

It will only improve the appearance and make the best of an obvious fault. Short nails do, however, emphasize the excellence of a good foot.

Some dogs keep their nails short by digging and friction. Their nails require little attention, but it is a rare dog whose foot cannot be bettered by artificially shortening the nails.

Nail clippers are available, made especially for the purpose. After using them, the sides of the nail should be filed away as much as is possible without touching the quick. Carefully done, it causes the dog no discomfort. But, once the quick of a dog's nail has been injured, he may forever afterward resent and fight having his feet treated or even having them examined.

The obvious horn of the nail can be removed, after which the quick will recede to permit the removal of more horn the following week. This process may be kept up until the nail is as short and blunt as it can be made, after which nails will need attention only at intervals of six weeks or two months.

Some persons clip the nails right back to the toes in one fell swoop, disregarding injury to the quick and pain of the dog. The nails bleed and the dog limps for a day or two, but infection seldom develops. Such a procedure should not be undertaken without a general anesthetic. If an anesthetic is used, this forthright method does not prejudice the dog against having his feet handled.

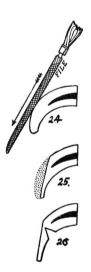

NAIL TRIMMING
ILLUSTRATED

The method here illustrated is to take a sharp file and stroke the nail downwards in the direction of the arrow, as in Figure 24, until it assumes the shape in Figure 25, the shaded portion being the part removed, a three-cornered file should then be used on the underside just missing the quick, as in Figure 26, and the operation is then complete, the dog running about quickly wears the nail to the proper shape.

122

Care for
the Old Dog

First, how old is old, in a dog? Some breeds live longer than others, as a general rule. The only regularity about dog ages at death is their irregularity breed to breed and dog to dog.

The dog owner can best determine senility in his canine friend by the dog's appearance and behavior. Old dogs "slow down" much as humans do. The stairs are a little steeper, the breath a little shorter, the eye dimmer, the hearing usually a little harder.

As prevention is always better than cure, a dog's life may be happily and healthfully extended if certain precautionary steps are taken. As the aging process becomes quite evident, the owner should become more considerate of his dog's weaknesses, procrastinations and lapses. A softer, drier, warmer bed may be advisable; a foam rubber mattress will be appreciated. If a kennel dog has been able to endure record-breaking hot or cold, torrential or desert-dry days, he may in his old age appreciate spending his nights at least in a warm, comfy human house. And if the weather outside is frightful during the day, he should—for minimum comfort and safety—be brought inside before pneumonia sets in.

The old dog should NOT be required or expected to chase a ball, or a pheasant, or one of his species of different sex. The old bitch should not continue motherhood.

If many teeth are gone or going, foods should be softer. The diet should be blander—delete sweet or spicy or heavy tidbits—and there should be less of it, usually. The older dog needs less fat, less carbohydrate and less minerals unless disease and convalescence dictate otherwise. DON'T PERMIT AN OLD DOG TO GET FAT! It's cruel. The special diet known as PD or KD may be in order, if the dog has dietary troubles or a disease concomitant with old age. The veterinarian should be asked about PD or KD diets. Vitamin B-12 and other vitamin reinforcements may help.

The dog diseases of old age parallel many of the human illnesses. Senior male dogs suffer from prostate trouble, kidney disease and cancer. Senior bitches suffer from metritis and cancer. Both sexes suffer blindness, deafness and paralysis. Dogs suffer from heart disease; I know one old dog that is living an especially happy old age through the courtesy of digitalis. If the symptoms of any disease manifest themselves in an old dog the veterinarian MUST be consulted.

Many dog owners are selfish about old dogs. In their reluctance to lose faithful friends, they try to keep their canine companions alive in terminal illnesses, such as galloping cancer. If the veterinarian holds little or no promise for recovery of a pet from an illness associated with old age, or if the pet suffers, the kindest act the owner can perform is to request euthanasia. In this sad event, the kindest step the owner may take in *his* interest is to acquire a puppy or young dog of the same breed immediately. Puppies have a wonderful way of absorbing grief!

Glossary of Dog Terms

Achilles tendon: The large tendon attaching the muscle of the calf in the second thigh to the bone below the hock; the hamstring.

A.K.C.: The American Kennel Club.

Albino: An animal having a congenital deficiency of pigment in the skin, hair, and eyes.

American Kennel Club: A federation of member show-giving and specialty clubs which maintains a stud book, and formulates and enforces rules under which dog shows and other canine activities in the United States are conducted. Its address is 51 Madison Ave., New York, N. Y. 10010.

Angulation: The angles of the bony structure at the joints, particularly of the shoulder with the upper arm (front angulation), or the angles at the stifle and the hock (rear angulation).

Anus: The posterior opening of the alimentary canal through which the feces are discharged.

Apple head: A rounded or domed skull.

Balance: A nice adjustment of the parts one to another; no part too big or too small for the whole organism; symmetry.

Barrel: The ribs and body.

Bitch: The female of the dog species.

Blaze: A white line or marking extending from the top of the skull (often from the occiput), between the eyes, and over the muzzle.

Brisket: The breast or lower part of the chest in front of and between the forelegs, sometimes including the part extending back some distance behind the forelegs.

Burr: The visible, irregular inside formation of the ear.

Butterfly nose: A nose spotted or speckled with flesh color.

Canine: (Noun) Any animal of the family *Canidae,* including dogs, wolves, jackals, and foxes.
(Adjective) Of or pertaining to such animals; having the nature and qualities of a dog.

Canine tooth: The long tooth next behind the incisors in each side of each jaw; the fang.

Castrate: (Verb) Surgically to remove the gonads of either sex, usually said of the testes of the male.

Character: A combination of points of appearance, behavior, and disposition

125

contributing to the whole dog and distinctive of the individual dog or of its particular breed.

Cheeky: Having rounded muscular padding on sides of the skull.

Chiseled: (Said of the muzzle) modeled or delicately cut away in front of the eyes to conform to breed type.

Chops: The mouth, jaws, lips, and cushion.

Close-coupled: Short in the loins.

Cobby: Stout, stocky, short-bodied; compactly made; like a cob (horse).

Coupling: The part of the body joining the hindquarters to the parts of the body in front; the loin; the flank.

Cowhocks: Hocks turned inward and converging like the presumed hocks of a cow.

Croup: The rear of the back above the hind limbs; the line from the pelvis to the set-on of the tail.

Cryptorchid: A male animal in which the testicles are not externally apparent, having failed to descend normally, not to be confused with a castrated dog.

Dentition: The number, kind, form, and arrangement of the teeth.

Dewclaws: Additional toes on the inside of the leg above the foot; the ones on the rear legs usually removed in puppyhood in most breeds.

Dewlap: The pendulous fold of skin under the neck.

Distemper teeth: The discolored and pitted teeth which result from some febrile disease.

Down in (or on) pastern: With forelegs more or less bent at the pastern joint.

Dry: Free from surplus skin or flesh about mouth, lips, or throat.

Dudley nose: A brown or flesh-colored nose, usually accompanied by eye-rims of the same shade and light eyes.

Ewe-neck: A thin sheep-like neck, having insufficient, faulty, or concave arch.

Expression: The combination of various features of the head and face, particularly the size, shape, placement and color of eyes, to produce a certain impression, the outlook.

Femur: The heavy bone of the true thigh.

Fetlock or Fetlock joint: The joint between the pastern and the lower arm; sometimes called the "knee," although it does not correspond to the human knee.

Fiddle front: A crooked front with bandy legs, out at elbow, converging at pastern joints, and turned out pasterns and feet, with or without bent bones of forearms.

Flews: The chops; pendulous lateral parts of the upper lips.

Forearm: The part of the front leg between the elbow and pastern.

Front: The entire aspect of a dog, except the head, when seen from the front; the forehand.

Guard hairs: The longer, smoother, stiffer hairs which grow through the undercoat and normally conceal it.

Hackney action: The high lifting of the front feet, like that of a Hackney horse, a waste of effort.

Hare-foot: A long, narrow, and close-toed foot, like that of the hare or rabbit.

Haw: The third eyelid, or nictitating membrane, especially when inflamed.

Height: The vertical distance from withers at top of shoulder blades to floor.

Hock: The lower joint in the hind leg, corresponding to the human ankle; sometimes, incorrectly, the part of the hind leg, from the hock joint to the foot.

Humerus: The bone of the upper arm.

Incisors: The teeth adapted for cutting; specifically, the six small front teeth in each jaw between the canines or fangs.

126

Knuckling over: Projecting or bulging forward of the front legs at the pastern joint; incorrectly called knuckle knees.

Leather: Pendant ears.

Lippy: With lips longer or fuller than desirable in the breed under consideration.

Loaded: Padded with superfluous muscle (said of such shoulders).

Loins: That part on either side of the spinal column between the hipbone and the false ribs.

Molar tooth: A rear, cheek tooth adapted for grinding food.

Monorchid: A male animal having but one testicle in the scrotum; monorchids may be potent and fertile.

Muzzle: The part of the face in front of the eyes.

Nictitating membrane: A thin membrane at the inner angle of the eye or beneath the lower lid, capable of being drawn across the eyeball. This membrane is frequently surgically excised in some breeds to improve the expression.

Occiput or occiputal protuberance: The bony knob at the top of the skull between the ears.

Occlusion: The bringing together of the opposing surfaces of the two jaws; the relation between those surfaces when in contact.

Olfactory: Of or pertaining to the sense of smell.

Out at elbow: With elbows turned outward from body due to faulty joint and front formation, usually accompanied by pigeon-toes; loose-fronted.

Out at shoulder: With shoulder blades loosely attached to the body, leaving the shoulders jutting out in relief and increasing the breadth of the front.

Overshot: Having the lower jaw so short that the upper and lower incisors fail to meet; pig-jawed.

Pace: A gait in which the legs move in lateral pairs, the animal supported alternatively by the right and left legs.

Pad: The cushion-like, tough sole of the foot.

Pastern: That part of the foreleg between the fetlock or pastern joint and the foot; sometimes incorrectly used for pastern joint or fetlock.

Period of gestation: The duration of pregnancy, about 63 days in the dog.

Puppy: Technically, a dog under a year in age.

Quarters: The two hind legs taken together.

Roach-back: An arched or convex spine, the curvature rising gently behind the withers and carrying over the loins; wheel-back.

Roman nose: The convex curved top line of the muzzle.

Scapula: The shoulder blade.

Scissors bite: A bite in which the incisors of the upper jaw just overlap and play upon those of the lower jaw.

Slab sides: Flat sides with insufficient spring of ribs.

Snipey: Snipe-nosed, said of a muzzle too sharply pointed, narrow, or weak.

Spay: To render a bitch sterile by the surgical removal of her ovaries; to castrate a bitch.

Specialty club: An organization to sponsor and forward the interests of a single breed.

Specialty show: A dog show confined to a single breed.

Spring: The roundness of ribs.

Stifle or stifle joint: The joint next above the hock, and near the flank, in the hind leg; the joint corresponding to the knee in man.

Stop: The depression or step between the forehead and the muzzle between the eyes.

Straight hocks: Hocks lacking bend or angulation.

Straight shoulders: Shoulder formation with blades too upright, with angle greater than 90° with bone of upper arm.

Substance: Strength of skeleton, and weight of solid musculature.

Sway-back: A spine with sagging, concave curvature from withers to pelvis.

Thorax: The part of the body between the neck and the abdomen, and supported by the ribs and sternum.

Throaty: Possessing a superfluous amount of skin under the throat.

Undercoat: A growth of short, fine hair, or pile, partly or entirely concealed by the coarser top coat which grows through it.

Undershot: Having the lower incisor teeth projecting beyond the upper ones when the mouth is closed; the opposite to overshot; prognathous; underhung.

Upper arm: The part of the dog between the elbow and point of shoulder.

Weaving: Crossing the front legs one over the other in action.

Withers: The part between the shoulder bones at the base of the neck; the point from which the height of a dog is usually measured.

(End of Part II. Please see Contents page for total number of pages in book.)